# The Democratic Rule of Law on Trial

This book examines selected high-profile U.S. First Amendment cases occurring during the Trump era as a vehicle for exploring a possible fundamental commonality in understanding the democratic rule of law globally. In each of these cases, the adjudicating body's analytical legal strategy is discussed in terms of how it reinforces or detracts from the democratic rule of law. It was and continues to be highly internationally anticipated as to what legal examples are being set by this established democracy when confronted by legal contests between the former Trump administration and those alleging their rights were somehow violated by the executive of that time. Thus, the book is instructive for an international audience on the essential role of the courts in protecting democracy through providing, where supported by the law and the facts, a remedy for the aggrieved comparatively powerless. The book will be essential reading for academics and researchers working in the areas of constitutional law, politics and human rights.

**Sonja Grover** is a full professor in the Faculty of Education, Lakehead University, Ontario, Canada. She graduated with a PhD from University of Toronto and has devoted the last 20 years of her career to law research. She has published extensively in peer-reviewed international and comparative law journals and has also single-authored numerous law books. Sonja is an associate editor with *The International Journal of Human Rights.*

Sonja is committed to improving the human rights situation of vulnerable groups, especially children, by exposing through her research publications where and how domestic and international legal systems have failed these groups and offering suggestions for remediation. She also has a keen interest in the fundamentals of the democratic rule of law, an area of study to which this book is a significant contribution.

# The Democratic Rule of Law on Trial

## First Amendment Cases of the Trump Era

**Sonja Grover**

Routledge
Taylor & Francis Group
LONDON AND NEW YORK

First published 2022
by Routledge
4 Park Square, Milton Park, Abingdon, Oxon OX14 4RN

and by Routledge
605 Third Avenue, New York, NY 10158

*Routledge is an imprint of the Taylor & Francis Group, an informa business*



*British Library Cataloguing-in-Publication Data*
A catalogue record for this book is available from the British Library

*Library of Congress Cataloging-in-Publication Data*
A catalog record for this book has been requested

ISBN: 978-0-367-72181-7 (hbk)
ISBN: 978-0-367-72184-8 (pbk)
ISBN: 978-1-003-15376-4 (ebk)

DOI: 10.4324/9781003153764

Typeset in Galliard
by Apex CoVantage, LLC

This book is dedicated to all those who are committed to the struggle for the democratic rule of law.

# Contents

# Acknowledgements

I wish to express my gratitude to Ms. Alison Kirk, Senior Editor, Routledge for her support of this work. I also extend my appreciation to my husband for his love and support which consistently provides me with much of the energy and confidence to pursue these scholarly challenges.

# Preface

This book examines selected high-profile U.S. First Amendment cases as a vehicle for exploring a possible fundamental commonality in understanding the democratic rule of law globally. That is democratic rule of law as signified in large part by the opportunity for marginalized or at least less powerful voices to receive a fair and robust hearing in the courts and in the process the protection they deserve. In the Trump era, it appeared to many that the democratic rule of law itself was on trial as those who contested the administration's positions were often vilified, including certain segments of the press and individual political "dissidents."

The world wondered how the U.S. courts would respond when these competing positions were fully litigated. It was and continues to be highly internationally anticipated as to what legal examples are being set by this established democracy when confronted by legal contests between the former Trump administration and those alleging their rights were somehow violated by the executive of that time. Thus, the book is instructive for an international audience on the essential role of the courts in protecting democracy through providing, where supported by the law and the facts, a remedy for the aggrieved comparatively powerless.

Interestingly, former U.S. President Trump's own First Amendment rights also came to be litigated both in the context of a legislative trial (the second impeachment trial addressing whether his speech on January 6, 2021, was protected speech or not) and in a judicial context (litigation concerning the temporary then permanent ban by Twitter of Trump from their platform for what Twitter contended was highly incendiary speech related to his claims regarding alleged election fraud in the 2020 U.S. Presidential election). The latter cases also are examined here.

The book addresses, in addition, recent landmark cases examining First Amendment religious freedoms and the equities involved in respecting the same while upholding the general public interest. Finally addressed are the free speech rights of schoolchildren in a contemporary era where the line between on-campus school speech and off-campus school speech is most often indecipherable given the reach of social media platforms. The snapchat case provided the U.S. Supreme Court the opportunity to consider this issue and whether students in any context have a First Amendment right to critique school authorities, even in offensive ways. The snapchat case then raises the issue of children's right to challenge power structures and the scope of such a right especially where school authorities are concerned.

In the final analysis, it is concluded that democracy is marked by all branches—the legislative, executive and the courts—serving the general public good and where often, it is only the courts that stand as the last barrier against authoritarianism.

# 1 The Democratic Rule of Law and Free Speech Examined in the Context of the Second Impeachment Trial of Donald J. Trump

## Introduction

Constitutional offences concern a breach of the public trust and of democratic values and, at their core, *subvert the democratic rule of law itself.* The U.S. Constitution, it is here argued, thus unsurprisingly allows for and demands accountability also in respect of living *former* federal civil officials who have allegedly committed constitutional offences while in office. There is then, it is here contended, no constitutional bar in the U.S. Constitution to impeachment proceedings in the House and Senate against a living former federal civil officer accused of "high crimes and misdemeanors" (the U.S. Constitution's term for constitutional offences) committed while still in office. In former U.S. President Trump's second impeachment case, the jurisdictional question was decided by the Senate in favor of the House Manager Prosecutors. Nevertheless, the majority of Republican senators continued to hold, and even after the second impeachment trial on the merits reached its conclusion in an acquittal, that the Senate had had no jurisdiction to try the case in the first instance. This, it is here argued, did damage the democratic rule of law in America and will continue to do so if left unchallenged. It created the erroneous impression for the U.S. public and globally that former federal civil officers of the United States can, on purported jurisdictional grounds, constitutionally escape accountability for alleged constitutional offences committed against that democracy while still in office.

We will here consider the issues commonly held to underlie the jurisdictional question whether living *former* U.S. federal civil officers are subject to impeachment and Senate trial. That is we will address the formulation by the Defence and the Prosecution in the Trump second impeachment case of the issues generally considered embedded in the jurisdictional question; formulations that lead to predictable arguments and counterarguments. This author will analyze the robustness of the contrary formulations of the issues which the Defence versus the Prosecution respectively contend are foundational to the jurisdictional question and consider the implications of that reassessment.

The overarching specific jurisdictional question in this case is whether a living *former U.S. President* was constitutionally still subject to Senate impeachment trial proceedings subsequent to the House having passed an impeachment article with

DOI: 10.4324/9781003153764-1

the exhibition of that article to the Senate occurring when President Trump was no longer holding office due to his term having expired. We will also consider whether historical precedent is in fact instructive on the fundamental jurisdictional question whether living federal *"civil officers"* (as that latter term is defined in the Constitution of the United States)—when no longer in office—are yet potentially subject to an impeachment legislative trial (i) their having been accused of high crimes and misdemeanours and (ii) impeachment articles(s) having been formulated by the House and passed by the House through a vote and advanced to the Senate. It will be argued that there is no such phenomenon factually or legally as "late impeachment" in such an instance as some have termed the Senate impeachment trial of a living U.S. former federal civil officer. This since, on the respectful view here, as will be argued, such impeachment processes are also timely and jurisdictionally constitutional.

We will consider then in particular here the arguments advanced by the Prosecution and the Defence on the jurisdictional question whether Donald J. Trump was subject to a second Senate impeachment trial as, at that time, a living *former President* of the United States for alleged high crimes and misdemeanours committed while in that aforementioned office. We will address the arguments as proffered both in the submitted briefs and the oral arguments of the parties. Let us begin, however, with (i) the text of the U.S. Constitution regarding impeachment of a President and (ii) the text of the single article of impeachment for alleged "incitement of insurrection" that was deliberated upon by the Senate in the second impeachment trial of the then *former* U.S. President, Donald J. Trump, 45th President of the United States of America:

> *Impeachment Clause: Article II, s. 4 (U.S. Constitution):* "The President, Vice President and all civil Officers of the United States, shall be removed from Office on Impeachment for, and Conviction of, Treason, Bribery, or other high Crimes and Misdemeanors"[1]

*The Impeachment Article in the Second Impeachment of Donald, J. Trump, Former President of the United States:*

> "H. Res. 24
>
> *In the House of Representatives, U. S.,*
>
> *January 13, 2021.*
>
> *Resolved,* That Donald John Trump, President of the United States, is impeached for high crimes and misdemeanors and that the following article of impeachment be exhibited to the United States Senate:

1 U.S. Const. Article II, s. 4. Note that by practice, no U.S. congressional members or senators or military personnel are impeachable as civil officers under Article II, s. 4. Federal judges are impeachable if they fall under the category of judges referenced by Article III s. 1 of the U.S. Constitution which states, "The Judges, both of the supreme and inferior Courts, shall hold their Offices during good Behavior." State judges can be impeached by their State legislative bodies. Congressional members and senators may be removed by expulsion by their own legislative body but not through impeachment.

Article of impeachment exhibited by the House of Representatives of the United States of America in the name of itself and of the people of the United States of America, against Donald John Trump, President of the United States of America, in maintenance and support of its impeachment against him for high crimes and misdemeanors.

**Article I: Incitement of Insurrection**

The Constitution provides that the House of Representatives "shall have the sole Power of Impeachment" and that the President "shall be removed from Office on Impeachment for, and Conviction of, Treason, Bribery, or other high Crimes and Misdemeanors." Further, s. 3 of the 14th Amendment to the Constitution prohibits any person who has "engaged in insurrection or rebellion against" the United States from "hold[ing] any office . . . under the United States." In his conduct while President of the United States—and in violation of his constitutional oath faithfully to execute the office of President of the United States and, to the best of his ability, preserve, protect, and defend the Constitution of the United States, and in violation of his constitutional duty to take care that the laws be faithfully executed—Donald John Trump engaged in high Crimes and Misdemeanors by inciting violence against the Government of the United States, in that:

On January 6, 2021, pursuant to the 12th Amendment to the Constitution of the United States, the Vice President of the United States, the House of Representatives, and the Senate met at the United States Capitol for a Joint Session of Congress to count the votes of the Electoral College. In the months preceding the Joint Session, President Trump repeatedly issued false statements asserting that the Presidential election results were the product of widespread fraud and should not be accepted by the American people or certified by State or Federal officials. Shortly before the Joint Session commenced, President Trump addressed a crowd at the Ellipse in Washington, DC. There, he reiterated false claims that "we won this election, and we won it by a landslide." He also willfully made statements that, in context, encouraged—and foreseeably resulted in—lawless action at the Capitol, such as: "if you don't fight like hell you're not going to have a country anymore." Thus incited by President Trump, members of the crowd he had addressed, in an attempt to, among other objectives, interfere with the Joint Session's solemn constitutional duty to certify the results of the 2020 Presidential election, unlawfully breached and vandalized the Capitol, injured and killed law enforcement personnel, menaced Members of Congress, the Vice President, and Congressional personnel, and engaged in other violent, deadly, destructive, and seditious acts.

President Trump's conduct on January 6, 2021, followed his prior efforts to subvert and obstruct the certification of the results of the 2020 Presidential election. Those prior efforts included a phone call on January 2, 2021, during which President Trump urged the secretary of state of Georgia, Brad Raffensperger, to "find" enough votes to overturn the Georgia Presidential election results and threatened Secretary Raffensperger if he failed to do so.

In all this, President Trump gravely endangered the security of the United States and its institutions of Government. He threatened the integrity of the democratic system, interfered with the peaceful transition of power, and imperiled a coequal branch of Government. He thereby betrayed his trust as President, to the manifest injury of the people of the United States.

Wherefore, Donald John Trump, by such conduct, has demonstrated that he will remain a threat to national security, democracy, and the Constitution if allowed to remain in office, and has acted in a manner grossly incompatible with self-governance and the rule of law. Donald John Trump thus warrants impeachment and trial, removal from office, and disqualification to hold and enjoy any office of honor, trust, or profit under the United States."[2]

## The Language of the Impeachment Article in the Trump Second Impeachment Case

In the aforementioned impeachment article (at paragraph five), the House Managers (the Prosecution) make several key contentious claims that give rise fundamentally to the jurisdictional question. That jurisdictional question is whether a living *former* U.S. President can be impeached and, if found guilty by the Senate, removed from office and potentially disqualified from holding future U.S. federal civil office. The Prosecution in the Trump second impeachment alleged that the President i) "will remain a threat to national security, democracy, and the Constitution *if allowed to remain in office*"; ii) "Donald John Trump thus warrants impeachment and trial, *removal from office* and iii) *disqualification* to hold and enjoy any office of honor, trust, or profit under the United States (emphasis added)."[3]

When the January 13, 2021, article of impeachment was drafted and voted on in the House, President Donald J. Trump was still in office. Hence the reference in the aforementioned impeachment article at paragraph five to the necessity for "removal" and "disqualification" (given the alleged continuing threat should President Trump remain in office or hold future federal civil office) was, on its face, straightforward. However, a central contentious aspect arises in that the article of impeachment was advanced to the Senate with the House Managers knowing that Trump's term as U.S. President would expire before the Senate trial for the second Trump impeachment could be held. Thus, the Senate trial and verdict in President Trump's second impeachment case involved Trump as a living *former President* of the United States. The questions thus arise as to (i) in what sense, if any, "removal" from office by the Senate is still applicable to a living *former* U.S. President and (ii) how a living *former* U.S. President can–if convicted by the Senate on the impeachment article—be disqualified from the opportunity in the future to "hold and enjoy any office of honor, trust, or profit under the

2 Congress.Gov H.Res.24—Impeaching Donald John Trump, President of the United States, for high crimes and misdemeanors. 117th Congress (2021–2022).

3 Second Impeachment Article Against Donald J. Trump paragraph five excerpts.

United States" if he or she cannot, in the circumstance, *factually* be removed from office in the first instance.[4] The quandary in that respect arises *if* the U.S. Constitution Article II s. 4 is interpreted to mean that (i) the President must be "removed from office" as a *factual matter* (implying the penalty is to be imposed only on a sitting President) and that (ii) *factual removal* is to occur before he or she can be disqualified from holding future U.S. federal civil office. On the foregoing Trump disputable Defence interpretation then, to recap, the Senate verdict in a case of disqualification can only be applied where (i) a sitting U.S. President was found guilty by the Senate of an impeachable offence(s) and *factually removed* from office and then, (ii) given the gravity of the alleged ongoing threat and/or other consideration, disqualified from holding future U.S. federal civil office. We will here, however, challenge the viability of that Trump Defence interpretation relating to the Senate jurisdictional matter. First though, let us recall some of the pre-trial events in Senate in the second impeachment Trump case.

## Pre-trial Machinations in Senate in the Second Impeachment of Donald J. Trump, 45th President of the United States

### *The Dismissal Attempt*

The House approved the article of impeachment in the second impeachment of President Trump and it was, as was here previously discussed, set out in House Resolution 24 of January 13, 2021, while President Trump was still in office. The vote was 232 to 197 with 222 Democrats and ten Republicans voting in favor of the impeachment article.[5] Donald J. Trump's term of office as President expired January 20, 2021, when Joseph Biden was inaugurated as the 46th President of the United States. The aforementioned single article of impeachment was delivered to the Senate by the House Managers on January 25, 2021, after President Trump's term as U.S. President had expired.

On January 26, 2021, there was a motion in the Senate to hold a vote to dismiss the second impeachment trial of former President Trump before it had even begun. This by way of Senator Rand Paul raising a point of order contending that (i) a living former President cannot be impeached as Article II s. 4 and Article I s. 3 of the U.S. Constitution, in referencing the impeachment of "the President," are purportedly referring exclusively to the *sitting President* and that (ii) the second impeachment trial of Donald J. Trump would allegedly be the unconstitutional impeachment of a *private citizen*. Senator Chuck Schumer asked for a vote to table the Rand dismissal motion and that request passed 55 to 45, with five Republicans voting with the Democrats. This then equated to a vote

4 Here, as mentioned, President Trump's term expired before the Senate trial was conducted and the impeachment *acquittal* verdict was rendered by the Senate.

5 Weiyi, C. A Step-by-Step Guide to the Second Impeachment of Donald J. Trump. *The New York Times* (February 13, 2021).

*against* dismissal of the trial.[6] On January 26, 2021, there was a summons issued to former President Trump to appear at his second Senate impeachment trial. On February 4, 2021, Mr. Trump was called/requested to testify under oath at his Senate trial, but he rejected that request through his counsel. On February 9, 2021, before the Senate, convened then as an impeachment court, the parties (the House Managers as the Prosecution and the Trump Defence) argued the question of the Senate's constitutional jurisdiction to impeach a living former U.S. President. The Senate voted 56 to 44 to proceed with the second impeachment trial of the former President as to the merits consideration holding that the trial of a living former President of the United States for alleged impeachable offences was within the Senate's jurisdiction.[7] Let us turn then to an in-depth consideration of the jurisdictional question (whether a living former U.S. President can be subjected to a Senate impeachment trial) and to some of the many issues embedded within that question (keeping in mind that this author does *not* presume to have deciphered all the implied issues underlying the jurisdiction question in the second impeachment of former President Trump).

## The Implications of Due Process for the Constitutionality of a Senate Impeachment Trial of a Living *Former* U.S. President

The Trump Defence maintained that it was *ipso facto* unconstitutional to try Trump in a Senate impeachment trial as the Senate trial would occur and the verdict would be rendered when the President was no longer in office due to his term having expired. The Trump Defence further argued that it was therefore unconstitutional to bring an impeachment article against Trump in the first instance even though he was a sitting President at the time the impeachment article was approved by the House.[8] The latter deduction is incorrect, on the

6 The question whether President Trump as a living *former* President could be impeached was the core question taken up in the phase of the second impeachment trial of President Donald J. Trump dealing with jurisdiction. It is here suggested that once the dismissal motion was defeated and it was announced by the President of the Senate that the Senate would reconvene *as an impeachment court*, the constitutionality of the Senate proceedings was already acceded to by the Senate regardless of the ultimate outcome of the jurisdiction question. The initial jurisdictional question to decide was whether the constitutional trial could move to consider the merits of the case where the accused was a living *former* U.S. President at the time the Senate trial was initiated. Unlike a civil non-legislative trial where jurisdictional arguments are heard only by the judge, here the senators as both judges and jurors heard and decided the jurisdictional question (as so happened, the senators were also witnesses to the alleged insurrection constituting an attempt to interfere with the certification of the 2020 election results proceedings that were taking place at the Capitol (January 6, 2021).

7 *Ibid.*, Weiyi, C. A Step-by-Step Guide to the Second Impeachment of Donald J. Trump. *The New York Times* (February 13, 2021).

8 On the view of the current author, where there is a dismissal blocking a Senate impeachment trial on the grounds that the impeached former civil officer is *at the time of trial* then a private citizen, the impeachment article itself is *erroneously* impugned as unconstitutionally brought.

view here, in that once an impeachment article(s) is/are approved by the House and advanced to the Senate, there must be a timely Senate trial. This given the exigency of the due process requirement being applicable also to the House and Senate impeachment process. Clearly, it cannot be that there is a bar on bringing impeachment articles against a U.S. President who allegedly committed constitutional offences while in that federal civil office and especially, moreover, one who, as was Trump, still sitting as President at the time the impeachment article was approved by the House. Further, it cannot be constitutionally permissible that a Senate trial is foreclosed because a U.S. President, for instance, the day before or on the day of the Senate impeachment trial decides, perhaps unexpectedly in some cases, to resign. The civil officer to be tried for high crimes and misdemeanours *committed while in U.S. federal civil office* cannot so-to-speak resign from his or her reckoning with the constitutionally defined accountability mechanism (i.e. where he or she is no longer in office at the time of the Senate trial and/or on the date anticipated for the rendering of the Senate verdict).

There is, it should be noted, and as will be here explained, no constitutional limitation set out in the U.S. Constitution on the House against bringing an impeachment article(s) against a living former U.S. President or other living former U.S. federal civil officer for alleged constitutional offences committed while in office. Where an impeachment article(s) is/are brought forth by the House to the Senate against a living former U.S. federal civil officer, including for instance a former U.S. President for high crimes and misdemeanours committed while in office, and those articles are left standing,[9] the Senate must thus proceed with the impeachment trial proceedings. That step is then inherently constitutional in meeting the due process requirement (the Senate first deciding on jurisdiction and, if that is affirmed, then moving to the merits of the case under consideration).

## On the Issue of Mootness in the Impeachment of a Living Former U.S. President

The House advancing an impeachment article(s) and the Senate impeachment trial of a living former U.S. President (or other former U.S. federal civil officer) raises, it is here argued, a *live consideration*. This given both the need for accountability and the issue of potential disqualification from holding *future* U.S. federal civil office as a viable penalty. The Senate impeachment trial of a living *former* civil officer, such as a former U.S. President, against whom articles of impeachment have been brought allows for the establishment of a legal record as to whether that former civil officer had been *eligible for factual removal* under Article II s. 4

9 Referring here to the situation in which the impeachment article(s) is/are neither withdrawn by the House (likely before exhibition of the article(s) to the Senate) nor dismissed by the Senate through a Senate motion before the Senate impeachment trial proceedings of the Senate (convened as a constitutional court) on the jurisdiction and merits issues would have begun.

of the U.S. Constitution (that is whether *factual removal* would have been *constitutionally warranted*) had he or she still been in office when convicted. If such is the case, then the Senate has a basis—an objective factual legal record and the argument of both the Prosecution and Defence—upon which to consider the issue of disqualification of the former President from holding a *future* civil office of trust under the U.S. Government including the U.S. presidency. The consideration as to *disqualification* from holding future U.S. federal civil office *always*, as indicated per the text of the U.S. Constitution, Article I s. 3,[10] concerns a living *former* U.S. President *or former* other U.S. federal civil officer and not one currently in office.

That disqualification from holding future federal civil office is an option as a remedy for constitutional offences arguably makes it clear that living *former* U.S. federal civil officers are *not* immune from the impeachment process and potentially conviction by the Senate. Recall in this regard that under U.S. criminal law, there is an imperfect but yet relevant analogy, the *mootness exception* re "*Conduct Capable of Repetition, Yet Evading Review*":

> Some disputes or injuries may arise in the short-term and have the potential for recurrence, but always fail to last long enough to permit federal judicial review. In such a situation, *federal courts have justified an exception to the mootness doctrine.*[11]
>
> However, the Court has held that this exception applies only in "exceptional situations," where the plaintiff "can make a reasonable showing that he will again be subjected to the alleged illegality (emphasis added)."[12]

The Trump second impeachment trial concerned an instance of alleged "incitement to insurrection" by a U.S. President *while still in office*. If the opportunity for accountability for that alleged incitement (here not through the federal court but through a Senate impeachment trial) were foreclosed due to the President no longer being in office, the risk of further incitement to insurrection—if such occurred in the first instance—would arguably, on the view of the Prosecution, be an ongoing threat. This given the continuing strong political influence of this former President with a large segment of the American public. The change in status of the accused (no longer being in Presidential office) on its own, out of a larger context, might appear, at first glance, to substantiate a claim that the case against President Trump in the second impeachment was moot (using the

10 "Judgement in Cases of Impeachment shall not extend further than to removal from Office, and disqualification to hold and enjoy any Office of honor, Trust or Profit under the United States." (Article I s. 3, U.S. Constitution).

11 Roe v. Wade, 410 U.S. 113, 125 (1973) Cited in Congressional Research Service. *Mootness: An Explanation of the Justiciability Doctrine* (February 7, 2007) at pp. 4–5.

12 City of Los Angeles v. Lyons, 461 U.S. 95, 109 (1983) Cited in Congressional Research Service. *Mootness: An Explanation of the Justiciability Doctrine* (February 7, 2007) at pp. 4–5.

imperfect analogy of mootness in a criminal proceeding).[13] However, on the analysis here, the fact that (i) disqualification from holding future U.S. federal civil office (including the U.S. presidency) was arguably still a live issue and that (ii) the Prosecution, on behalf of the House and the American public as plaintiff, argued a *continuing threat* to democracy should the former U.S. President, President Trump, not be convicted in a Senate impeachment trial and then disqualified are relevant considerations as to whether the impeachment case was moot even if constitutionally brought.

On the analysis here the second impeachment case against former U.S. President Trump was *not* moot. This since the disqualification remedy was still available and the Prosecution was arguing relevant alleged facts *requiring a legal determination* by the senators namely (i) that former President Trump had purportedly incited an insurrection on January 6, 2021, while he was still President and hence his said conduct *met the constitutional standard for factual removal from office* had his term not expired before a possible Senate conviction could be returned and that (ii) the former President allegedly posed a continuing threat to the U.S. democracy and the democratic rule of law, including through purported further ongoing and anticipated continuing incitement to insurrection, and, therefore, should be disqualified from holding future U.S. federal civil office.

## On Whether the U.S. Constitution Bars Impeachment for the Constitutional Offences of Living Former Federal Civil Officers

### *On the Minimum Mandatory Penalty for Constitutional Offences Being Removal; Not Removal and Disqualification*

In the more usual course, one would expect that the impugned U.S. federal civil officer accused of high crimes and misdemeanours while in office would still be in office when the impeachment Senate trial occurs and a guilty verdict (if that is the case) is rendered. However, it is here contended that it is *not* a requirement for the holding of a Senate impeachment trial that the accused U.S. civil officer still be in office at the time of the trial. This since disqualification, by constitutional design, never occurs simultaneous/in parallel with factual removal from office (factual removal occurring where the accused federal civil officer is still in office at the time the Senate guilty verdict is rendered). Rather disqualification occurs *sequentially* in all instances *after* a determination on whether the accused's conduct while in office *warrants/warranted* factual removal from office even if that could not practically be effected as he or she was already out of office. That this sequential two-step process separated in time is the case by constitutional design is reflected in the following: (i) The Senate vote required for a disqualification

13 See Congressional Research Service. *Mootness: An Explanation of the Justiciability Doctrine*, 'Change in Status of the Parties' (February 7, 2007) at p. 2.

(simple majority) is different from and occurs after the vote required for a finding that removal is/was warranted and for an actual factual removal from office occurring where the Senate-convicted individual is still in office. Two-thirds of the Senate convened as a constitutional court must vote guilty to uphold a finding that the conduct warrants/warranted removal from office and to effect a factual removal should the civil officer still be in office when the Senate guilty verdict is reached; (ii) disqualification of the Senate-convicted individual *always* applies to a *former* U.S. federal civil officer regardless of the mechanism of his or her departure from office (factual removal for constitutional offences committed while in office, resignation or expiry of his or her term); and (iii) a finding in favor of disqualification from holding future federal civil office is a discretionary one and hence is a completely separate issue from that of the mandatory removal upon Senate conviction in an impeachment trial (where the individual was still in office when convicted by the Senate for constitutional offences).

Both the living *former* U.S. federal civil officers considered for disqualification from holding future federal civil office who were (i) removed from office upon a guilty verdict by the Senate for an impeachable offence(s) *committed while in office* and (ii) those who were found guilty by the Senate of the same when they were already out of office (due to expiry of their term or resignation) are on a level equitable playing field in terms of consideration of the merits of the disqualification from future office remedy in their particular case. That is the vulnerability to and eligibility for "disqualification" from holding future U.S. federal civil office of a former U.S. federal civil officer found guilty of an impeachable offence by the Senate is *not* affected by whether they became a *former* federal civil officer through removal, expiry of the term of office or resignation. *The critical factor is rather the finding by the Senate of guilt in regard to the impeachment article(s)—a declaration in essence that removal was constitutionally warranted whether or not it could factually be carried out. That determination lays the groundwork for potential disqualification from holding future U.S. federal civil office.* Hence, disqualification from holding future federal civil office as a potential constitutional remedy in regard to a living former U.S. federal civil officer found guilty of high crimes and misdemeanours committed while in office is applicable regardless of whether (i) that federal civil officer—including a U.S. President—became a *former* federal civil officer on account of resignation or expiry of his or her term before the guilty verdict was rendered by the U.S. Senate on the impeachable offences(s) or (ii) became a *former* federal officer upon factual removal subsequent to the finding of guilt on the impeachable offence(s).

The U.S. Constitution stipulates a *minimum mandatory penalty* upon a finding of guilt on impeachable crimes of factual removal from office should the convicted federal civil officer still be in office at the time that Senate judgement is rendered. Where the convicted is not still in office there is, as here previously argued, still, upon a Senate finding of guilt, the correlated determination that factual removal was *constitutionally warranted* had the Defendant's term not expired or there been no resignation before the Senate conviction. Further, disqualification from holding future U.S. federal civil office is *not* predicated on there having been a *factual removal* from current office but rather only on (i) the civil officer being a former civil officer and (ii) a finding that removal was *constitutionally warranted* even though in certain cases it could not practically be effected (the finding that removal was *constitutionally warranted* being the inherent indisputable implication of every Senate conviction as per the U.S. Const. Article II, s. 4). As a consequence, former U.S. federal civil officers whose term expired or who resigned before the Senate guilty verdict was rendered are *not* immune from disqualification from holding future U.S. federal civil office. Hence, the discretionary application of disqualification from holding future U.S. federal civil office as a penalty is a live issue at the Senate trial for *all former civil officials impeached by the House and found by the Senate to have been guilty* regardless of the mechanism of their becoming former federal civil officers.

A group of legal constitutional experts came to the same conclusion as here argued but as a result of a somewhat different analysis:

> Impeachment is the exclusive constitutional means for removing a President (or other officer) before his or her term expires. *But nothing in the provision authorizing impeachment-for removal limits impeachment to situations where it accomplishes removal from office.* Indeed, such a reading would thwart and potentially nullify a vital aspect of the impeachment power: the power of the Senate to impose disqualification from future office as a penalty for conviction. In order to give full effect to both Article I's and Article II's language with respect to impeachment, therefore, *the correct conclusion is that former officers remain subject to the impeachment power after leaving office, for purposes of permitting imposition of the punishment of disqualification.* . . . The Framers . . . would surely disagree that a person who sought to overthrow our democracy could not be disqualified from holding a future office of the United States because the plot reached its crescendo too close to the end of his or her term (emphasis added).[14]

Impeachment, it is here agreed with the aforementioned constitutional experts, is *not* a mechanism limited to or defined as "impeachment-for removal"—referring to factual removal from office of the Senate-convicted federal civil officer. It is here argued rather that impeachment is, in the first instance, directed to determining whether removal—even if it could not be factually effected—was warranted. *The latter determination is arguably as essential for the protection of the democracy where the accused is no longer in office at the time of the Senate verdict as is actual factual removal from office upon a guilty verdict by Senate where that removal penalty can be imposed.* This is the case, on the view here, whether or not the Senate then goes on to apply the disqualification remedy to a Senate-convicted *former* civil officer whose term expired before the Senate guilty verdict was rendered or who resigned before the verdict. The availability of the

14 Constitutional Law Scholars on Impeaching Former Officers (January 21, 2021).

disqualification from future U.S. federal civil office as a remedy pursuant to the conviction of any former civil officer convicted by the Senate, however, of course adds another layer of import to the guilt determination. This also in the case of a former civil officer who was found guilty but not susceptible to factual removal from office given him or her already being out of office at the time of the Senate verdict.

Hence, it is here contended that the Senate impeachment trial is fundamentally about establishing and exposing the truth of the risks, if any, to the preservation of the democracy posed by the accused civil officer during the time he or she was in office and the potential ongoing and/or future risks that individual may represent. It will furthermore be up to the American public to decide, in considering the factual and legal record created through the House impeachment and Senate trial, whether the Senate, acting as a constitutional court, conducted itself with honor and fidelity to the Constitution in its handling of the particular impeachment case and the determinations made.

### *The Implication of the Minimum Mandatory Constitutional Penalty of Removal From Office for Impeachable Offences: The Defence Versus Prosecution View*

Let us consider more closely the implication of the obligatory U.S. constitutional remedy of "removal from office" of a federal civil officer[15] for treason, bribery or other high crimes and misdemeanours. The wording of Article II s. 4 of the U.S. Constitution discusses in effect *a minimum mandatory penalty* where (i) in the most straightforward case, the offending U.S. federal civil officer is still in office at the time of the Senate guilty verdict on impeachable offences and (ii) hence a factual removal can be effected subsequent to conviction by the Senate. The question arises, however, whether, as the Defence argues, the minimum mandatory penalty for a sitting impeached civil officer means that the accused civil officer must *in every case* be in civil office at the time of the Senate trial and of the Senate verdict to be constitutionally impeached. If that is the correct interpretation, then it renders impeachment (the very bringing of an impeachment article) *necessarily* conditional upon the potential *factual removal* of the civil officer (that is impeachment is then considered to be a function of the possibility of removal upon conviction such that where removal cannot be effected factually; there can be no impeachment article(s) brought).

The opposing view is that impeachment articles are *not* solely applicable where a *factual removal* from office can be practically effected subsequent to a Senate guilty verdict (the opposing view then challenging the notion of so-called "impeachment for *factual removal*" as the only constitutional scenario in an impeachment case). Instead, a guilty verdict by Senate on the impeachment

15 Note that according to the practice of impeachment in the United States, members of Congress are not subject to impeachment (see Constitution Annotated ArtII.S4.1.1 Impeachment and Removal from Office: Overview).

article(s) establishes that removal from office was warranted. However, the two matters—a finding that removal was warranted and actual factual removal—are distinct and may or may not co-occur depending on whether the convicted federal civil officer was still in office at the time of the Senate conviction. That is there could be a conviction in a Senate impeachment trial without the *factual removal* of the convicted federal civil officer as when the civil officer's term expired or the accused Party resigned before the Senate guilty verdict was rendered. In other words, on the latter analysis, as the Prosecutors argued in the Trump second impeachment case, the U.S. Constitution permits Senate conviction for impeachable constitutional offences by a living *former* U.S. federal civil officer[16] who committed those impeachable offences while in office but who is not in office at the time of a Senate guilty verdict.

The Prosecution position then is, in effect, that impeachment is *not* equivalent to impeachment for the *factual removal* from office in every impeachment case scenario. The article(s) of impeachment will in every impeachment scenario, however, reference impeachable acts committed *while the offending civil officer was still in office*, and therefore, the impeachment article(s) itself will always reference the need, at a minimum, for factual removal from that office. This was indeed the case in regard to the impeachment article also in the Trump second impeachment.[17] In the second impeachment against Donald J. Trump, the Defence nevertheless appeared to contend that the article of impeachment of January 13, 2021, was unavoidably "defectively drafted."[18] This since the article makes reference to the necessity for removal from office of the 45th President of the United States though he was already out of office at the time the impeachment article was exhibited to the Senate and the Senate impeachment proceedings were underway in the second impeachment case

It is here contended, in opposition to the Defence position, that the wording of the January 13, 2021, impeachment article referencing "removal" from civil office is *not* defectively drafted, nor is it ostensibly so unavoidably. Rather, it is here argued that the impeachment article in the second impeachment case against Donald J. Trump simply sets out the Prosecution position that Donald J. Trump's conduct *while in Presidential office*—as delineated in the January 13, 2021, impeachment article—"warrants impeachment and trial, removal from office, and disqualification to hold and enjoy any office of honor, trust, or profit under the United States."[19] Consider then the wording of the January 13, 2021,

16 Civil officers as referred to in Article II s. 4 of the U.S. Constitution.

17 "Donald John Trump thus warrants impeachment and trial, *removal from office*, and disqualification to hold and enjoy any office of honor, trust, or profit under the United States." (January 13, 2021, impeachment article against Donald J. Trump.)

18 In the Proceedings Before the United States Senate Re The Impeachment of Former President Donald J. Trump, Trial Memorandum of Donald J. Trump, 45th President of the United States of America at p. 1.

19 Congress.Gov January 13, 2021, impeachment article against Donald J. Trump.

impeachment article referencing conduct that "warrants" impeachment and trial, removal from office and disqualification from future civil office. In other words, the impeachment article references a need for a finding by the Senate of impeachable conduct such that the constitutional remedy available could be applied. The Prosecution is maintaining then in the January 13, 2021, impeachment article that the President *met the standard for "removal from Presidential office" during his tenure and subsequent to his alleged commission of the constitutional offences* (his conduct met the test *warranting* removal and in fact, in the Prosecution's view, disqualification from *future* U.S. federal civil office as well). That Prosecution claim made in the January 13, 2021, impeachment article that Donald J. Trump's conduct *warranted* removal and disqualification is *not* vitiated as a legal position based simply on the fact that Trump would no longer be President of the United States at the time of the Senate proceedings including at the point the verdict would be rendered, his term having expired before then. This is the case in that whether or not the conduct of civil officers while in their office *warranted removal (triggered constitutional liability)* does *not* change based on whether the civil officers in question effectively avoided the possibility of *factual removal* (the latter given that their term of office expired or they resigned before a possible Senate conviction and practical removal could be effected).

Article II s. 4 of the U.S. Constitution sets out that no U.S. President (or other "civil officer" as that term is understood in that clause) is to be left in office subsequent to their having committed an impeachable offence once accorded a Senate impeachment trial and found guilty. Article II s. 4 thus sets out the ineligibility of such a Senate-convicted civil officer to continue to hold his or her office (it sets out a penalty, at a minimum, of being barred from continuing in the current federal civil office should the term not have expired yet and there has been no resignation). The January 13, 2021, impeachment article against Donald J. Trump, on the view here (i) makes just such an *ineligibility claim* against Donald J. Trump to continue to hold his Presidential office once having allegedly committed the constitutional crimes while in office (that is the claim was that constitutionally, Trump was removable after January 6, 2013, pending a Senate conviction) and (ii) makes a claim also for disqualification of Donald J. Trump from holding *future* civil office, including the U.S. Presidency, once out of office *based on his allegedly having engaged in conduct warranting removal from office in his first term and the alleged continuing threat to democracy he posed.*

Article II s. 4 of the U.S. Constitution textually authorizes that pursuant to a Senate impeachment trial and conviction, the civil officer, having been *deemed removable from office*, shall be removed if still in office as per the obligatory requirements of Article II s. 4. However, the current author would argue that (i) impeachment was not contemplated by the Framers to be applicable only when there is a sitting factually "removable President or other federal civil officer" at the time of Senate conviction (so-called impeachment for removal) and that (ii) this is evident from Article I s. 3 of the U.S. Constitution which specifies that the range of penalties available for constitutional offenses committed in office include also "disqualification" from future federal civil office of a *former* civil officer including a former U.S. President. It would make no sense in terms of protecting the democracy from an alleged internal domestic threat to restrict potential disqualification from future office to only those former federal officers removed through an impeachment conviction by the Senate as opposed to having disqualification as an available remedy also regarding those former civil officers impeached by the House who resigned or had their term expire before the Senate guilty verdict was rendered. This since both categories of former civil officers would presumably potentially pose the same continuing threat to the security and integrity of the Republic.

Likewise, on the Prosecution view in the Trump second impeachment, if the civil officer resigns or his or her term expires before the Senate impeachment trial begins and/or the verdict is rendered, upholding of the impeachment by the Senate is still possible. This is due to the discretionary constitutional remedy of disqualification from holding *future* office for which the U.S. Constitution also provides and which is available as a remedy in the case of an impeached *former* civil officer found guilty by the Senate of a constitutional offence(s). On this analysis then, disqualification from *future* civil office through the U.S. Senate impeachment trial process requires that (i) the U.S. federal civil officer accused was found guilty by the Senate of the impeachable offence(s) and hence found to have been ineligible to have continued to hold the office were he or she is still in office at that time *and* (ii) is out of office—whether through removal, resignation or expiry of the term—at the time the discretionary remedy of being barred from holding *future* civil office is imposed. In this regard, it should be noted that the U.S. Constitution does *not* set out a limitation on disqualification from holding *future* civil office to only those offending *former* federal civil officers who were in office when the Senate guilty verdict was rendered and then removed.

On the analysis here, (i) a Senate guilty verdict regarding a living *former* U.S. federal civil officer[20] in an impeachment case *where that former civil officer was one whose term expired or who resigned before the Senate guilty verdict was pronounced* is a declaration of that former civil officer having been *"constitutionally removable"* from office (ineligible/disqualified to have held that office any longer once the constitutional offences were committed while in office and the guilty verdict rendered though not *factually* removable due to the practical impossibility in the aforementioned circumstances) while (ii) the disqualification finding in such a case is akin to a declaration of ineligibility to serve in *future civil office* under the United States due to having been found guilty of committing past impeachable constitutional offences while in U.S. federal civil office and based on the assessed continuing threat.

In the next section, we examine in further depth how we may consider the issue of "removal from office" and disqualification in a case of an impeachment

20 Under the U.S. Constitution, disqualification from future office only applies to *former* civil officers per Article I s. 3 who have been impeached, Senate-convicted and removed if still in office on conviction.

under U.S. Constitution Article II s. 4 of a *former* civil officer who was out of office at the time of the Senate conviction. We will consider the legal concepts of "legal fictions" versus "legal nullities" and what they can contribute to the analysis of the issue.

## On Legal Fictions, Legal Nullities and the "Removability" of a *Former* U.S. President From Office

The Defence, as discussed here, argued that the impeachment article of January 13, 2021, did not apply to the 45th President, Donald J. Trump, as he was no longer in office at the time of the second impeachment Senate trial. The Defence based this reasoning on Article II s. 4 of the U.S. Constitution which states: "The President, Vice President and all civil Officers of the United States, *shall be removed* from Office on Impeachment for, and Conviction of, Treason, Bribery, or other high Crimes and Misdemeanors (emphasis added)."[21] The Defence in this regard contended that:

> The constitutional provision requires that a person actually hold office to be impeached. Since the 45th President is no longer "President," the clause "shall be removed from Office on Impeachment for . . ." is impossible for the Senate to accomplish, and thus the current proceeding before the Senate is *void ab initio* as a legal nullity that runs patently contrary to the plain language of the Constitution.[22]

The Defence for the former President Donald J. Trump thus advanced the argument in its answer to the Impeachment Article in the second impeachment that the proceeding before the Senate in its entirety, including the planned jurisdictional proceedings, were legally invalid from their inception—a "legal nullity."[23] This, the Defence argued, was the case since the President was no longer in office, his term having expired. It is here argued, in contrast, that while *factual removal* of a living *former* U.S. President upon conviction by the Senate for an impeachable offence(s) is a *factual* nullity and a *legal fiction*, it is by no means a *legal* nullity. This is the case in that impeachment Senate trial proceedings against a living *former* U.S. President serve to allow for a decision as to whether, in the view of two-thirds of the Senate, the former President is guilty or not guilty of the impeachable offence(s) committed while in office as charged by the House. If that be the case, then removal *would have been warranted* had the President still been in office at the time of the Senate conviction. In a *conviction* by the Senate

21 Constitution Annotated ArtII.S4.1.1 Impeachment and Removal from Office: Overview.

22 In the Senate of the United States of America, Answer of the President Donald John Trump, 45th President of the United States, to Article I:Incitement of Insurrection at pp. 1–2 (Defence Counsel: Bruce L. Castor and David Schoen (February 2, 2021).

23 In the Senate of the United States of America, Answer of the President Donald John Trump, 45th President of the United States, to Article I:Incitement of Insurrection at pp. 1–2.

of a living *former President* no longer in office for an impeachable offence(s) *committed while in office* is thus embedded "a retrospective eligibility for removal" judgement on the former President. The actual removal of a President whose term expired or who resigned before the Senate impeachment trial and/or guilty verdict was rendered is, of course, *factually* impossible. It is, nevertheless, it is here argued, a useful "legal fiction" grounded in essence on a finding of constitutional eligibility for that removal had he or she still been in office at the relevant time for factual removal. That finding then in turn is key to consideration of the disqualification from holding future federal civil office as a potential remedy for conviction on impeachable offences. So consequential is the Senate finding in itself (on a minimum two-thirds vote) of the convicted having met the constitutional standard for removal from office for impeachable offences (even if in the circumstance that *factual* removal could not practically be effected), that the Constitution requires only a simple majority to disqualify the convicted former U.S. federal civil office from holding future U.S. federal civil office.

A Senate guilty verdict[24] on the impeachment article against a living *former* U.S. President (whose term had already expired or who resigned before the verdict) is, it is here contended then, viable and of great import given the *legal finding* of "removability" though actual removal is something that cannot be effected in the circumstance. The Senate guilty verdict against a living former U.S. President (or other former federal civil officer) constitutes then rather, practically and legally speaking, a finding of *eligibility for removal as a* ***legal fact*** *not a fact that can be actualized in practical reality.* It is a finding of "removability" that constitutionally would have necessitated per Article II s. 4 factual removal had the circumstances allowed for such removal (had the offending civil officer i.e. the former President been found guilty by the Senate while still in office). Put differently, the *legal reality* is constituted of the finding by the Senate that the President was, subsequent to committing the impeachable offence(s) while in office (i), no longer eligible to hold the Office of the President and (ii) hence not only *removable* but subject to mandatory removal per Article II s. 4 of the U.S. Constitution once found guilty through an impeachment trial and saved from that fate *as a practical matter* only due to the timing of the expiry of his or her term or resignation.

Thus, *factual removal* from civil office of a Senate-convicted living *former* U.S. federal civil officer per Article II s. 4 is a *legal fiction.* The finding of "removability" of a living *former* U.S. federal civil officer in a Senate impeachment trial is, however, a legal fact; one that arguably morphs into the *legal fiction* of actual removal per Article II s. 4. However, *legal fictions are not akin to legal nullities though the Defence in the Trump second impeachment trial conflates the two.* Legal fictions instead are (i) legally valid concepts and (ii) have important real world consequences.[25] The law is replete in North America, including the United

24 Found guilty by the required two-thirds Senate vote.

25 See Kelsen, H. Chapter 1 On the Theory of Juridic Fictions. In Maksymilian, Del Mar and Twining, William (Eds.) *Legal Fictions in Theory and Practice* (Berlin: Springer, 2015)

States, with legal fictions which are recognized and routinely operative in the law and which have important implications for determining the rights and obligations of parties at that time and into the future.[26] In the second impeachment of *former* U.S. President Donald J. Trump (out of office at the time of the Senate trial), a guilty verdict would have meant that the former President had been found *constitutionally eligible for removal from office* though this could not be effected due to the expiry of his term of office prior to the Senate verdict being rendered. That finding of "removability" combined with the fact of the President no longer in fact holding office (his term having expired) would then meet the pre-conditions set out in Article II s. 4 of the Constitution for a *consideration* of the Prosecution's demand for imposition of the discretionary remedy of disqualification of the former President from holding future U.S. civil office. The two pre-conditions for consideration of the disqualification remedy are then that (i) the U.S. federal civil officer was found unfit to have continued to hold his or her office subsequent to committing the impugned impeachable constitutional offences while in office and (ii) that he or she was no longer in that office (due to removal, expiry of his or her term or resignation) when the disqualification from holding *future* federal civil office remedy is considered and potentially imposed by the Senate.

Conviction by the Senate of a living *former U.S. President* for impeachable offences while in office entails the legal fiction of "removing" that civil officer factually who is already no longer in office (the latter due to expiry of his or her term or resignation). This is legally supportable in that the U.S. Constitution does *not* contemplate any circumstance wherein an impeached living current *or former* federal civil officer would not be formally tried by and potentially be found guilty by the Senate. The latter given the due process exigencies previously here discussed. Were this not the case, the former federal civil officer would

---

discussing the legal fiction of the child born to a married woman as the result of an adulteress affair being regarded as the child of the husband. It is not that the law presumes the husband to be the child's father as a matter of fact in certain instances but rather the legal fiction "regulates for certain reasons and for certain ends, that under certain circumstances the husband has the same duties and rights in relation to the child which was conceived by his wife in an adulterous relation and that this child has the same duties and rights in relation to this husband as they exist between the husband and his own children which were conceived in wedlock" at pp. 10–11 (See as a U.S example on this point, for instance, Michigan law on this matter: "Sometimes a married woman gives birth to a child whose biological father is not her husband. Although the husband is not the child's biological parent, he is the child's legal parent under Michigan law. The husband is the legal parent of every child born or conceived during the marriage." https://michiganlegalhelp.org/self-help-tools/family/non-marital-children-born-or-conceived-during-marriage (accessed March 26, 2021).

26 One such legal fiction is that of the corporation as legal person. In Canada, for instance, the corporation as legal person has certain constitutional rights limited only as necessary to be consistent with democratic values (i.e. freedom of commercial expression) and not others (the right to be protected from cruel and unusual punishment where a fine for instance is regarded as grossly excessive). This issue was recently addressed by the Supreme Court of Canada in Quebec (Attorney General) v. 9147–0732 Québec Inc.

have no legislative mechanism for defending himself or herself against the House impeachment charge(s). The Senate conviction (for impeachable offences committed while in office) of a living *former President* no longer in office at the time of the conviction is, as explained, a declaration that the former President was "removable" constitutionally and would have been so factually but for the circumstance.

Where culpability of the living *former* President (or other former federal civil officer) for constitutional offences that he or she committed while in office is found by two-thirds of the Senate to be a *legal fact*, there is then a modicum of *accountability* in that regard. This even though the practical remedy in the form of factual removal from office is not available. This situation in that respect is somewhat akin to a declaratory remedy issued by a non-legislative court in a civil case.[27] This in that

> Declaratory relief refers to a court's judgement stating the rights of parties without ordering any specific action. . . . When a Party is requesting a declaratory judgment, the Party is seeking an official declaration regarding the status of the controversy in issue.[28]

Here *factual* removal is not a consequence entailed in the Senate conviction for impeachable offences since the Senate-convicted living *former* federal civil officer is already out of office at the time of the conviction. The impeached former federal civil officer thus *no longer poses an imminent threat to the Republic through the power of that office.* The out-of-office requirement is met and legal accountability established for the impeachable offences through the Senate finding of guilt warranting removal had the former civil officer still been in office.

To summarize then, the Senate trial judgement on the article of impeachment against a living *former* U.S. President no longer in office at the time of the Senate verdict can be considered somewhat analogous to a declaratory remedy in a non-legislative civil court. This in that a declaratory judgement by a non-legislative civil court clarifies the rights of the complainant and the Party complained against without necessarily accompanying that with an order for relief requiring that certain practical concrete actions be taken. Thus, it is the case that though *former*

27 The Senate being part of the legislature is here referred to as a "legislative court" while a "non-legislative court" is one that, as the term is used here, does not, as part of its jurisdictional mandate draft and articulate law. However, the non-legislative courts (criminal and civil) may at times provide novel interpretations of law (statutory and constitutional) that may be perceived to advance the understanding and implementation of the law better consistent with the values underlying the democratic rule of law.

28 Legal Information Institute (Cornell University) Declaratory Relief. Note that the controversy to be settled through declaratory relief in a non-legislative civil court must be justiciable. The impeachability of a former U.S. President or other U.S. federal civil officer is clearly a judiciable one given that there are innumerable U.S. Senates which have been seized of such a matter including the Senate that determined it had jurisdiction over the second impeachment trial of former President Donald J. Trump.

President Trump could not, *as a matter of fact*, have been removed from Presidential office in the second impeachment even if he would have been found guilty by the Senate,[29] that does *not* imply—contrary to the contention of the Defence—that the Senate trial was unconstitutional or that the Senate's judgement on the article of impeachment was barred from being rendered.[30] A Senate verdict of guilt or innocence regarding alleged impeachable conduct while in office of a *former* federal civil officer is a pronouncement on whether that conduct met the standard for an impeachable offence rendering him or her constitutionally *removable* from office. It is a declaration, in the proper case, of removability and ineligibility at some point to have held that federal civil office given impeachable conduct during the term of office. That declaration, on the view here, has import in (i) allowing for accountability for impeachable conduct that occurred while in office by a living *former* civil officer declaring the conduct to have been unconstitutional and by (ii) setting the necessary determination of impeachable past conduct while in office allowing for a *possible disqualification* from holding future U.S. federal civil office where the threat may be ongoing.

In the next section, we examine (i) what is established in an impeachment of a *former* U.S. President and (ii) the Trump Defence contentions in the second impeachment case regarding the purported only proper and constitutional purpose of impeachment.

## On the Purpose of Impeachment Proceedings Against a Living *Former* U.S. Civil Officer

For the reasons here previously discussed, the Senate impeachment trial of a living *former* U.S. President or other former U.S. federal civil officer who is no longer in office when the Senate verdict is rendered is *not* moot. This in part, as mentioned, in that the U.S. Senate is still left with the live issue in such a case—if there is a guilty verdict—as to whether the former civil officer's conduct while in

29 This given that Trump's term of Presidential office had expired before the Senate trial began.

30 The current author thus *contests* the Trump Defence view that "The text then is very clear: Conviction at an impeachment trial requires the possibility of a removal from office. Without that possibility, there cannot be a trial. In the civil law analogue, this case would be summarily dismissed under Federal Rules of Civil Procedure 12(b)(6), for "failure to state a claim upon which relief can be granted." (In the Proceedings before the United States Senate Re the Impeachment of Former President Donald J. Trump, Trial Memorandum of Donald J. Trump, 45th President of the United States of America (February 8, 2021) at p. 18. On the contrary view here, on the Trump second impeachment, had former President Trump been convicted by the Senate, relief would have been entailed in the Senate finding of guilt for impeachable offences in itself and in eligibility for consideration for disqualification from future federal civil office and possible such disqualification. Further, the impeachment claim is properly articulated (the "cause of action" in the civil non-legislative court analogy) with factual elements of the claimed (alleged) constitutional offence (incitement to insurrection) cited. Further, the claim of alleged incitement to insurrection as a constitutional offence is grounded in U.S. constitutional law and hence recognized in law as a potential cause of action (here impeachment proceedings).

office merits disqualification from holding future civil office. In the Trump second impeachment trial, the proceedings were directed to determining whether the former President was to be declared to have committed, while in office, the impeachable offence of inciting insurrection against the U.S. government in violation of his oath to uphold the U.S. Constitution and to faithfully execute the laws of the United States.[31] A finding of guilt or innocence on that aforementioned impeachment article by the Senate constitutes then a declaration that Mr. Trump respectively did or did not commit an impeachable offence worthy of removal. A guilty verdict would have been a kind of legal fiction only insofar as Mr. Trump could not as a former President any longer be factually removed. However, a Senate verdict of guilty would have been—just as with the actual verdict of innocence—a legally valid (constitutional) declaratory judgement and of historical, precedential and moral import for the public of today and for posterity.[32] *That declaratory Senate judgement as to whether or not the former President had been eligible for removal had his term not expired before the Senate rendered judgement is then in itself a legitimate purpose of the Senate impeachment trial.* This author for that reason respectfully contests the Trump Defence position (articulated in the next quote) that impeachment is only legally viable when the impeached civil officer is still in office when the Senate guilty verdict is rendered so that he or she can be factually removed:

> *The purpose of impeachment is to remove someone from office*, and unequivocally, this impeachment trial is not about removing someone from office, as Mr. Trump left office on January 20, 2021. *He is now, both factually and legally, a private citizen* (emphasis added).[33]

It is here argued that *factual removal* from office is but one possible outcome of a constitutional impeachment ending in a Senate guilty verdict. This since it is an outcome precluded in the impeachment trial of a *former* civil officer. *Factual removal, it is here argued in opposition to the Trump Defence position is, furthermore, not the purpose of impeachment. Removal is rather one vehicle to execute on the purpose of impeachment in those instances where the offending federal civil officer is still in office when the Senate convicts.* The purpose of impeachment under the U.S. Constitution is to protect the American public from threats to the democratic rule of law and to the democratic values and institutions upon which it is grounded. A declaratory Senate judgement as to whether a *former* U.S. President

31 The U.S. Presidential Oath: "I do solemnly swear (or affirm) that I will faithfully execute the Office of President of the United States, and will to the best of my Ability, preserve, protect and defend the Constitution of the United States." (U.S. Constitution Article II s. 1 clause 8.1).

32 As it turns out, the second impeachment of Donald J. Trump was of paramount interest internationally—as was the first—it being likewise highly instructive as to the actual and/or potential strengths and weaknesses of the U.S. democratic system.

33 In the Proceedings before the United States Senate Re the Impeachment of Former President Donald J. Trump, Trial Memorandum of Donald J. Trump, 45th President of the United States of America (February 8, 2021) at p. 18.

committed an impeachable offence worthy of removal from office serves to protect the public by informing the public as to the Senate's view of the degree of risk, if any, that the former President presented while in office to the health and viability of the American democracy and its institutions. Such information could, for instance, moderate the lens through which the public assesses the former President's next political moves and communications while out of office. Further, as will be discussed, a guilty verdict on the impeachment article in relation to a *former* President (something which is legally viable as has here been argued) contributes to potential application of the constitutional protective mechanism of disqualification from holding further U.S. federal civil office.

On the analysis here, the fact that Donald J. Trump was factually and legally a private citizen at the time of his second impeachment trial is irrelevant to the constitutionality of his second Senate impeachment trial. Respectfully, on the view here, the Defence *incorrectly* contends and infers from the constitutional text (Article II s. 4 of the U.S. Constitution) that impeachment upon Senate conviction of a U.S. President not currently holding the office (a *former* President) is a "late impeachment" and as such an impeachment of a "private citizen."[34] The Defence goes so far as to argue that the second impeachment of former President Trump post his having left office at the end of his first term constitutes a "Bill of Attainder" which the Defence defines as an impeachment of *any* private citizen. It is here argued in rebuttal *that the conviction* of a living *former President* of the United States of America by the Senate is (i) in law akin to providing declaratory relief for the American public by setting for the record the guilt of the former President for his or her impeachable offences *committed while in Presidential office* and (ii) does *not* concern that Party's acts committed as a private citizen. This since a private citizen who has *never held civil office* cannot commit constitutional impeachable high crimes and misdemeanours under Article II s. 4. *Constitutional offences are predicated on holding or having held civil office during the time of the commission of the impeachable conduct.* Such offences under the Constitution can be committed only by perpetrators who abused the public trust while holding the office of the President, the Vice President or some other federal civil office as understood under Article II s. 4 of the U.S. Constitution.

Article I s. 3 of the U.S. Constitution does *not* preclude disqualification of a federal civil officer convicted by the Senate of impeachable offences while holding office where that Party was already out of office at the time of the conviction. Such a disqualification amounts, in practice, to a kind of *prospective impeachment* before the

34 In the Proceedings before the United States Senate Re the Impeachment of Former President Donald J. Trump, Trial Memorandum of Donald J. Trump, 45th President of the United States of America (February 8, 2021) at pp. 19–20. The Defence does concede, however, that "There is little discussion in the historical record surrounding the framing and ratification of the Constitution that treats the precise question of whether a person no longer a civil officer can be impeached." (In the Proceedings before the United States Senate Re the Impeachment of Former President Donald J. Trump, Trial Memorandum of Donald J. Trump, 45th President of the United States of America (February 8, 2021) at pp. 20–21).

convicted former civil officer, that is, for instance, a former President has or could even assume that future U.S. federal civil office such as the presidency. Disqualification is, as the Prosecution in the Trump second impeachment argued, an act grounded in the Constitution. It entails in essence a prospective impeachment of a person deemed to be an ongoing threat to ***democratic government*** who is a member of a discrete and small group—*former* federal civil officers ***convicted*** by the U.S. Senate of a constitutional high crime and misdemeanour committed while in past U.S. federal civil office.[35] It is a disqualification then based on the finding by the Senate of, in its view, an established continuing risk to the democracy should that former civil officer, for instance, former President, assume federal civil office in future, especially the presidency. That continuing risk has been deduced from both the Senate conviction for impeachable offences committed during the previous Presidential term of that particular living former offending former President and additional evidence regarding the further constitutional threats he or she poses. To disqualify an impeached Senate-convicted living former federal civil officer from future civil office reflects, it can be argued, the perspective embodied in Shakespeare's phrase "What's past is prologue; what to come, in yours and my discharge." That is the past will also be the future destiny unless that destiny is reshaped by making certain necessary choices. Here then a destiny of future constitutional offences by the convicted former federal civil officer is deemed a certainty if he or she is not disqualified from holding future such office.

Factual removal from office of a federal civil officer who committed constitutional offences ***while in office*** and so violated the public trust is not the purpose nor the *sine qua non* of impeachment under the U.S. Constitution. This since factual removal, as previously here discussed, is but the necessary mechanism for protecting the democracy where the Senate-convicted civil officer is still in office. Thus, the fact that a living former President at the time of the Senate guilty verdict is not *factually* subject to removal (due to his or her term of office having expired or he or she having resigned before the Senate verdict was rendered) does *not* morph the impeachment, Senate conviction and disqualification from future civil office into a Bill of Attainder. Rather, the legislative penalty is properly constitutionally applied to the conduct of the living Senate—convicted *former* civil officer for ***constitutional offences committed while in office*** (conduct that is by definition an abuse of power and beyond the jurisdiction of that or any civil officer). Recall also that the penalty of "disqualification" from holding future civil office (in consideration of past constitutional offences and an assessed continuing risk of the same) is, when applied, always imposed on a living Senate-convicted *former* civil officer. This given that disqualification never occurs simultaneous with factual removal. Thus, the Framers did *not* consider the legislative penalty of

35 "The trial of a *former official* for abuses he *committed as an official*—arising *from an impeachment that also occurred while he was in office*—poses no risk of subjecting private parties to punitive legislative action targeting their private conduct (emphasis added)." (In the Senate of the United States of America, Trial Memorandum of the House of Representatives in the Impeachment Trial of President Donald J. Trump (February 2, 2021) at p. 70).

disqualification for constitutional offences committed in office by a living *former* civil officer to be a Bill of Attainder though the disqualification is applied whilst the convicted person is no longer in office.

The purpose of impeachment proceedings under the U.S Constitution is the protection of the democracy vested in the people and grounded on the democratic rule of law. That purpose is to be realized by whatever of the following constitutional means is practically available whether that be (i) factual removal from office; (ii) factual removal from office and disqualification from holding future civil office or (iii) disqualification alone; the latter as when a former federal civil officer is found guilty of the constitutional offences charged that were committed while in office, but the convicted individual is no longer in office at the time the Senate guilty verdict is rendered.

While Commissions of Inquiry into alleged unconstitutional conduct by a former civil officer provide the public with important information, so do impeachment trials. The latter in the context of an adversarial process that allows for the public's assessment of the arguments and counter-arguments on the law and the facts. The public is thus provided the opportunity to decide for itself after listening to the Prosecution and Defence during the Senate impeachment proceedings (i) whether impeachable offences were committed by the former federal civil officer while in office, (ii) how this was allowed to happen if it did and (iii) what needs to be done in the future to protect the Republic from these types of impeachable acts where those impeachable offences were deemed to have been committed by the former civil officer. The public may then let its voice be heard on these matters in terms of its perception of what reforms are necessary and in what domains. The U.S. public has the constitutional right to know (i) what evidence may be proffered by the House, and tested during a Senate trial, which evidence the House alleges substantiates the impeachment article(s) in respect of a *former* federal civil officer, that is, for instance, a living former *President* (just as with a current President or other federal civil officer) and (ii) the holding of the Senate on the issue of the guilt or innocence of the living former federal civil officer as to the charged constitutional offence(s) and whether the Senate considers that such conduct merits disqualification.[36]

Removal from office *as a factual matter* as the purpose of impeachment and, in essence, *synonymous* with impeachment (as the Defence framed the matter in former President Trump's second impeachment trial) respectfully, on the current analysis, is *not* the inference to be drawn from Article II s. 4 of the U.S. Constitution. Rather Article II s. 4 stating that "The President, Vice President and all civil Officers of the United States, *shall be removed* from Office on Impeachment for, and Conviction of, Treason, Bribery, or other high Crimes and Misdemeanors (emphasis added)"[37] sets out that no impeached civil officer, including

36 In an effort to keep our focus on the pure legal constitutional issues, we will not here consider whether or not the Senate in Donald J. Trump's second impeachment trial rendered impartial justice given the facts and the law.

37 U.S. Constitution Article II s. 4.

a President, is to be left in office should he or she still be in office at the time of the Senate conviction for an impeachable offence(s). *Article II s. 4* thus *sets the minimum mandatory penalty upon conviction for an impeachable offence of the convicted civil officer still in office. No lesser penalty such as censure by the Senate upon conviction for the impeachable offence is constitutionally permissible per Article II s. 4.* The operative word in the Article II s. 4 provision—"shall"—articulates the mandatory directive requiring removal from office should the civil officer in question, that is the President who is convicted of an impeachable offence by the Senate still be in office at the time the Senate's judgement on the merits of the case is rendered. Where the impeached (Senate-convicted) civil officer is out of office (either through (i) removal or (ii) through expiry of his or her term or through resignation) at the time of the impeachment trial and/or Senate guilty verdict, the maximum penalty guideline set out at Article I s. 3[38] provides for possible disqualification from holding future civil office. Whether that discretionary remedy is applied will depend (assuming an impartial Senate deliberating and deciding on the matter) on the objectively assessed continuing risk posed by the former civil officer to the Republic and to the democratic rule of law upon which it stands.

On the view here, Article II s. 4 of the U.S. Constitution does *not* contemplate a President (or other federal civil officer) impeached by the House having the option to avoid constitutional accountability (penalty) due to his or her term expiring or he or she resigning before a Senate impeachment trial begins and/or before a Senate guilty verdict is rendered. Instead Article II s. 4, it is here argued, is premised on the assumption that the impeachment trial will go forward irrespective of a resignation or the term of office of the House-impeached civil officer expiring before the Senate trial or verdict.[39] This is the proper inference, it is here held, in that Article II s. 4 was *not* designed with the intent to afford immunity to potential constitutional penalty (that is *mandatory removal* from office if still in office and *potential disqualification* of—where disqualification is considered—a House-impeached living *former* federal civil officer). This since the entire purpose of Article II s. 4 is to protect the Republic and to ensure that a civil officer who committed a constitutional offence(s) *while in office* is no longer a threat (this through mandatory removal from office if still in office and also

38 U.S. Constitution Article I s. 3: "Judgement in Cases of Impeachment shall not extend further than to removal from Office, and disqualification to hold and enjoy any Office of honor, Trust or profit under the United States."

39 There is precedent for an impeachment and Senate trial of a living former U.S. federal civil officer. William Belknap, a secretary of war was impeached in 1876 by the House *after he resigned*. Senate was convened as a constitutional court to hear the case and the Senate decided 37 to 29 that it had jurisdiction to hear the case. Belknap was, however, ultimately acquitted with the majority of the senators who voted for acquittal, citing their belief that Senate did not have jurisdiction to try Belknap (note that a majority of Senate had voted to convict but this was not the two-thirds necessary for a conviction). See NPR "There Is Precedent for Trying a Former Government Official, Established 145 Years Ago" (January 29, 2021) (author Domenico Montanaro).

disqualification from future office where there is a continuing threat posed by the then former civil officer). Given the purpose of Article II s. 4, the Framers would have been more than unlikely to have contemplated that the living former U.S. federal civil officer accused of constitutional offences *committed while in office* enjoys a bulwark against constitutional accountability by way of his or her being out of office (through resignation or expiry of his or her term) before the House adopts the impeachment article(s) by simple majority and/or before the Senate trial and/or verdict.[40] Thus, former President Trump, though his term had expired before the Senate impeachment trial, was, on this analysis, still properly subject to the constitutional accountability mechanism to determine the Senate's position on his guilt or innocence regarding the alleged constitutional offence in his case: Incitement to insurrection purportedly committed January 6, 2021, during his tenure as President.

A living *former* President (or other *former* federal civil officer) *convicted* by the U.S. Senate of an impeachable offence(s) committed *while in office* is one who will thus have been deemed for the record (i) to have been subject, based on that constitutional offence (or offences), to mandatory removal from holding office and (ii) a former civil officer who would have been factually removed *but for* the fact that he or she was already out of the office at the time of the Senate trial and/or conviction due to the date of the expiry of his or her term of office or as a result of his or her resignation. There is then no mechanism in the U.S. Constitution for the avoidance—through resignation or expiry of the accused's term of office—of an impeachment trial of a living former federal civil officer pursuant to articles of impeachment for constitutional offences that are accepted by the House. Nor is there a mechanism in the U.S. Constitution for the avoidance, *upon a Senate conviction*, of being considered for disqualification from holding future civil office where the remedy of disqualification from future civil office is a remedy articulated in the impeachment article(s) that were advanced by the House in the particular case.

Article II s. 4 of the U.S. Constitution, it is here argued, is *not* (contrary to the Defence view in the Trump second impeachment) *in effect* also "a statute of limitations" on when a Senate impeachment trial can be held and a conviction rendered. There is no constitutional requirement that the Senate impeachment trial and conviction occur when the House-impeached civil officer is still in office.[41] If Article II s. 4 was, in effect, a "statute of limitations" on the impeachment trial (to the time the House-impeached civil officer was still in office), then the discretionary disqualification remedy could never be applied to a former civil officer who would have been convicted but for the fact that he or she was already out of office before a Senate trial and/or Senate conviction could take place. Disqualification from future U.S. federal civil office is, however, essential

40 A delay in advancing the resolutions to the Senate may leave time for resignation or there may be an expiry of the term of office of the House-impeached civil officer in the interim as there was in Trump's second impeachment.

41 The offending conduct (the constitutional offences), however, must have occurred while the accused was still in office.

to protect the American public from any ongoing threat from, for example, a living *former* President guilty of an impeachable offence(s) while in office that betrayed the public trust and his or her Presidential oath. In fact, the Article I s. 3 bar, where imposed, to holding future federal civil office is applicable by constitutional design only to *former federal civil officers* found guilty by the Senate of an impeachable offence(s). Yet disqualification is *not* moderated by the mechanism which resulted in the former civil officer in question no longer being in office. Were it otherwise, the living former President or other living former federal civil officer who has in fact committed egregious constitutional offences while in office but who was out of office (through resignation or the expiry of his or her term) before the alleged time window for trial and conviction by the Senate could continue to be a threat to the democratic system by returning to U.S. federal civil office. Instead, Article I s. 3, through providing for possible disqualification from future federal civil office, protects against Senate-convicted living *former* civil officers (regardless of the mechanism of their not being in office at the time of conviction) who might otherwise be a threat if they regained power. This is only possible since Article II s. 4 is not a statute of limitations on House impeachment or a Senate impeachment trial of living former federal civil officers.

In sum then, the in effect, 'statute of limitations' interpretation of U.S. Constitution Article II s. 4 proffered by the Defence in the Trump second impeachment case would render only those Presidents (or other civil officers) convicted of constitutional offences through an impeachment trial held while he or she was still in federal civil office subject to disqualification from future office. Those living former presidents who may have committed high crimes and misdemeanours—*including even potentially treason*—but who left office before an impeachment trial and/or Senate guilty verdict (due to expiry of the term or resignation) would be immune to disqualification from future office. The erroneous (on the view here) Defence interpretation of the Article II s. 4 "minimum mandatory penalty" upon Senate conviction as, in essence, a "statute of limitation" would prevent disqualification for living *former* civil officers who have committed constitutional offences covered under Article II s. 4 but who were out of office before the Senate verdict was rendered. That would greatly diminish the protection the Framers intended through their affording, by way of Article I s. 3, a discretionary disqualification remedy as applicable to those convicted as living *former* U.S. federal civil officers of constitutional offences committed while in office.

## On Whether the Criminal Process Is a Substitute for the Impeachment of a Living Former President Out of Office Before a Senate Impeachment Verdict Can Be Rendered

On the analysis here, it is no answer to say that the criminal justice process is the proper and only available venue for achieving accountability for constitutional offences where the accused is a former federal civil officer whose term expired or who resigned before he or she could be convicted of an impeachable offence(s) and removed from office. The wording of Article I s. 3 of the U.S. Constitution itself indicates that this is incorrect. Article I s. 3 states

> Judgement in Cases of Impeachment ***shall not extend further than to removal from Office, and disqualification*** to hold or enjoy any Office of honor, Trust or Profit under the United States: ***but the Party convicted shall nonetheless be liable*** and subject to Indictment, Trial, Judgment and Punishment, according to Law.[42]

The wording thus indicates that a Senate conviction on impeachment is not equivalent to conviction on trial in the judicial system (If that were the case, then "Judgement in Cases of Impeachment" would in fact "extend further than to removal from Office, and disqualification"). Rather, Article I s. 3 makes it clear that in the proper case, a Party convicted of impeachable offences is ***not precluded*** from liability under the criminal code and hence not precluded either from potential indictment and punishment if convicted of a crime(s) (where the constitutional offence or offences overlap with a codified crime(s)).

Arguably, the penalty under Article I s. 3 for constitutional offences does not extend to imprisonment in part since the Framers considered that a legislative trial may not always offer the same full array of basic necessary due process and fairness protections guaranteed (theoretically at least) in a criminal trial in the judicial system. An additional reason may be that, contrary to the Defence position in the Trump second impeachment, not all constitutional offences worthy of impeachment are necessarily crimes. Consider in this regard also that only one constitutional offence is actually defined in the U.S. Constitution and that is "treason." Thus, arguably many constitutional impeachable offences may not have analogues in the criminal code or at least not substantively comparable analogues. Treason as it is set out in the U.S. Constitution is a high crime defined substantively and as to procedural requirements at Article III s. 3 and with a specified associated constitutional remedy set out at Article II s. 4.[43] The constitutional remedy for treason is limited to removal and disqualification while the federal treason statute, 18 U.S.C. § 2381[44] has a more expansive penalty range.[45]

42 Article I s. 3 of the U.S. Constitution.

43 Article III s. 3 U.S. Constitution: "Treason against the United States, shall consist only of levying War against them, or in adhering to their Enemies, giving them Aid and Comfort. No Person shall be convicted of Treason unless on the Testimony of two Witnesses to the same overt Act, or on Confession in open Court."

44 Legal Information Institute (Cornell University)18 U.S. Code § 2381—Treason:

> Whoever, owing allegiance to the United States, levies war against them or adheres to their enemies, giving them aid and comfort within the United States or elsewhere, is guilty of treason and shall suffer death, or shall be imprisoned not less than five years and fined under this title but not less than $10,000; and shall be incapable of holding any office under the United States.

45 18 U.S.C. § 2381.

Conviction through the criminal justice system pertains to violation of the criminal code while impeachment pertains to the violation of the Constitution and the oath of office. Each process serves a different purpose[46] and has a different range of penalties, and it is for that reason also, it is here contended, that while impeachment does not preclude criminal prosecution, the latter cannot be a substitute for the former.[47]

In the second impeachment case brought against former President Donald J. Trump, incitement of insurrection was charged by the House. The charge was brought against the former President as articulated in the impeachment article as a *constitutional offence* and not a criminal offence.[48] The standards of proof required, rules for conduct of the trial, purpose etc. are different in each venue—the judicial versus legislative trial forum. It is essential to note on this point that the Constitution does not define the *constitutional crime* of "insurrection" or "incitement to insurrection" nor does it set out the elements of those crimes. Therefore, how specific facts in a particular case may be construed by a jury in a criminal trial considering the same charge(s) may be quite different from how the same facts will be construed by senators acting as jurors in an impeachment trial. Thus, the same outcome in terms of a finding of guilt versus innocence on incitement to insurrection is not guaranteed on the same facts in a criminal proceeding versus a Senate impeachment proceeding. Given the foregoing, it is clear that accountability via impeachment versus a criminal justice process for "incitement to insurrection" cannot be equated nor ensured under either mechanism. It has here been argued nevertheless that both mechanisms (trial by legislative and judicial process) are available also as to constitutional offences committed by a former President where the constitutional offence is also articulated as a criminal offence in the federal and/or relevant State criminal code.

Those who argue that a U.S. living *former* civil officer cannot be subjected to an impeachment trial maintain that the judicial criminal process offers the appropriate remedial mechanism in such a case. The Aaron Burr case is an example of turning to the criminal courts for accountability of a former civil officer. That case involved a *former* U.S. federal civil officer—a former U.S.

46 Impeachment is more a preventive measure than punitive while the criminal process is designed both to protect the public and to penalize.

47 In conviction for treason through an impeachment, the Constitution at Article III s. 3 *bars* a Bill of Attainder that would deprive the heirs of the impeached convicted treasonous Party from collecting a fee for the sale of the property upon that convicted Party's death or otherwise collecting inheritance but not including any title under the United States "only a life estate terminating with the death of the offender could be sold." (Constitution Annotated Article III, Section 3, Clause 2: Punishment of Treason Clause).

48 Legal Information Institute (Cornell University) 18 U.S. Code § 2383—Rebellion or insurrection (criminal law definition): "Whoever incites, sets on foot, assists, or engages in any rebellion or insurrection against the authority of the United States or the laws thereof, or gives aid or comfort thereto, shall be fined under this title or imprisoned not more than ten years, or both; and shall be incapable of holding any office under the United States."

Vice-President (1801–1805)—tried in *a criminal court* for treason.[49] The trial was presided over by then Chief Justice of the U.S. Supreme Court John Marshall, who was at the time also a federal judge for the U.S. Circuit Court for Virginia.[50] Burr was acquitted in that the facts proffered by the Prosecution did not fulfill the elements for treason as set out in Article III s. 3 mirrored in the federal criminal code.[51] ("Marshall acquitted Burr on the ground that acts of treason against the United States by definition require the existence of a state of war (Article III, Section 3 of the U.S. Constitution)"[52] which was not the case at the time Burr's alleged constitutional offence/crime occurred. Though a trial on treason in Burr's case was not conducted in the Senate, that fact cannot, on the analysis here, be taken as proof of the proposition that an impeachment trial would have, *on account of his being a former civil officer*, been constitutionally precluded. As the case involved treason and treason is ***defined*** in mirrored fashion in the Constitution and the U.S. criminal code, this was a rare instance where one could reasonably expect that the outcome of the trial in either proceeding should have been the same as to a finding of guilt or innocence assuming due process prevailed. However, in most instances, the constitutional offence is not defined in the Constitution and thus not mirrored in the U.S. criminal code as an offence defined nor as to the stipulated elements of the offence.

## Recap Concerning Disqualification of a Living Former Civil Officer and the Question Whether Such Is a Bill of Attainder

To recap then, the notion that there is a "statute of limitations" in essence on when an impeachment trial can be held, on the view here, respectfully, is the erroneous inference of the Defence in the Trump second impeachment. That inference was (on this current analysis) incorrectly drawn by the Defence from the "mandatory minimum penalty" of "removal" upon conviction of a sitting President or other sitting civil officer for an impeachable offence. What amounts

49 It is open to debate why the criminal court venue was chosen for the Burr trial on treason. It may be that some wanted to see Burr in prison by any means possible (an outcome that constitutionally cannot flow from an impeachment trial). This given that some felt Burr was responsible for a wrongful death—that of Alexander Hamilton whom Burr had shot in a duel (See National Constitution Centre: Aaron Burr's trial and the Constitution's treason clause (September 1, 2020, by Scott Bomboy).

50 See National Constitution Centre Aaron Burr's trial and the constitution's treason clause (September 1, 2020, by Scott Bomboy). Note also that at the time of the Burr criminal trial, "circuit courts had original jurisdiction to try treason cases" (see Editors of Encyclopedia Britannica, Encyclopedia Britannica, Aaron Burr, Vice-President of the United States).

51 Constitution Annotated, U.S. Constitution Article III s. 3 Clause 1: "Treason against the United States, shall consist only in levying War against them, or in adhering to their Enemies, giving them Aid and Comfort. No Person shall be convicted of Treason unless on the testimony of two Witnesses to the same overt Act, or on Confession in open Court."

52 See Editors of Encyclopedia Britannica, Encyclopedia Britannica, Aaron Burr, Vice-President of the United States.

to the setting out of a ***minimum mandatory penalty*** (at Article II s. 4) for a convicted sitting civil officer does ***not***, however, preclude the Senate (i) determining whether a living ***former President*** or other living former civil officer met the criteria for conviction on an impeachment article(s) relating to the constitutional offence(s) alleged to have occurred during his or her time in office and (ii) imposing upon Senate conviction the allowable penalty available in that case of disqualification from future civil office. Put differently, Article II s. 4 is ***not*** a limitation imposing a bar on an impeachment trial by the Senate of a living ***former*** President ***or*** living ***former*** other civil officer but rather a limitation setting a bar on a remedy less than removal of a current President or sitting other civil officer found guilty by the Senate of the impeachment article(s) charged. Article II s. 4 ***does not speak to*** the issue of the minimum penalty for a living former President or other living former civil officer convicted through the impeachment process while out of office—Article I s. 3 instead does so in providing for the discretionary remedy of disqualification from holding future office.

Recall that the discretionary application of disqualification is ***always*** in respect to a former civil officer, that is, for example, a living former President, not a sitting President. Article II s. 4 (a minimum mandatory penalty) does not set out or speak to any requirement as to when the Senate ***conviction*** for impeachable constitutional offences must have occurred, that is during the President's (or other civil officer's) term or after. Nor does Article I s. 3 (stipulating the maximum penalty upon conviction through impeachment for constitutional offences) condition disqualification from future office upon a Senate conviction that occurred during the former civil officer's term of office. Thus, a living former President whose term expired or who resigned before the Senate impeachment conviction verdict was rendered would still be subject to potential disqualification upon conviction through a Senate (legislative) impeachment trial. Furthermore, the disqualification mechanism in an impeachment trial is a separate penalty process from removal with a different required Senate vote (a simple majority vote of the Senate is required for disqualification from future U.S. civil office compared to the two-thirds Senate vote required to convict on impeachable offences and, where the convicted is still in office, then to immediately remove him or her from current office).

One can reasonably argue that a Senate conviction in an impeachment context is in U.S. constitutional law in effect legally equivalent to a removal since no separate vote on removal is required upon conviction.[53] Hence, by convicting a living ***former*** President, the Senate is essentially retrospectively deeming that Party to have been legally eligible for factual removal had she or he still been in office. Furthermore,

53 U.S. Constitution Article II s. 4: "The President, Vice President and all civil Officers of the United States, shall be removed from Office on Impeachment for, and Conviction of, Treason, Bribery, or other high Crimes and Misdemeanors." The point of Article II s. 4 is that where the Senate-convicted impeached civil officer is still in office, removal is mandatory and automatic requiring no separate vote (See the Committee on the Judiciary Impeachment Resolution Regarding Judge Halsted Ritter at p. 2245).

since disqualification is discretionary and can only be applied to a living former President or other former federal civil officer (one convicted of an impeachable offence), removal and disqualification occur at different times for the convicted Party in the penalty phase. Since disqualification is applicable as a discretionary impeachment penalty to *any living former President convicted of an impeachable offence*, there is no requirement that the former President was convicted while in office as opposed to after or that he or she be out of office then due to removal. The limitation on maximum penalties (set out in Article I s. 3) does not specify how a convicted President should have left office to be susceptible to disqualification or require that both penalties (removal and disqualification) *must* be imposed.

Since disqualification is discretionary, it is clear that the several possible iterations of the penalties include (i) factual removal alone where the President is a sitting President when convicted of the constitutional offence(s); (ii) removal from office where the President is a sitting President when convicted of the constitutional offence(s) and then, as a former President, disqualification from future office; or (iii) disqualification alone where, at the time of the Senate conviction, the former President is no longer in office due to expiry of his or her term or resignation. Article II s. 4 sets out the minimum mandatory sentence available upon conviction of a sitting federal civil officer for bribery, treason and/or other high crimes and misdemeanours *not* a temporal requirement for when an impeachment trial may be held, and a conviction result. As explained here, the available discretionary constitutional remedy of disqualification thus may also be applied to a living former President who was already out of office at the time of the Senate conviction for an impeachable offence(s). Were it otherwise, the Framers would have addressed the current threat posed by a sitting federal civil officer who had committed constitutional offences in office but not any ongoing such threats he or she might pose where convicted by the Senate while out of office.

That the Framers intended the protection of the democracy through the impeachment clauses of the U.S. Constitution to extend also to protection from the influence, sway and political power of living former Presidents who committed constitutional offences while in office but were convicted by the Senate while out of office is evidenced by the Constitution's disqualification clause. Indeed, a conviction in a Senate impeachment trial of a *former* President who was out of office before he or she could be convicted allows for establishing the record as to (i) when and how the impeachable constitutional offences occurred and (ii) given the guilty verdict, also a record that had the impeachment trial and guilty verdict taken place during the President's term, he or she would have been *ineligible* to complete the remainder of his or her term.

The conviction of a living *former* federal civil officer through the Senate impeachment trial serves the important purpose of providing the basis for the consideration of and potential discretionary application of a *disqualification* of that former civil officer,[54] that is former President from holding any federal office

54 As that term "civil officer" is understood in the U.S. Constitution.

of public trust in future. Indeed, a ***disqualification***—barring the convicted former President under Article I s. 3 of the U.S. Constitution[55] from holding "any Office of honor, Trust or Profit under the United States"[56] such as the Presidency in future—is a *pre-emptive* impeachment and conviction of sorts. That disqualification, where imposed, is grounded on the Senate-assessed threat that the Senate convicted former civil officer, that is former U.S. President, continues to pose to the Republic. Disqualification, on the analysis here, is a potential remedy in regard to a living *former* civil officer, that is, for example, a former U.S. President convicted and removed from office *or* a former U.S. President tried by the Senate and found guilty by the Senate while out of office.

The pre-emptive barring from future civil office through the Constitution's disqualification clause of a Senate-convicted living former civil officer (regardless whether that convicted Party was removed or already out of office at the time of the Senate conviction) is itself arguably, in a sense at least, a *legal fiction.* This in that it is a remedy for ***anticipated future harms that have not yet occurred and may never have occurred and for harms expected to occur while occupying an office not yet assumed.*** Disqualification is a remedy based on an ongoing risk to democracy assessed to be posed by the former civil officer, that is, for example, a living former President and one therefore justifiably to be avoided even if, in the moment, theoretical.

At the time the *former* President is ***disqualified*** from holding a future U.S. federal civil office (through a Senate conviction on impeachment and the discretionary application of the constitutional remedy/penalty of disqualification), he or she is *in every case* already a private citizen.[57] Thus, the Constitution contemplates that constitutional remedies can be applied to *former* civil officers and this must include Senate conviction as well in that the latter is in itself a level of accountability. Once convicted on the impeachment article(s), it is irrelevant to the discretionary application of disqualification how the former President came to be out of office; through removal, expiry of the Presidential term or resignation. The Constitution does *not* specify that a former President (or other former civil officer) must be out of office due to removal to be considered for disqualification. Rather, the Constitution leaves open the possibility that disqualification may, where the Senate deems constitutionally appropriate, be a penalty applied to a living former President or other former civil officer convicted through a Senate impeachment trial (Article I s. 3; the maximum penalty clause). In any case, as discussed, a Senate conviction in an impeachment case is constitutionally equivalent to removal in law if not

55 Article I, s. 3 U.S. Constitution "Judgment in Cases of Impeachment shall not extend further than to removal from Office, and disqualification to hold and enjoy any Office of honor, Trust or Profit under the United States; but the Party convicted shall nevertheless be liable and subject to Indictment, Trial, Judgment and Punishment, according to Law."

56 Article I, s. 3 U.S. Constitution.

57 Upon convictions by the Senate, the convicted Party would be removed from office per Article II s. 4.

necessarily so factually.[58] This since no separate vote is required for removal upon Senate conviction by a two-thirds Senate vote. The Senate conviction of a *former* civil officer, as here previously explained, is a declaration of that Party having been removable constitutionally but not factually due to the practical circumstances leaving then the possibility of disqualification as also the constitutional remedy still available. Were a separate vote to remove be required upon Senate conviction, it would create, at a minimum, a procedural conundrum in the case of a Senate-convicted living *former* civil officer in an impeachment case, a procedural complexity that, however, in fact does not exist.

## *Disqualification as Always Only Applicable to Former Civil Officers*

A Senate impeachment trial of a former civil officer no longer in office (due to the expiry of the term of office or resignation) where the accused is convicted establishes that that Party had been ineligible to continue to hold that office subsequent to committing the impeachable offence(s) while in office. Such a finding is akin, as here previously discussed, to a declaration marking a retrospective factual removal as a legal fiction but one that allows for consideration of the live issue of disqualification from holding future civil office. The convicted, that is former U.S. President then can be constitutionally pre-emptively barred from a future federal civil office through a finding of guilt through the Senate impeachment trial process and the discretionary imposition of disqualification.

It is important to recognize that disqualification—when it is imposed—applies *always* only to the convicted Party *who is out of federal civil office* (now a private citizen having been found guilty of an impeachable offence and removed if sitting or found *to have been removable* though now already out of office due to expiry of the term of office or resignation). *The disqualification remedy does not in any way pertain to the Party's conduct as a private citizen though in practice it is always applied to a private citizen no longer in federal civil office who was convicted in an impeachment trial for constitutional offence(s) committed while in office.* Thus, on the respectful analysis here, it is entirely misleading to contend, as the Defence did in Trump's second impeachment, that (i) the former President, Donald J. Trump, as a private citizen was immune from the impeachment process for alleged impeachable conduct during his time in office and that (ii) the application of the penalty of disqualification upon conviction by the Senate would in his case constitute a Bill of Attainder:

> The 45th President believes and therefore avers that as a private citizen, the Senate has no jurisdiction over his ability to hold office and for the Senate to take action on this averment would constitute a Bill of Attainder in violation of Art. I, Sec. 9. Cl. 3 of the United States Constitution.[59]

58 As when the civil officer is already out of office due to expiry of the term of office or resignation before the Senate guilty verdict is rendered.

59 In the Senate of the United States of America, Answer of President Donald John Trump, 45th President of the United States, to Article I:Incitement of Insurrection at p. 2.

Discretionary disqualification,[60] per the Framers' design, when imposed is then always applied to a *former civil officer* not one currently sitting in office.[61] This fact is consistent with the view that disqualification of a former President (or other former civil officer) for impeachable offences committed while in office *was not considered by the Framers to be a Bill of Attainder* for private conduct. The Prosecution in the second impeachment trial of Donald J. Trump made the point thus that the trial of a former civil officer is not a Bill of Attainder:

> The trial of a former official for abuses he committed as an official—arising from an impeachment that also occurred while he was in office—*poses no risk of subjecting private parties to punitive legislative action targeting their private conduct* (emphasis added).[62]

The Prosecution, however, on the view here, failed to bolster its argument of the constitutional legitimacy of a Senate trial of a living *former* civil officer (here one impeached by the House while still in office) by highlighting the fact that the U.S. Constitution contemplates such a possibility through its very design. This in that the Constitution provides for (i) disqualification being always of an impeached Senate-convicted *former* civil officer (one no longer in office), (ii) the discretionary call for a vote on disqualification being initiated only after Senate conviction and automatic removal from office where the Party is not already out of office through expiry of the term of office or resignation and (iii) applicability of disqualification to Senate-convicted living former civil officers regardless of the mechanism of their not being in office (to the latter point, recall that a separate vote on factual removal upon Senate-conviction is not required as the conviction itself establishes the ineligibility to continue to hold the office if still in office).

### *On the Issue of Criminality and Bills of Attainder*

It is here argued that the second impeachment of Donald J. Trump as a former U.S. President did *not* (contrary to the contention of the Defence) amount to a Bill of Attainder because (i) Bills of Attainder most often relied on *ex post facto* law that criminalized a high offence that was not criminal at the time it was committed and (ii) Bills of Attainder imposed punishment by the legislature for the criminalized conduct rather than through a judicial criminal process.[63] For-

60 Disqualification is a discretionary penalty upon Senate conviction for impeachable constitutional offences committed while in office (see Article I s. 3 U.S. Constitution).

61 It would make no legal or logical sense to remedy any future threat to democracy posed by the Senate-convicted civil officer while that convicted civil officer still posed a current threat in office. Hence, Senate conviction in an impeachment case is synonymous with removal from office where the convicted party is still in office at the time of the conviction.

62 In the Senate of the United States of America, Trial Memorandum of the House of Representatives in the Impeachment Trial of President Donald J. Trump (February 2, 2021) at p. 70.

63 Compare Black, C.L. and Bobbitt, P. *Impeachment a Handbook*, New Edition (New Haven: Yale University Press, 1974) at p. 29.

mer President Trump's second impeachment involved a single charge of alleged "incitement to insurrection" as a *constitutional offence* constituting a high crime and misdemeanour. Furthermore, incitement to insurrection was not an *ex post facto* criminal offence at the time of President Trump's second impeachment trial. In any case, the second Senate trial of Donald J. Trump, 45th President of the United States, was not directed to considering any statutory crime(s), and the article of impeachment therefore did not set out a criminal offence nor its elements under the U.S. federal Criminal Code nor under any State Criminal Code. The Prosecution in the second impeachment of Donald J. Trump (in the following excerpt from the Prosecution trial memorandum) distinguished its task as different from that of establishing criminality by the former President during his tenure of office thus:

> The Constitution authorizes impeachment and conviction for "high Crimes and Misdemeanors." As Alexander Hamilton explained in the Federalist Papers, impeachable offenses "are of a nature which may with peculiar propriety be denominated POLITICAL, as they relate chiefly to injuries done immediately to the society itself. Therefore, whether President Trump's conduct violated the criminal law is a question for prosecutors and courts; "offenses against the Constitution are different than offenses against the criminal code (emphasis in the original)."[64]

Hence, the second impeachment of Donald J. Trump, 45th President of the United States did *not*, it is here argued, involve a verdict on a criminal offence based on *ex post facto* or then current criminal law rendered through a legislative non-judicial trial. Thus, there was also for that reason no violation of the U.S. Constitution's prohibition against Bills of Attainder: "No Bill of Attainder or ex post facto Law shall be passed."[65]

In respect of a Senate trial concerning a constitutional offence (as was former President Trump's second impeachment trial), the Framers themselves adjudged that the Constitution and the Senate rules formulated and applied by the Senate trying the case would ensure adequate due process in the normal course. Hence it is, on the view here, misleading to first erroneously classify or equate the second impeachment charge against former President Trump with a "Bill of Attainder" and from that incorrect underlying proposition then maintain that he was not afforded due process. Former President Trump was in fact accorded due process through the relevant constitutional provisions and agreed upon Senate rules for the impeachment trial (trial rules agreed to by the Democrat majority and Republican minority Senate leaders). Further, not only was former President Trump (through his impeachment trial counsel) able to give what appears, in his estimation, to have been a full and

64 In the Senate of the United States of America, Trial Memorandum of the House of Representatives in the Impeachment Trial of President Donald J. Trump, February 2, 2021, at p. 43.
65 Constitution Annotated; U.S. Constitution Article I s. 9 Clause 3.

adequate exonerating answer to the Prosecution case but he had been afforded the opportunity to testify under oath at the impeachment trial, an opportunity he declined to seize.

## Constitutional Offences and the Misnomer Termed "Late Impeachments"

### *The Relevance of the Disqualification Remedy as Applied to a Living Former President*

The Prosecution in the second impeachment of Donald J. Trump, 45th President of the United States, alleged he, while in office, violated the Fourteenth Amendment s. 3, which states:

> No person shall . . . hold any office . . . under the United States . . . who, having previously taken an oath . . . as an officer of the United States . . . to support the Constitution of the United States, shall have engaged in insurrection or rebellion against the same, or given aid or comfort to the enemies thereof. But Congress may by a vote of two-thirds of each House, remove such disability.[66]

The constitutional remedy that was requested, had the former President, Donald J. Trump, been found guilty of the alleged constitutional offence charged ("incitement to insurrection" committed while in Presidential office) was "disqualification." Given that disqualification is a pre-emptive barring from holding future civil office applied to a former civil officer, the judgement of disqualification is a constitutional remedy in itself (akin to declaratory relief in civil court, as here previously discussed) and requires no further concrete real world action. Since, furthermore, disqualification of a living *former* U.S. President (or other U.S. *former* federal civil officer) convicted of high crimes and misdemeanours committed while in office is a live issue also in such cases, it is, on the respectful view here, erroneous to refer to such impeachments as "late impeachments." A remedy (potential disqualification) still available renders the impeachment of a living former civil officer who resigned or whose term expired before the Senate guilty verdict was rendered still timely in the circumstance and not a "late impeachment." That the President was "both factually and legally a private citizen"[67] at the time of the Senate second impeachment proceedings regarding jurisdiction and on the merits is irrelevant to the issue of "timeliness" since the U.S. Constitution contemplates disqualification considerations to be applied to Senate-convicted *former* civil officers.

66 U.S. Constitution Fourteenth Amendment s. 3.

67 In the Proceedings before the United States Senate Re the Impeachment of Former President Donald J. Trump, Trial Memorandum of Donald J. Trump, 45th President of the United States of America (February 8, 2021) at p. 18.

### *Due Process Considerations and the Notion of a So-Called Late Impeachment*

The former President, having been accused of an impeachable offence committed while in office, was entitled to a Senate trial as a matter of due process. The Senate had no jurisdiction, both under the U.S. Constitution and current Senate rules, to decline to consider the article of impeachment once delivered by the House and exhibited to the Senate as it was in Mr. Trump's second impeachment process. Of course, there may be motions to attempt to block the impeachment trial but even then, the article(s) of impeachment is being addressed by the Senate. Since the Senate cannot constitutionally simply ignore the article of impeachment exhibited to it by the House, the impeachment process also in that regard cannot be considered late.

### *Controversy About Textual Interpretation of Article II s. 4 of the U.S. Constitution*

In its trial brief, the Defence for former President Trump in the second impeachment case challenges the Prosecution's alleged textual interpretation of the term "the President" as it appears in Article II s. 4 of the U.S. Constitution. That Article sets out that "*The President*, Vice President and all civil Officers of the United States, shall be removed from Office on Impeachment for, and Conviction of, Treason, Bribery, or other high Crimes and Misdemeanors (emphasis added)."[68] The Defence argued that the Prosecution, with "no authority," was attempting to "legally redefine "former Presidents" as "Presidents" for some constitutional provisions and not others":[69]

> Mr. Trump has held the Office of the President of the United States; his service was not terminated by removal pursuant to section 4 of article II of the Constitution (and even if this sham late impeachment were to result in a conviction, he *still* would not have been thus removed). . . . He is therefore *legally* in the separate category of "former President" and is statutorily *not* the President of the United States referred to in the Impeachment Clauses of the Constitution. . . . The text of the Constitution simply does not contain language allowing for the impeachment of a former President and does not address "late impeachments," i.e., an impeachment of a former officer (emphasis in the original).[70]

On the analysis of the current author, in contrast, the Prosecution was not attempting to redefine the meaning of "the President" in Article II s. 4 but

68 U.S. Const. Article II, s. 4.

69 In the Proceedings before the United States Senate Re the Impeachment of Former President Donald J. Trump, Trial Memorandum of Donald J. Trump, 45th President of the United States of America (February 8, 2021) at p. 18.

70 In the Proceedings before the United States Senate Re the Impeachment of Former President Donald J. Trump, Trial Memorandum of Donald J. Trump, 45th President of the United States of America (February 8, 2021) at pp. 19–20.

rather argue that living *former* Presidents are subject to impeachment for high crimes and misdemeanours committed while in their civil office and, upon Senate conviction, can be considered for disqualification. This author has addressed here previously the issue of a Senate conviction of a former President whose term had expired or who resigned before that Senate verdict was rendered. A Senate conviction in such a case is akin to a *declaration of the removability* of that President had he or she still been in office upon conviction/a removal in law then though not factually. This then sets the precondition (under Article II s. 4) allowing for a possible discretionary imposition of disqualification (per Article I s. 3) from holding future civil office as a live issue.

Since the U.S. Constitution provides for discretionary imposition *specifically as upon former civil officers* of disqualification from holding future office, the conviction of former civil officers for impeachable offences committed while in office arguably was contemplated by the Framers. This view is bolstered by the fact that being removed *as a factual matter* from civil office is *not* a precondition for disqualification. Rather, the requirement is that the Senate-convicted Party is out of office when Senate deliberations about possible disqualification occur. That is the U.S. Constitution does *not* stipulate at Article I s. 3 that disqualification can only be imposed on former civil officers (such as a former U.S President) convicted of impeachable offences committed while in office if that Party were out of office due to removal. Disqualification then is a safeguard against any significant ongoing threats to democracy posed by impeached and Senate-convicted former civil officers regardless of the circumstances of their being out of office (removal, expiry of the term of office or resignation).

The Defence in the Trump second impeachment argued that the phrase "former President" is "actually a term of art with legal ramifications, as, in the Defence view, evidenced by the Former Presidents Act (3 U.S.C. § 102 note)."[71] Ironically, the federal statute known as "The Former Presidents Act," *for the purposes of that particular statute*, relies on a *legal fiction*. The latter legal fiction is one that defines "former President of the United States" as a category that includes *only* previous U.S. Presidents "whose service in such office shall have terminated *other than by removal pursuant to section 4 of Article II of the Constitution of the United States of America* (emphasis added)."[72] Clearly, it is the case that *factually* former Presidents of the United States of America *would include* also any who have been impeached and removed from office upon Senate conviction. It is evident that the "Former Presidents Act" seeks to exclude from eligibility for a lifetime monetary allowance as "former U.S. President" those Presidents who have been found guilty by the Senate of violating their oath of office while in office and therefore were impeached and if still in office removed. It would be contrary to the intent of the federal statute in question to provide a lifetime allowance to a former U.S. President who was found by the

71 Trial Memorandum of Donald J. Trump, 45th President of the United States of America (February 8, 2021) at p. 19.

72 Former Presidents Act (3 U.S.C. § 102 note) (f)(2).

Senate to have violated his or her oath of office having committed an impeachable offence while in office. The latter would be the case, however, regardless of whether the Senate judgement rendering a verdict of guilty as to the impeachment articles was rendered while the accused was still in Presidential office or after he or she no longer occupied that office (the latter due either to the expiry of the term of office or resignation).

In interpreting a statute, the intent of the statute must be considered. In this case, the "Former Presidents Act" was designed to *preclude* those former Presidents who had been *found guilty by the Senate* of constitutional offences while in office from receiving a lifetime allowance when out of office. This then would prevent such a former civil officer in essence being rewarded for his or her constitutional offence(s). Thus, the current author would dispute the Defence's notion that (i) former President Trump would have to be considered a "former President" as defined under the "Former Presidents Act" (hence eligible for the lifetime allowance) as he was no longer in office and (ii) he would be eligible for the lifetime allowance regardless of whether he had been convicted by the Senate in his second impeachment trial or acquitted, as ultimately was the case, since he could not be factually removed in any case (already being out of office due to expiry of his term).[73] If convicted by the Senate, former President Trump would have been (i) deemed to have been removable from his office while he was in office on the facts and the Constitution (Article II s. 4) and to have been so removed but for the expiry of his term and (ii) would have been still subject to potential disqualification from future U.S. federal civil office per Article I s. 3. Certainly, had he been convicted by the Senate in his second impeachment trial, and especially if also disqualified, it is difficult to envision Donald J. Trump not being considered *excluded* from the category of "former Presidents" for the purposes of "The Former Presidents Act" and a lifetime allowance intended in part to reward the faithful service to the Constitution of a former President.

To recap then, it is here argued that though a conviction by the Senate in this second impeachment proceeding would not have removed former President Trump *factually* (since his term had already expired), it would have, however, essentially done so in law. This given that the Senate would, through a conviction, have rendered a verdict that (i) Mr. Trump's conduct as President of the United States while in office (per the specific acts in question articulated in the

73 "[E]ven if this sham late impeachment were to result in a conviction, he *still* would not have been thus removed and he does not currently hold such office. He is therefore legally in the separate category of 'former President' and is statutorily not the President of the United States referred to in the Impeachment Clauses of the Constitution (emphasis in the original text)." In the Proceedings before the United States Senate Re the Impeachment of Former President Donald J. Trump, Trial Memorandum of Donald J. Trump, 45th President of the United States of America (February 8, 2021) at p. 19. Hence, Trump would still, on the Defence analysis, erroneous on the view here, be a 'former President' *as defined under the 'Former Presidents Act'* even if he had been convicted by the Senate in the second impeachment trial post expiry of his term of office."

impeachment article of January 13, 2021) met the criteria for impeachment pursuant to his committing what the Senate would have then determined to be a high crime and misdemeanour and (ii) in that Senate conviction scenario (which did not occur), Mr. Trump's would have been deemed to have been constitutionally ineligible to continue in office had he still been a sitting President at the time. These findings would have constituted a form of *declaratory relief* (i) setting out retrospectively the former President's eligibility for mandatory removal from office during the waning days of his presidency, and the constitutional offences held to have occurred in January 2021 the last month of the first term[74] as well as (ii) established the constitutional basis for considering disqualification from holding future U.S. civil office.

### On the Defence View of the Meaning of "the" President

The Defence avers (erroneously on the view here) that the term "the President" in Article II s. 4 of the U.S. Constitution refers exclusively to the current President—the sitting President as it allegedly does in every other clause of the Constitution where it appears. The Defence on this point argues that "This provision does not state 'a' President or 'a former' President, it unequivocally states 'the' President. And when one refers to 'the' President, the reference is clearly to the current President."[75] On the view here, however, the use of the article "the" in Article II s. 4 of the U.S. Constitution can be intended to refer to the particular President in question—that is the President who has been convicted of an impeachable offence.[76] Hence, "the" in the phrase "[t]he President, Vice President and all Civil Officers of the United States, shall be removed from Office on Impeachment . . ." in Article II s. 4 of the U.S. Constitution references the particular President, the particular Vice-President or specific other civil officer who is subject to removal if still in office. Article II s. 4 simply makes clear that an impeached and Senate-convicted civil officer must be removed from office where not already out of office as a minimum mandatory penalty and constitutional remedy for the sake of the integrity of the democracy. Article II s. 4 does *not* accord immunity to former civil officers found guilty by the Senate of impeachable offences committed while in office simply because they are out of office when the Senate guilty verdict is rendered. It is in part for that reason that Article I s. 3 of the U.S. Constitution does *not* bar a disqualification remedy in the case of a Senate-convicted former civil officer who was out of office when the guilty verdict was rendered.

74 Congress.Gov See the House Manager's January 13, 2021, article of impeachment H.Res.24.

75 In the Proceedings before the United States Senate Re the Impeachment of Former President Donald J. Trump, Trial Memorandum of Donald J. Trump, 45th President of the United States of America (February 8, 2021) at p. 19.

76 Stevenson, A. (Ed.), Elliot, J. and Jones, R. *Oxford English Dictionary*, 2nd Edition (Oxford: Oxford University Press, 2002).

### *Contentious Inferences From Who Presides Over the Impeachment Trial*

The Defence in Trump's second impeachment trial references Article I s. 3 of the Constitution, which reads in part:

> The Senate shall have the sole Power to try all Impeachments. . . . When the President of the United States is tried, the Chief Justice shall preside (emphasis added).[77]

The Defence *infers* from the fact that the Chief Justice of the United States Supreme Court did *not* preside over that second impeachment Senate trial that the *former President*, who did not hold the U.S. presidency at the time of the Senate second impeachment trial, was not and could not constitutionally be subject to a Senate impeachment trial. This Defence analysis oddly seems to suggest that who presides determines who amongst those civil officers accused of constitutional offences while in office may be subjected to an impeachment trial. However, Article I s. 3 of the Constitution upon which the Defence relies in making this argument begins with the proviso that "The Senate shall have the sole Power to try *all* impeachments (emphasis added)."[78] The Prosecution in part relies on (i) the word "all" to counter that this includes also impeachments of former Presidents and (ii) on the fact that the Senate makes the rules as to whether a living former President can be tried through its practice which does include the trials of former civil officers (though this second impeachment trial of Donald J. Trump was the first time a *former President* has been tried by the Senate). Where a *sitting President* is tried, the Chief Justice *must* preside while where a living *former* civil officer (including a *former* President) is tried, the President of the Senate may preside. That this is permitted is clear from the authority over the Senate rules for the trial that Article I s. 3 of the Constitution provides: "The Senate shall have the sole Power to try all Impeachments."[79]

## The Contentious Viability of a First Amendment Defence to Impeachment and the Implications for the Democratic Rule of Law

In this section, we will consider (regarding the second impeachment case against Donald J. Trump, 45th President of the United States) the Defence reliance, in part, on the First Amendment to argue that Mr. Trump's speech to a crowd near the Capitol on January 6, 2021, was "protected speech" and not an "incitement to insurrection." We will not concern ourselves, however, with whether the Trump January 6, 2021, speech was in fact an "incitement to insurrection" but,

77 U.S. Constitution Article I s. 3.
78 U.S. Constitution Article I s. 3.
79 U.S. Constitution Article I s. 3.

for the limited purpose here, with instead the implications of a First Amendment alleged bar to impeachment at least for purely inflammatory speech as the Trump Defence would have it. The Prosecution in the second Trump impeachment, in contrast, argues that:

> Most fundamentally, the First Amendment protects private citizens from the government; it does not protect government officials from accountability for their own abuses in office. Therefore, as scholars from across the political spectrum have recognized, the First Amendment does not apply at all to an impeachment proceeding. As one scholar writes,[80] "the First Amendment does not shrink the scope of the impeachment power or alter what conduct would fall within the terms of high crimes and misdemeanors (emphasis added)."[81]

On the analysis of the current author, to countenance a First Amendment defence to impeachment is to undercut the First Amendment rights of the American public as expressed through their House of Representatives by way of articles of impeachment. That is the First Amendment defence, if considered a viable one in an impeachment case, renders the articles of impeachment potentially ineffectual from the onset where the issue centres on the official's conduct through speech.

Recall that *constitutional offences* need not meet the standard of a criminal law (criminal code) definition nor meet the elements of a statutory crime.[82] Inquiring of senators in an impeachment context whether the impugned speech of the civil officer while in office was protected by the First Amendment would thus, in most instances, be akin to asking for the interpretation of a Rorschach inkblot. With such a defence (if accepted *even though not applicable for the reasons already discussed*), any contested speech—so long as two-thirds of the Senate are agreeable for whatever reason—may be deemed to have been "protected speech" even if, in practice, it posed and perhaps continues to pose a threat to the democratic rule of

80 Whittington, K.E. Is There a Free Speech Defense to an Impeachment? *Lawfare* (January 19, 2021). Cited in the Trial Memorandum of the House of Representatives in the Impeachment Trial of President Donald J. Trump (February 2, 2021) at p. 45. Whittington in the same Lawfare blog makes the point that the Senate can convict also for lawful behaviour that it deems yet to meet the criterial for High Crimes and Misdemeanors. Hence, the First Amendment defence will be of no avail in that circumstance, that is for a former civil officer impeached for *constitutional offences* committed while in office. Whittington thus makes the point that criminal liability and liability through impeachment are completely distinct and the one is not conditioned on the other.

81 In the Senate of the United States of America, Trial Memorandum of the House of Representatives in the Impeachment Trial of President Donald J. Trump (February 2, 2021) at p. 45.

82 Whittington also explains that "Violence is not a necessary predicate for impeaching officers for their speech, nor need speech be the proximate cause for violence to be condemnable through the mechanism of impeachment." (Whittington, K.E. Is There a Free Speech Defense to an Impeachment? *Lawfare* (January 19, 2021)). Thus, incitement to insurrection as a constitutional offence may be judged on a standard that is not entirely aligned with the criminal standard for establishing the offence under statute.

law. A First Amendment defence arguably could result in anti-democratic demagoguery that threatens the Republic being *erroneously* relegated at best to the category of "mere maladministration" rather than impeachable abuse of power that betrays the public trust and the impugned Party's oath of office. Absent a First Amendment defence in an impeachment case concerning speech that allegedly threatens the Republic, the civil officer at the centre of the impeachment trial is, on the analysis here, at least under a more stringent test for what constitutes speech that does not betray the public trust and the Office. In sum then, the First Amendment cannot constitutionally, it is here contended, be available in an impeachment trial context as a potential shield for high crimes or misdemeanours committed, at least in part, through speech which directly attacks and seriously undermines the democratic rule of law.

The question can be raised as to whether Donald J. Trump's January 6, 2021, speech to a crowd at the ellipse (a crowd that then largely advanced on the U.S. Capitol building with the intent to stop the counting of electoral college votes for U.S. President) was, if not a direct "incitement to insurrection," at a minimum, an attempt ironically (given the purported First Amendment shield for Trump's January 6, 2021, impugned speech argument advanced by the Defence) to interfere with the freedom of expression of the American public made manifest through the counting of the electoral college vote.

Since January 6, 2021, former President Trump has been the key focal point of an important First Amendment case but one, in the view of the current author, too often underestimated as to its broad consequence for the democratic rule of law and the role of the judiciary in upholding democratic values. That is the Trump Twitter case discussed in the next chapter.

## References

### *Literature*

Black, C.L. and Bobbitt, P. *Impeachment a Handbook*, New Edition (New Haven: Yale University Press, 1974).

Kelsen, H. Chapter 1 On the Theory of Juridic Fictions: With Special Consideration of Vaihinger's Philosophy of the As-If. In Maksymilian, Del Mar and Twining, William (Eds.) *Legal Fictions in Theory and Practice* (Berlin: Springer, 2015) pp. 3–29.

Maksymilian, Del Mar and Twining, William (Eds.). *Legal Fictions in Theory and Practice: Legal and Philosophy Library*, Volume 110 (Berlin: Springer, 2015).

### *Materials*

Congress.GOV Constitution Annotated ArtII.S4.1.1 Impeachment and Removal from Office: Overview) https://constitution.congress.gov/browse/essay/artII-S4-1-1/ALDE_00000282/ (accessed March 26, 2021).

Congress.Gov H.Res.24—Impeaching Donald John Trump, President of the United States, for High Crimes and Misdemeanors. 117th Congress (2021–2022) www.

congress.gov/bill/117th-congress/house-resolution/24/text (accessed March 25, 2021).

Congressional Research Service. *Mootness: An Explanation of the Justiciability Doctrine* (February 7, 2007) www.everycrsreport.com/reports/RS22599.html (accessed April 7, 2021).

Constitutional Law Scholars on Impeaching Former Officers (January 21, 2021) www.politico.com/f/?id=00000177-2646-de27-a5f7-3fe714ac0000 (accessed April 2, 2021).

Constitution Annotated; U.S. Constitution Article I s. 9 Clause 3 https://constitution.congress.gov/browse/article-1/section-9/ (accessed March 29, 2021).

Constitution Annotated; U.S. Constitution Article III, Section 3, Clause 2: Punishment of Treason Clause https://constitution.congress.gov/browse/essay/artIII-S3-C2-1/ALDE_00001227/ (accessed April 10, 2021).

Editors of Encyclopedia Britannica, Encyclopedia Britannica, Aaron Burr, Vice President of the United States www.britannica.com/biography/Aaron-Burr (accessed March 30, 2021).

Former Presidents Act (3 U.S.C. § 102 note), National Archives www.archives.gov/about/laws/former-Presidents.html (accessed March 28, 2021).

In the Proceedings before the United States Senate Re the Impeachment of Former President Donald J. Trump, Trial Memorandum of Donald J. Trump, 45th President of the United States of America (February 8, 2021) https://int.nyt.com/data/documenttools/trump-defense-impeachment-trial/3a17fbb266bf3bf5/full.pdf (accessed March 26, 2021).

In the Senate of the United States of America, Answer of the President Donald John Trump, 45th President of the United States, to Article I: Incitement of Insurrection (Defence Counsel: Bruce L. Castor and David Schoen (February 2, 2021) https://int.nyt.com/data/documenttools/trump-brief-defense-impeachment/bd873567d385cdcc/full.pdf (accessed March 26, 2021).

In the Senate of the United States of America, Trial Memorandum of the House of Representatives in the Impeachment Trial of President Donald J. Trump (February 2, 2021) https://judiciary.house.gov/uploadedfiles/house_trial_brief_final.pdf?utm_campaign=5706-519 (accessed April 13, 2021).

The Committee on the Judiciary Impeachment Resolution Regarding Judge Halsted Ritter https://www.govinfo.gov/content/pkg/GPO-HPREC-DESCHLERS-V3/pdf/GPO-HPREC-DESCHLERS-V3-5-5-5.pdf (accessed March 13, 2022).

Legal Information Institute (Cornell University) 18 U.S. Code § 2381—Treason (Criminal Law Definition) www.law.cornell.edu/uscode/text/18/2381 (accessed March 31, 2021).

Legal Information Institute (Cornell University) 18 U.S. Code § 2383—Rebellion or Insurrection (Criminal Law Definition) www.law.cornell.edu/uscode/text/18/2383 (accessed March 31, 2021).

Legal Information Institute (Cornell University) Declaratory Relief www.law.cornell.edu/wex/declaratory_relief#:~:text=Declaratory%20relief%20refers%20to%20a,of%20the%20controversy%20in%20issue (accessed March 26, 2021).

National Constitution Centre Aaron Burr's Trial and the Constitution's Treason Clause (September 1, 2020 by Scott Bomboy) https://constitutioncenter.org/blog/the-great-trial-that-tested-the-constitutions-treason-clause (accessed March 30, 2021).

Stevenson, A. (Ed.), Elliot, J. and Jones, R. *Oxford English Dictionary*, 2nd Edition (Oxford: Oxford University Press, 2002).

United States Senate: Impeachment Trial of William Belknap www.senate.gov/about/powers-procedures/impeachment/impeachment-belknap.htm (accessed April 2, 2021).

U.S. Constitution (The National Archives) www.archives.gov/founding-docs/constitution-transcript (accessed March 26, 2021).

Weiyi, C. A Step-by-Step Guide to the Second Impeachment of Donald J. Trump. *The New York Times* (online, updated February 13, 2021) www.nytimes.com/interactive/2021/02/08/us/politics/trump-second-impeachment-timeline.html (accessed March 26, 2021).

Whittington, K.E. Is There a Free Speech Defense to an Impeachment? *Lawfare* (January 19, 2021) www.lawfareblog.com/there-free-speech-defense-impeachment (accessed April 14, 2021).

www.npr.org/2021/01/29/961330810/there-is-precedent-for-trying-a-former-government-official-established-145-years (accessed October 7, 2021).

### *Cases*

Quebec (Attorney General) v. 9147–0732 Québec Inc. Supreme Court of Canada Judgment 2020 SCC 32 (Judgement November 5, 2020) https://scc-csc.lexum.com/scc-csc/scc-csc/en/item/18529/index.do (accessed March 27, 2020).

# 2 The Trump First Amendment Twitter Case

## Blocking the Public's Political Speech on Government Social Media Accounts

### Selected Overview of the Procedural History and Context of the Trump Twitter Case

The Trump Twitter First Amendment case originated with seven individual plaintiffs who were blocked from Donald J. Trump's Twitter account @realDonaldTrump while he was President of the United States. These persons were blocked from the account according to the Court of Appeals "because they expressed views he [President Trump] disliked."[1] The first lawsuit in the case was filed July 11, 2017, and brought by the Knight First Amendment Institute, Columbia University on behalf of the seven individual plaintiffs. The plaintiffs contended that:

> the @realDonaldTrump account is a "public forum" under the First Amendment, from which the government may not exclude people based simply on their views . . . the White House is violating the seven individual plaintiffs' First Amendment right to petition their government, and . . . by purging critics from the @realDonaldTrump account, the White House is depriving those who remain in the public forum the opportunity to hear critical voices.[2]

It is to be noted that the @realDonaldTrump was set up by Mr. Donald J. Trump in 2009 as a private citizen. However, after becoming U.S. President,

1 Knight First Amendment Institute at Columbia University, Rebecca Buckwalter, Philip Cohen, Holly Figueroa, Eugene Gu, Brandon Neely, Joseph Papp, and Nicholas Pappas (Plaintiffs) v. Donald J Trump, President of the United States and Daniel Scavino, White House Director of Social Media and Assistant to the President (Defendants) and Sarah Huckabee Sanders (Defendant) In the United States Court of Appeals for the Second Circuit (Decided July 9, 2019) at p. 2.

2 Knight Institute v Trump, (July 11, 2017). See In the United States District Court for the Southern District of New York, Knight First Amendment Institute at Columbia University et al. v Donald J Trump, President of the United States et al., Complaint for Declaratory and Injunctive Relief https://knightcolumbia.org/cases/knight-institute-v-trump (accessed May 10, 2021).

DOI: 10.4324/9781003153764-2

Mr. Trump continued to use the account not simply to express his opinions on contemporary issues as before but also "to communicate with the public about official actions and policies of his administration."[3]

> Since his inauguration in January 2017, he has used the Account, according to the parties, "as a channel for communicating and interacting with the public about his administration. . . . The President's tweets from the Account can be viewed by any member of the public without being signed into a Twitter account. However, if a user has been blocked from the Account, they cannot view the Account's tweets when logged in to their account. At the time of the parties' stipulation, the Account had more than 50 million followers. The President's tweets produce an extraordinarily high level of public engagement, typically generating thousands of replies, some of which, in turn, generate hundreds of thousands of additional replies."[4]

President Trump's account grew over the years to having 89 million followers on his @realDonaldTrump account in spring 2021.[5]

The plaintiffs in the first lawsuit prevailed at trial in the United States District Court for the Southern District of New York (J. Buckwald presiding). The then President was ordered to unblock the appellees from the @realDonald Trump account. The President then appealed to the United States Court of Appeals for the Second Circuit where the trial judgement was affirmed by the Appeals Court holding of July 9, 2019. That Appeals Court judgement held that the President had violated the First Amendment rights of the plaintiffs by blocking them on a platform that he was using largely as a public platform. The President was denied an *en banc* Second Circuit Appeal rehearing of the case.

On July 31, 2020, there was a second lawsuit filed by the Knight First Amendment Institute triggered by the fact that the then President Trump, though he had unblocked certain followers, continued to block particular categories of followers of his @realDonaldTrump on account of their views namely "those that cannot identify the specific tweet that prompted their blocking, and those blocked before President Trump's inauguration."[6] The appellees in this second lawsuit likewise maintained that their First Amendment rights had been abridged by the then U.S. President by way of his blocking of their access to the @realDonaldTrump Twitter account. The

3 Donald J. Trump, President of the United States et al. (Petitioners) v Knight First Amendment Institute at Columbia University et al. (Respondents) Petition for a writ of Certiorari to the United States Court of Appeals for the Second Circuit (In the Supreme Court of the United States) at pp. 4–5.

4 Donald J. Trump, President of the United States et al. (Petitioners) v Knight First Amendment Institute at Columbia University et al. (Respondents) Petition for a writ of Certiorari to the United States Court of Appeals for the Second Circuit (In the Supreme Court of the United States) Appendix A: Appeals Court for the Second Circuit Judgement at p. 5a).

5 Fritze, J. and Wolf, R. Supreme Court Dismisses as Moot Case Questioning Donald Trump's Blocking of Critics on Twitter. *USA Today* (April 5, 2021).

6 Knight First Amendment Institute at Columbia University, Knight Institute v Trump.

President of the United States (then Donald J. Trump) appealed to the Supreme Court of the United States in August 2020 for a writ of certiorari quashing the lower court decision in Columbia University, Knight Institute that required him to *unblock* on his @realDonaldTrump account the seven plaintiffs in the Knight Institute case. Trump formulated what was the central question *from his perspective* as follows: "Whether the First Amendment deprives a government official of his right to control his personal Twitter account by blocking third-party accounts if he uses that personal account in part to announce official actions and policies."[7]

On January 6, 2021, after the President's speech to a crowd at the Capitol complex ellipse in Washington, D.C. (which speech became the subject of a January 13, 2021, impeachment article for alleged incitement to insurrection): (i) Twitter temporarily suspended the Twitter account in question and (ii) issued a warning to the then President Trump that he had, in their estimation, violated Twitter rules and that further violations would result in a permanent suspension of his @realDonaldTrump Twitter account. Twitter then took the position that two further tweets the President posted January 8, 2021, on the topic of the election and those who supported him violated Twitter's "Glorification of Violence Policy" and he was permanently banned from the service.[8]

After Biden's inauguration as the 46th President of the United States, he became the petitioning party in the Petitioners v Knight First Amendment Institute at Columbia University et al. On January 19, 2021, the Justice Department under Biden petitioned the United States Supreme Court (USSC) to vacate the judgement of the Court of Appeals for the Second Circuit asking the Court to find the case moot. The USSC vacated the judgement below and the case was remanded to the United States Court of Appeals for the Second Circuit with instructions to dismiss the case as moot. In this chapter, we consider in the Trump Twitter case (i) certain relevant facts and selected key Trump arguments to the USSC for certiorari, (ii) the aggrieved party's selected key arguments on reply and (iii) the implications of the various formulations of the issues for the democratic rule of law and the First Amendment principle.

## The Petition to the United States Supreme Court for Certiorari

It is to be understood that the Trump petition for certiorari acknowledged that at the time:

> In certain instances, President Trump receives assistance from Daniel Scavino, an Assistant to the President, in posting tweets to the @realDonaldTrump

7 Donald J. Trump, President of the United States et al. Petitioners v Knight First Amendment Institute at Columbia University et al. Petition for a writ of Certiorari to the United States Court of Appeals for the Second Circuit (In the Supreme Court of the United States) 'Question Presented' at p. I.

8 Permanent suspension of @realDonald Trump, Twitter Inc. (January 8, 2021).

> account. . . . The White House and White House staff also separately operate two government Twitter accounts: @POTUS and @WhiteHouse.[9]

The @realDonaldTrump account thus was operated in a manner likewise to the government accounts in the involvement of government officials normally involved in the President's official communications. The question arises as to why then President Donald J. Trump retained his @realDonaldTrump account for the purpose in large part of communicating policy and administrative moves to the public when there were already available social media accounts easily acknowledged by the public as official government accounts given their name tags @POTUS and @WhiteHouse. Arguably, the @realDonaldTrump account would more likely be perceived by the public as an interactive platform where the public would be welcomed to respond to the President's tweets given its more informal name compared to the monikers which referenced the Presidential office and the White House. Certainly, then President Trump did little if anything to (i) diminish his use of the @realDonaldTrump for making official Presidential pronouncements or (ii) to discourage public interaction on the @realDonaldTrump regarding his administration's policy moves save for the extremely limited numbers of persons overall he blocked on the *site* (that blocking preventing them then from interacting directly with him by replying to his tweets or retweeting while logged into their blocked account).

The very fact that then President Trump's blocking of certain persons from @realDonaldTrump was so selective arguably suggests that it was not the interaction *per se* by those blocked that was objectionable to him but rather *the content of their speech,* which was critical of the President. In fact, the President stipulated as much.[10] Thus, it is reasonable to conclude that President Trump intended the @realDonaldTrump to be an interactive public forum for discussion of contemporary issues and *support* generally of the administration's response to them as well as a forum to assess, from the administration's perspective, critically the stance of the Democrats on those same matters. The analysis here leads to a conclusion consistent with that of the Appeals Court in the case. That conclusion is that the @realDonaldTrump account was *intentionally used as a public forum* such that excluding persons from @realDonaldTrump due to the content of their opposing views was unconstitutional:

> The court of appeals determined that, in light of Twitter's default settings, under which any unblocked Twitter user can see and reply to any published tweet, *the government had "intentionally opened [the account] for*

9 Donald J. Trump, President of the United States et al. Petitioners v Knight First Amendment Institute at Columbia University et al. Petition for a writ of Certiorari to the United States Court of Appeals for the Second Circuit (In the Supreme Court of the United States) at p. 5.

10 Donald J. Trump, President of the United States et al. Petitioners v Knight First Amendment Institute at Columbia University et al. Petition for a writ of Certiorari to the United States Court of Appeals for the Second Circuit (In the Supreme Court of the United States) at p. 7.

> *public discussion when the President, upon assuming office, repeatedly used the Account as an official vehicle for governance* (emphasis added)."[11]

While it is true that the blocking function is available to any Twitter user, it can be reasonably argued that when blocked by Donald J. Trump from an account that is being used largely as a public forum *by the 45th President of the United States* (as was @realDonaldTrump), the blocking is most likely perceived by those blocked and the general public as an official act. This is all the more the case given that members of the administration helped manage the account. *The Appeals Court for the Second Circuit "rejected the argument that the blocking was not state action, concluding that because the President 'acts in an official capacity when he tweets' he must be acting in the 'same capacity' when he blocks other users' accounts* (emphasis added)."[12] Recall in this regard that "Press Secretary Sean Spicer confirmed that the President's tweets are official statements of the President."[13] Furthermore, the President's tweets are considered official records that must be preserved for the National Archives and Records Administration as per the Presidential Records Act.[14] Hence, though the account was registered to Donald J. Trump in his private capacity, it was, it is here contended, being used by him at the relevant time largely if not entirely in his official capacity as the U.S. President (the latter referring to tweeting official government communications and *selectively blocking* some Twitter accounts).

The Appeals Court in the case held that the interactive feature of Twitter whereby unblocked participants in @realDonaldTrump created much content on that account (through their reactions to Trump's tweets regarding certain official government actions and policies of his administration) resulted in that virtual space allowing interaction being a public forum. Hence a public forum was *operationalized* through @realDonaldTrump by the then President *as President* by way of giving full access for direct participation to the unblocked followers

11 Donald J. Trump, President of the United States et al. Petitioners v Knight First Amendment Institute at Columbia University et al. Petition for a writ of Certiorari to the United States Court of Appeals for the Second Circuit (In the Supreme Court of the United States) at p. 8.

12 Donald J. Trump, President of the United States et al. Petitioners v Knight First Amendment Institute at Columbia University et al. Petition for a writ of Certiorari to the United States Court of Appeals for the Second Circuit (In the Supreme Court of the United States) at p. 8. The District Court had found it unnecessary in deciding the case to determine whether the blocking of certain members of the public from the @realDonaldTrump was a State action.

13 Donald J. Trump, President of the United States et al. Petitioners v Knight First Amendment Institute at Columbia University et al. Petition for a writ of Certiorari to the United States Court of Appeals for the Second Circuit (In the Supreme Court of the United States) at p. 96a.

14 Donald J. Trump, President of the United States et al. Petitioners v Knight First Amendment Institute at Columbia University et al. Petition for a writ of Certiorari to the United States Court of Appeals for the Second Circuit (In the Supreme Court of the United States) at p. 96a.

via their retweets, replies and mentions. The latter content was protected non-governmental private speech under the First Amendment.[15]

Trump was making public his administration's important domestic and international moves, and millions of followers had the opportunity to directly engage in the conversation regarding these matters by accessing the interactive virtual space on the @realDonaldTrump account. Thus, the @realDonaldTrump account, though registered as a personal account, was being used (i) to promote "governmental speech" through Trump's initial tweets on the site constituting official government statements and (ii) to host a public forum for discussion of the then President's official statements posted via tweet on the account. Hence, the @realDonald Trump account, on the analysis here, was used by the administration as an official government social media platform. While Trump's initial tweets may have been immune to First Amendment challenge as "governmental speech,"[16] his blocking of certain users as a governmental action was, it is here contended, *not* likewise immune. This since he was now not blocking certain users as a private person but as the most consequential government official (the U.S. President). In fact, he was blocking *dissenters* from the said Twitter account digital interactive space as the highest U.S. government official. This he did since he objected to certain users' views expressed on the @realDonaldTrump public forum site though this was their First Amendment liberty (freedom of expression) right. That is Trump blocked those with particular views that challenged his administration's positions and policy.

The Court of Appeals in the case held, and this author concurs, that the @realDonaldTrump account was *not* being used as a private account[17] given that it was being used to regularly communicate matters of governance and its interactive feature was wide open to the general public to react to that information. Respectfully, it would appear then to be erroneous to contend, as did the Dissent in the Appeals Court holding in the second lawsuit in this case, that President Trump had simply "continued to use Twitter's features the same way he did before taking office" and that therefore "the government had not *created* a public forum on the account (emphasis in the original)."[18]

15 Donald J. Trump, President of the United States et al. Petitioners v Knight First Amendment Institute at Columbia University et al. Petition for a writ of Certiorari to the United States Court of Appeals for the Second Circuit (In the Supreme Court of the United States) at pp. 8–9.

16 Donald J. Trump, President of the United States et al. Petitioners v Knight First Amendment Institute at Columbia University et al. Petition for a writ of Certiorari to the United States Court of Appeals for the Second Circuit (In the Supreme Court of the United States) at Appendix A: Appeals Court for the Second Circuit Judgement p. 21 a "The Free Speech Clause restricts government regulation of private speech; it does not regulate government speech."

17 Donald J. Trump, President of the United States et al. Petitioners v Knight First Amendment Institute at Columbia University et al. Petition for a writ of Certiorari to the United States Court of Appeals for the Second Circuit (In the Supreme Court of the United States) at Appendix A: Appeals Court for the Second Circuit Judgement p. 15a.

18 Donald J. Trump, President of the United States et al. Petitioners v Knight First Amendment Institute at Columbia University et al. Petition for a writ of Certiorari to the United States Court of Appeals for the Second Circuit (In the Supreme Court of the United States) at p. 9.

Mr. Trump, after becoming U.S. President, was using his @realDonaldTrump Twitter account in a novel way (i) making official pronouncements in the name of the U.S. government and (ii) allowing an enormous following of millions to react to these official government pronouncements in the public forum facility provided by Twitter. These uses of the account arguably rendered the account at issue *functionally* a government account. Thus, President Trump did, on the analysis here, in one practical sense, create the public forum for discussion of his policy moves as President, though Twitter had originated the public forum possibility through the nature of its service facilities. There is no indication that then President Trump worked to actively discourage use as a public forum of the interactive space on his @realDonaldTrump Twitter account. Indeed, it would appear that quite the opposite occurred. The extraordinarily high usage per day by then President Trump of the @realDonaldTrump account and the tremendous extent of the public's participation in the interactive space on that account suggests that Mr. Trump kept a running dialogue with that segment of the public which generally endorsed him and continuously generated replies, retweets and commented on his ongoing high-volume official tweets.

The then President held that his decision to block certain followers "from his own account" was a personal decision—private conduct—and not a State action. His position was then that it was Donald J. Trump in his personal capacity, not the U.S. government that blocked access for certain users to @realDonaldTrump when logged into their Twitter accounts.[19] However, if the President had wanted to distinguish for the public his "personal speech" from "governmental speech," he could have used accounts more easily recognizable as government accounts, that is @POTUS to make governmental pronouncements instead of relying so heavily on the @realDonaldTrump. That intentional heavy reliance on the @realDonaldTrump Twitter account (an account registered to Mr. Trump in his personal capacity), on the analysis here, should *not* serve to shield the then President from scrutiny regarding possible First Amendment violations when he blocked certain users from accessing @realDonald Trump from their own Twitter accounts based on those users' political views. Then President Trump took the position, however, that:

> the court of appeals wrongly concluded that the government had created a public forum for speech within the interactive features of the President's personal Twitter account, even though *the President uses his account to speak to the public, not to give members of the public a forum to speak to him and among themselves* (emphasis added).[20]

19 Donald J. Trump, President of the United States et al. Petitioners v Knight First Amendment Institute at Columbia University et al. Petition for a writ of Certiorari to the United States Court of Appeals for the Second Circuit (In the Supreme Court of the United States) at pp. 10–11.

20 Donald J. Trump, President of the United States et al. Petitioners v Knight First Amendment Institute at Columbia University et al. Petition for a writ of Certiorari to the United States Court of Appeals for the Second Circuit (In the Supreme Court of the United States) at p. 11.

Given that the interactive space on @realDonaldTrump was, throughout Mr. Trump's presidency, *in practice* used by millions of his followers "to speak to him and among themselves" through their replies, retweets and comments *in response to his official government tweets*, the claim that there was no intention to host such a public forum on the account would appear to be seriously undercut. Then President Trump continued to consistently use @realDonaldTrump *registered* as a personal account, on the view here, to interact with the public *as President* about his governance positions and, at points, to selectively shut out the political dissent he found intolerable.

On the respectful analysis here, particularly of concern is President Trump's contention through counsel in his application to the United States Supreme Court for certiorari that:

> if the President's tweets somehow transformed his blocking decisions into *governmental action*,[21] then *those tweets likewise transformed his blocking decisions into acts of government speech*—namely, an official refusal to consider respondents' speech (emphasis added).[22]

The President's previously mentioned analysis on that point essentially, on the view here, *erroneously* renders *suppression* of speech by the government to be in itself "government speech" and hence immune[23] from all First Amendment challenge. It is here argued, in contrast, that *suppression of speech* by a government official on a public forum as a reaction to the response of certain members of the public to official statements (content-based discrimination) *cannot* be considered an exercise of government's unfettered right to its *own* speech. To so consider such *suppression of private speech* as "itself government speech" is to, it is here contended, eviscerate any and all of the substantive meaning that constitutes the First Amendment free expression right of the U.S. Constitution.

Clearly, the Appeals Court in the second lawsuit in this case (on the view here) properly did *not* equate the *suppression* (blocking) by President Trump of responses generated by certain private persons to his government speech *as*

21 That the President's tweets transformed his blocking decisions into governmental action was the contention of the Appeals Court in the second lawsuit in this case.

22 Donald J. Trump, President of the United States et al. Petitioners v Knight First Amendment Institute at Columbia University et al. Petition for a writ of Certiorari to the United States Court of Appeals for the Second Circuit (In the Supreme Court of the United States) at p. 12.

23 "That 'Congress shall make no law . . . abridging the freedom of speech, or of the press' is a restraint on government action, not that of private persons." Columbia Broad. Sys. Inc. v. Democratic Nat'l Comm., 412 U.S. 94, 114 (1973) (opinion of Burger, C.J.) Cited in Donald J. Trump, President of the United States et al. Petitioners v Knight First Amendment Institute at Columbia University et al. Petition for a writ of Certiorari to the United States Court of Appeals for the Second Circuit (In the Supreme Court of the United States) at p. 12.

*itself* "government speech." Rather, the Appeals Court held what it framed as "governmental action" (then President Trump blocking of certain persons and categories of persons from the @realDonaldTrump account when logged into their own Twitter accounts) as an unconstitutional infringement on the personal liberty of private citizens in respect of their freedom of expression right. The *suppression of protected private speech* through government action is in any case, it is here suggested, *not* in itself "*government* speech" also in that such suppression is beyond the jurisdiction of the government in its being inconsistent with the First Amendment. That is, if the "government action" of the blocking by a government official of speech generated by selected political dissenters on Twitter—the suppression of speech by a government official—is speech at all, such would be (i) *"extra-governmental" speech* meaning *ultra vires* the lawful scope of "government speech"[24] and hence (ii) subject to First Amendment challenge as unconstitutional.

On the analysis here, the Appeals Court framed the matter properly in designating as "government action," in violation of the First Amendment, the blocking by then President Trump of the speech of certain private citizens on the @ realDonaldTrump interactive space generated from their own Twitter accounts. Afterall, the speech by selected private citizens then President Trump objected to as *President* and blocked on his account *as President* was constituted of oppositional responses to his *official government* tweets posted on @realDonaldTrump concerning *his* government's policies and administrative moves. The public would hence interpret his blocking from @realDonaldTrump of certain accounts linked to political dissenters as the action of Donald J. Trump as President and not as action by Donald J. Trump in his private capacity.

Mr. Trump arguably had a habit of making public pronouncements as to the purported lack of legitimacy of certain opposing narratives to that of his administration and *as President*, for instance, labelled certain mainstream media such as CNN and their affiliated reporters as "enemies of the people." His action in blocking certain opponents' accounts from generating responses to official government tweets posted by the then President to @realDonaldTrump thus is, one could reasonably argue, entirely consistent with then President Trump contending that his narrative *as President* should predominate without serious challenge. It would arguably seem that President Trump's view as expressed was that his narrative on most if not every governmental issue was beyond serious critique. For instance, in 2020 there was "an effort by President Donald Trump to *narrow*

24 Compare "The Supreme Court has urged 'great caution' *to prevent* the government from 'silenc[ing] or muffl[ing] the expression of disfavored viewpoints' under the guise of the government speech doctrine" [which gives immunity from First Amendment challenge to government speech]. See Donald J. Trump, President of the United States et al. Petitioners v Knight First Amendment Institute at Columbia University et al. Petition for a writ of Certiorari to the United States Court of Appeals for the Second Circuit (In the Supreme Court of the United States) at Appendix A: Appeals Court for the Second Circuit Judgement p. 22a (emphasis added).

the ability *of social media companies* to remove objectionable content and require new transparency rules (emphasis added)."[25] President Trump's effort in this regard was triggered by certain steps Twitter had taken: "The Republican president in May directed the U.S. Commerce Department to file the petition *after Twitter Inc.* warned readers to fact-check his posts about unsubstantiated claims of fraud in mail-in voting (emphasis added)."[26] The Federal Trade Commission, however, took no action in that regard perhaps in consideration of the First Amendment quagmire the administration might step into should such limitations on fact-checking by social media be instituted.

This desire by the Trump administration to challenge the scope of fact-checking by social media on its platforms raises the general issue of the public's right to the truth on the potential or realized implications of particular State policy and practice especially in regard to possible various fundamental human rights violations. The United Nations has commented on the right to truth in that regard as follows:

> the right to the truth about gross human rights violations and serious violations of human rights law is an inalienable and autonomous right, linked to the duty and obligation of the State to protect and guarantee human rights, to conduct effective investigations and to guarantee effective remedy and reparations. This right is closely linked with other rights[27] and has both an individual and a societal dimension and should be considered as a non-derogable right and not be subject to limitations.[28]

The State honoring the public's right to the truth in general, and in particular in regard to actual or potential State violations of human rights, it is here contended, is one indicia of the operation of the democratic rule of law.

Mr. Trump argued in his application to the United States Supreme Court to have the Appeal Court's decision in the Twitter case quashed, however, that the @realDonaldTrump was his personal property to be managed as he saw fit including in respect of the use of the blocking function:

25 Shepardson, D. No Action Yet on Trump Social Media Liability Proposal. *Insurance Journal* (online) (October 8, 2020).

26 Shepardson, D. No Action Yet on Trump Social Media Liability Proposal. *Insurance Journal* (online) (October 8, 2020).

27 "The right to the truth is closely linked to the right to an effective remedy; the right to legal and judicial protection; the right to the family life; the right to an effective investigation; the right to a hearing by a competent, independent, and impartial tribunal; and the right to obtain reparation." See United Nations Economic and Social Council E/CN.4/2006/91 Promotion and Protection of Human Rights: Study on the right to the truth. Report of the Office of the United Nations High Commissioner for Human Rights (February 8, 2006) at p. 12.

28 United Nations Economic and Social Council E/CN.4/2006/91 Promotion and Protection of Human Rights: Study on the right to the truth. Report of the Office of the United Nations High Commissioner for Human Rights (February 8, 2006) at p. 2.

> The President's use of his own property (his personal Twitter account) in a manner available to all private citizens (applying Twitter's blocking function) does not constitute state action to which the First Amendment applies.[29]

Recall that while technically @realDonaldTrump *was registered* to Mr. Trump as a personal account, it was not, as was discussed, used primarily as such once he became President nor would a personal account normally be managed by government personnel as was @realDonaldTrump. Rather, the @realDonaldTrump Twitter account was used to officially announce, via Presidential tweets, various of his administration's positions, policies and actions and the account allowed for, as explained, interaction with the public in that regard. There is every indication then that Mr. Trump perceived himself, and wished to be perceived by his followers on @realDonaldTrump, as operating on that social media platform in his communications under the federal power of the Presidency and under colour of federal law when (i) tweeting on that account about his governance perspectives and decisions and (ii) permitting public responses to his official statements (made via tweets) in the interactive space on that same account. Importantly, in no other case would the blocking of someone from a Twitter account have the same gravitas as being blocked by the President of the United States who was tweeting on a social media account (i.e. @real Donald Trump) whilst inviting the public to consider his tweets as official government statements of the President. Mr. Trump as President, on the view here, intentionally communicated his tweets and hosted a public forum on @real Donald Trump in his official and not his personal capacity. Hence, his White House press secretary unsurprisingly confirmed in June 2017 that President Trump's tweets should be considered "official statements by the President of the United States."[30]

Mr. Trump argued in his application for certiorari to the United States Supreme Court that since the blocking function on Twitter was not the result of "power 'possessed by virtue of [federal] law,' such that his actions are "made possible only because [he] is clothed with the authority of [federal] law,"[31] his blocking of certain uses on his personal Twitter account was not government action. However, only President Trump could have used his @realDonaldTrump account *in his official capacity as then President* which, it is here contended, is exactly what

29 Donald J. Trump, President of the United States et al. Petitioners v Knight First Amendment Institute at Columbia University et al. Petition for a writ of Certiorari to the United States Court of Appeals for the Second Circuit (In the Supreme Court of the United States) at pp. 12–13.

30 Donald J. Trump, President of the United States et al. Petitioners v Knight First Amendment Institute at Columbia University et al. Petition for a writ of Certiorari to the United States Court of Appeals for the Second Circuit (In the Supreme Court of the United States) Appendix A: Appeals Court for the Second Circuit Judgement at p. 6a.

31 Donald J. Trump, President of the United States et al. Petitioners v Knight First Amendment Institute at Columbia University et al. Petition for a writ of Certiorari to the United States Court of Appeals for the Second Circuit (In the Supreme Court of the United States) at p. 13.

he decided to do subsequent to his inauguration. This *both* by (i) generating ongoing tweets as official statements concerning his governance as President and (ii) allowing for public response on his @real DonaldTrump Twitter platform to those Presidential tweets which, all are agreed, constituted official government statements by the President of the United States. On the analysis here then, persons blocked from @real Donald Trump when logged into their accounts were hence being blocked from an account being used as a Presidential government account akin to @POTUS. As such, on the view here, the content-based blocking of certain private speech on the @real DonaldTrump public forum feature of the platform was, by Donald Trump's own design, also government action by Donald Trump *as President*. In this regard, it is relevant to note that "*the fact that any Twitter user can block another account does not mean that the President somehow becomes a private person when he does so* (emphasis added)."[32]

Counsel for the then President tried to draw a distinction (before Trump was permanently banned by Twitter from its service) between the @realDonaldTrump account and clearly *designated government accounts* thus:

> He created and began frequent use of that account in 2009, well before taking public office. In contrast to the @WhiteHouse and @POTUS accounts, over which he may exercise control only by virtue of his office, he will continue to have control over the @realDonaldTrump account after his term of office has completed.[33]

To that point, the current author would respectfully respond that only by virtue of his office as then President of the United States (post the election of 2016 and inauguration) was Donald J. Trump able to control/manage the @realDonald Trump Twitter account in important ways as if it were a registered government account such as @POTUS. This specifically by way of communicating his governance decisions as President of the United States regarding foreign and domestic affairs on @realDonaldTrump and hosting a public forum *for public discussion on those official Presidential statements* on the same account. President Trump's tweets *automatically* were official statements under the Presidential Records Act, and hence, his speech on @realDonaldTrump could not be divorced from his office. It is here contended that Mr. Trump's particular use of the @realDonald Trump Twitter account as then U.S. President in (i) posting official statements by the President there in the form of tweets and (ii) in the management of the

32 Donald J. Trump, President of the United States et al. Petitioners v Knight First Amendment Institute at Columbia University et al. Petition for a writ of Certiorari to the United States Court of Appeals for the Second Circuit (In the Supreme Court of the United States) at Appendix A: Appeals Court for the Second Circuit Judgement p. 15a.

33 Donald J. Trump, President of the United States et al. Petitioners v Knight First Amendment Institute at Columbia University et al. Petition for a writ of Certiorari to the United States Court of Appeals for the Second Circuit (In the Supreme Court of the United States) at p. 13.

public forum interactive feature of the account (including blocking) was not, could not and was not expected to be divorced from his office as President of the United States in the perception of the public.[34] It would be incongruous, to say the least, to contemplate that the public at once (i) perceived Mr. Trump to be making official government statements on @realDonald Trump through his tweets but then (ii) considered him suddenly to somehow be acting as if he were a private citizen simply utilizing a facility on his personal Twitter account when monitoring the public's reaction on the interactive public forum of that account including when blocking certain user accounts.

In communicating *as President* on the @realDonaldTrump platform, Mr. Trump was exercising his authority under federal law to *officially inform the public as President of his governance actions as President of the United States.* He was also, on the view here, signalling that @realDonaldTrump was being used as a government and not a private personal account. Consider that *if* some of that information that Mr. Trump officially shared with the public as U.S. President on @realDonaldTrump through tweets (constituting official statements of the President) had been classified as Top Secret (by the U.S. National Security Service), Mr. Trump would still have had the authority under federal law to communicate it on *@realDonaldTrump*. This since he could, *as then President* (i) declassify the material automatically by, for instance, his simply speaking about it to the public and (ii) allow public reaction to it (the thus declassified material) on his @realDonald Trump public forum site. It is hence (i) the particular use made by Donald J. Trump of the account @realDonaldTrump *as President* as if it were a registered government account and (ii) the public's perception of the account as a source of official governmental statements from the 45th President of the United States and as a platform for the discussion of the same with the President that is at issue. The issue is *not* the accessibility of these various accounts to Donald J. Trump once his Presidential term expired (only the account @realDonaldTrump still being accessible to him as a private citizen not the @POTUS and @the WhiteHouse accounts had he not been permanently barred from Twitter). While not all acts by a State official are government acts, it is fair, it is here argued, to contend that then President Trump's official communications to the public of his governance decisions and his hosting of a public forum by way of the Twitter account @realDonaldTrump was conduct executed in his official capacity as President of the United States and intended to be perceived as such.

Then President Trump's speech via tweets on @realDonaldTrump did not represent the opinions of a private person expressed on social media but rather, as previously mentioned, constituted (as his White House press secretary at the

34 Contrast the position of the then President on this issue: "Accordingly, President Trump's ability to use the features of his personal Twitter account, including the blocking function, are independent of his presidential office." See Donald J. Trump, President of the United States et al. Petitioners v Knight First Amendment Institute at Columbia University et al. Petition for a writ of Certiorari to the United States Court of Appeals for the Second Circuit (In the Supreme Court of the United States) at p. 14.

time in 2017 made clear) his *official communications as President* regarding his administration's governance decisions. Opening up this platform on @realDonaldTrump to the public for comment is thus *not* akin to simply opening up private property to public speech (a public forum) which speech then can be in part selectively and arbitrarily excluded by the holder of the private property used primarily as private property.[35] Rather, Donald J. Trump, as then President, invited all of the public to view and react to his tweets constituting *official government pronouncements* on his governance decisions and positions on @realDonaldTrump. The latter is a social media platform with a *public forum function* that has no space limitations regarding number of participants and all of these, on the view here, had a First Amendment right to participate where they abided by Twitter rules.[36]

Donald J. Trump was at the relevant time the then President of all the people of the United States, not just of those who were fervent supporters of most if not all decisions he made as President. All Americans therefore have and had a First Amendment right to learn of and lawfully express opinions on the Trump administration's policy moves and unclassified decisions. There was then *no constitutional basis*, centred as it was (on this analysis) in viewpoint discrimination to exclude certain persons from the @realDonaldTrump public forum virtual space that provided and was intended to provide easy access for the public to a discussion virtual space concerning the then President's governance decisions. That the account @realDonaldTrump was technically registered to Mr. Trump in his personal capacity is, it is here argued, no lawful shield from the First Amendment challenge to his blocking political dissenters to his views from his account when accessed through their personal Twitter accounts. This since it was uncontested in the case that (i) the @realDonaldTrump account was used mostly by Donald J. Trump in his official capacity as President and that (ii) certain members of the public were excluded *based on their views* opposing that of the Trump administration.

It must be recalled that the U.S. President is constitutionally obligated to govern in such a way as to preserve the democratic rule of law and democratic values. All Americans then—whether holding views favorable or not to the administration, where lawfully expressed, have a right under the First Amendment to

35 Compare Donald J. Trump, President of the United States et al. Petitioners v Knight First Amendment Institute at Columbia University et al. Petition for a writ of Certiorari to the United States Court of Appeals for the Second Circuit (In the Supreme Court of the United States) at p. 15: "As this Court has recently confirmed, 'private property owners and private lessees often open their property for speech,' and still retain the right to exclude speech or speakers on the basis of viewpoint."

36 This then is not akin to Presidents excluding certain persons from their physical personal property which has space limitations and to which the entire public was *not* invited. Compare *Id. supra* Donald J. Trump et al. v Knight First Amendment Institute at Columbia University et al. at p. 17: "Surely Franklin D. Roosevelt, John F. Kennedy, or George W. Bush did not forfeit the right to exclude people, including political critics, from the Hyde Park estate, the Hyannis Port compound, or the Crawford ranch by conducting official business or giving official addresses there."

(i) access the administration's official pronouncements on any social media platform being used to convey that information and (ii) to respond to that information on that platform from their own accounts where an interactive public forum is provided for the same. Furthermore, the official pronouncements of the President via tweets were *not* themselves private property. Hence placing them on @realDonaldTrump (which also provides a public forum interactive space) is an invitation, as previously mentioned, to the entire American public to comment, retweet or otherwise reply in response. It is to be highlighted that the U.S. President, furthermore, has an obligation to communicate in his official capacity with the American public on governance (as reflected for instance also by expected regular White House press briefings and State of the Union speeches). To block certain members of the public from the @realDonaldTrump platform *for their opposing views* is to essentially treat the government's official pronouncements as private property through the particular form of regulation of the account (that is by preventing certain persons (selected dissenters) from viewing the President's tweets and from responding to the tweets when attempting either from their own blocked social media accounts).

It is relevant to recall on the issue of limiting selected members of the public's exercise of their First Amendment right to access official Presidential statements and the opportunity to respond publicly to them (such as via questions raised); the exclusion in November 2018 by President Trump of CNN's Jim Acosta from White House briefings (by revoking his "hard" press pass that allows access to the Whitehouse press facilities). This after Acosta questioned the President's use of the word "invasion" to describe a caravan of migrants approaching the U.S.-Mexico border.[37] When Acosta kept asking the question and not relinquishing his microphone when first requested to do so, then U.S. President Trump hurled pejoratives at him, accused him of reporting fake news and being (as a CNN reporter) an enemy of the people.[38] The Acosta case was only one of the many attempts of the Trump administration to strip the press credentials of various reporters and exclude or limit somehow the participation and access of particular members of the press in regard to official government briefings.[39] Curtailing press access by certain media outlets is, in effect, to limit, to some extent at least, full public access for a segment of the public that relies heavily if not exclusively on those particular media outlets. That these various attempts were ultimately

37 First Amendment Watch at New York University "What Rights Do Reporters Have When Covering Official Press Briefings?" There was some debate as to whether Acosta had aggressively touched or grabbed the hand or arm of an intern working for the White House Press Office during the briefing, but the consensus based on video of the incident seems to have been that this was not the case.

38 In the United States District Court for the District of Columbia Cable News Network Inc. et al. (Plaintiffs) v Donald J. Trump et al. (Defendants) Transcript of a Motions Hearing Held Before the Honorable Timothy J. Kelly, United States District Judge (Heard November 16, 2018) at p. 3.

39 First Amendment Watch at New York University "What Rights Do Reporters Have When Covering Official Press Briefings?"

limited in their effect does not alleviate the concern that, on the view here, First Amendment rights were seriously abridged and that such a practice if unchecked by the courts could lead to initiatives by the executive for broader suppression of public speech.

In the Acosta aforementioned case, CNN requested a temporary restraining order which was granted. The latter on the basis that the plaintiffs likely would win on their argument that Acosta had been denied due process. This denial of due process had occurred even though, on the court's view, Acosta's right to a White House press pass was protected by the First Amendment and any denial of that right would require due process as stipulated under the Fifth Amendment.[40]

The District Judge in the Acosta revocation of the press pass case made the point that though there was case law that established that there was *no First Amendment general right of the public to enter the White House*, the facts here were compelling. The Judge held that since the White House had granted access to a part of that site to reporters to do their professional work in reporting, a limited First Amendment liberty right was thereby established in that regard with an accompanying due process right protecting that liberty interest.[41] It is here argued that, similarly, once then President Trump as President allowed replies, comments and retweets on the @realDonaldTrump interactive public forum from the *general public*[42] (in response to his official communications about his administration's governance decisions and policy; the latter made via his tweets on @ real Donald Trump), a limited First Amendment liberty interest protected by a due process right is created in respect of those members of the public who wish to post replies, comments and retweets on that site,[43] (namely a First Amendment liberty interest guaranteeing access to that public forum interactive space on @ realDonaldTrump permitting discussion of the Trump administration's governance, this then including also expressive speech, retweets etc. by those who held views that dissented from those of the then President).

It is here argued that the revocation (later restored)[44] of Mr. Acosta's press pass due to his challenging questions regarding the official Trump position as

40 In the United States District Court for the District of Columbia Cable News Network Inc. et al. (Plaintiffs) v. Donald J. Trump et al. (Defendants) Transcript of a Motions Hearing Held Before the Honorable Timothy J. Kelly, United States District Judge (Heard November 16, 2018) at pp. 6–7.

41 In the United States District Court for the District of Columbia Cable News Network Inc. et al. (Plaintiffs) v. Donald J. Trump et al. (Defendants) Transcript of a Motions Hearing Held Before the Honorable Timothy J. Kelly, United States District Judge (Heard November 16, 2018) at p. 8.

42 Access was not filtered by, for instance, party affiliation.

43 Compare In the United States District Court for the District of Columbia Cable News Network Inc. et al. (Plaintiffs) v. Donald J. Trump et al. (Defendants) Transcript of a Motions Hearing Held Before the Honorable Timothy J. Kelly, United States District Judge (Heard November 16, 2018) at p. 8.

44 The press pass was restored after a District Judge (one as fate would have it appointed by President Trump) ruled that Jim Acosta and CNN were likely to succeed on the argument that Acosta's Fifth Amendment right to due process had been violated. The Judge made it

President on a certain issue of public importance relating to governance (i.e. migration) is in some ways akin to the then President's exclusion of certain persons from the public forum on the @realDonaldTrump Twitter platform. This in that in both these cases there was, on the view here, a restriction or attempted restriction of a segment of the public's access to official Presidential pronouncements and to participation in discussion of these in a particular public forum. On the analysis here, reductively such moves to restrict, to an extent, access for some *in effect* transforms the official unclassified information itself into the President's personal property. The latter to be handled arbitrarily in terms of the manner and scope of its dissemination and the opportunities for public discussion about it. Such an approach is, on the view here, inconsistent with the President's obligation to uphold and protect the First Amendment rights of *all* American private citizens and to communicate with the American public as a whole on Presidential governance.

The President's counsel in the petition for certiorari to the United States Supreme Court in the Knight First Amendment Institute case then, on the respectful view here, misstates the case when he argues that:

> The individual respondents can no more insist on being given access to the President's tweets on @realDonaldTrump than they could insist on being given entry to Trump Tower if the President chose that as the venue where he made important official announcements to *preferred* members of the public and press (emphasis added).[45]

However, Trump Tower, in contrast to @realDonaldTrump, is *not* a social media virtual public platform with unlimited space for interactive public forum discussion participation. That is the Trump Tower space itself is/was *not* and *could not logistically* be used for communicating official governance statements where the *public as a whole* was invited free in that space to discuss and comment. The latter through the availability of an open public forum *physical facility* that would implausibly need to have capacity then to accommodate unlimited public attendance and participation.[46] Thus, (i) being given access to a particular *social media* platform account (@realDonaldTrump), and to the *virtual* interactive public forum (with unlimited capacity) on that platform, to learn of and discuss *official government communications* intended for the general American public (communications conveyed in the form of the President's tweets) is, on the view here, not

---

clear that he had not ruled on the First Amendment issue. See Wheeler, L The Hill "Judge orders White House to reinstate Acosta's press credentials" (November 16, 2018).

45 Donald J. Trump, President of the United States et al. Petitioners v Knight First Amendment Institute at Columbia University et al. Petition for a writ of Certiorari to the United States Court of Appeals for the Second Circuit (In the Supreme Court of the United States) at p. 21.

46 The public being in one's private physical space also poses security challenges that are not in the same way present through public participation on a virtual platform hosted on a personal social media account.

fairly analogized to (ii) being given *in-person entry* into a *private physical space* such as Trump Tower as a *preferred guest* to hear certain Presidential speech and to discuss his communications.[47]

President Trump had an obligation to communicate his official governance positions to the entire American public and to allow for the public's unfettered lawful responses consistent with their First Amendment rights. This no less is the case especially since the @realDonaldTrump interactive virtual public forum was initially open to the seven plaintiffs in the Knight First Amendment case[48] for their lawful speech[49] in response to President Trump's official government communications tweeted on that account. This is then, on the analysis here, quite contrary to what ultimately transpired. On the view here, what occurred is that then President Trump honoured the First Amendment rights *of only preferred users* of the @realDonaldTrump account by *blocking* at least some of the presidentially deemed non-preferred users. It is here contended that there is, under the First Amendment, no constitutionally permissible requirement of endorsement of the President's views and his administration's decisions for granting access to (i) official unclassified government communications regularly posted via tweet by the then President in his official capacity as President and thus under his federal authority as President (with assistance from certain of his White House staff) using the specific virtual social media space at issue and/or access to (ii) the virtual interactive public forum hosted for discussion concerning the official government communications on that same particular social media account.[50] This is the case, it is here argued, even where that public forum is hosted on an

47 On the view here, the President would still have an obligation then to use a venue (i.e. a White House press conference, a virtual social media platform etc.) where the same government statements/communications could be communicated to the American public as a whole.

48 Persons whose Twitter accounts were blocked from @realDonaldTrump based on content, namely those users' dissenting political views, with the blocking having occurred *prior to* Donald J. Trump becoming President, arguably also had a constitutional First Amendment right to access the @realDonaldTrump interactive public forum once the account was used by the then President for official government communications.

49 Lawful speech refers here to those categories of speech fully protected under the First Amendment as not all speech is so protected.

50 The Appeals Court in the Trump Twitter case determined that "@realDonald Trump is a designated public forum because it has been "repeatedly used as an official vehicle for governance" and is "accessible to the public without limitation." Cited in Donald J. Trump, President of the United States et al. Petitioners v Knight First Amendment Institute at Columbia University et al. Petition for a writ of Certiorari to the United States Court of Appeals for the Second Circuit (In the Supreme Court of the United States) at p. 22. While the government did not technically need to create the space on @realDonaldTrump as the public forum facility was already available on the Twitter platform, it is at the same time the case that (i) the government, through the then President Trump, opened that facility to the public so that he could communicate official U.S. government statements to the entire American public and globally and (ii) kept it open to all through their Twitter accounts until such time as President Trump, as the preeminent U.S. government official, chose to block some users.

account technically *registered* to the President in his personal capacity. Were it otherwise, social media accounts registered as *private but used for State speech* (the latter being official government communications made official under the federal authority of the government official i.e. the President) could (on the view here) be used to shield the administration and the general public, through State action (blocking certain user accounts) from hearing dissenting speech on a public forum virtual interactive space on that media platform in contravention of the President's obligation to uphold the First Amendment.

President Trump argued in his application for certiorari to the Supreme Court of the United States that the @realDonaldTrump account persisted after his inauguration as a personal private account used for the President's speech—often in communicating official governmental matters—but "not as a forum created by the government for the public to speak to the President and among themselves."[51] On the respectful view here, that position is belied by the fact that then President Trump purged only selectively certain users from the @realDonaldTrump public interactive forum. Those accounts blocked from @realDonaldTrump were held by persons who expressed vehement dissent to aspects of the Trump administration's governance. Generally, if not always, those who, for the most part, heartily endorsed President's Trump's official government communications and concurred with his administration's decisions, policy, statement of the purported facts and worldview were (i) permitted continued access to @realDonaldTrump to there view the President's tweets and (ii) the opportunity to comment, reply and/or retweet in response to the President's tweets such that these responses could be seen on the President's account timeline. There was then a back and forth with the general public through Presidential tweets constituting official government communications posted on @realDonaldTrump followed by the public response in some form through the interactive space as well. In addition, there was a Presidential response to public reaction on the platform to the President's tweets including the President's selective blocking decisions. This resulted in *some* users (those holding accounts then blocked from @realDonald Trump) not being able to any longer directly speak to the President on the @realDonald Trump platform by replying to, commenting on or retweeting his tweets using their preferred accounts.[52] On the analysis here, the First Amendment rights of the blocked users were violated and, as the Court of Appeals in the case explained, the fact that those blocked users had other vehicles for expressing

51 Donald J. Trump, President of the United States et al. Petitioners v Knight First Amendment Institute at Columbia University et al. Petition for a writ of Certiorari to the United States Court of Appeals for the Second Circuit (In the Supreme Court of the United States) at p. 23.

52 "[B]locking's only material effect on respondents' speech is that they may not speak directly to or on the President's own platform for speech by replying to or retweeting his tweets using their preferred accounts in a manner that appears on his account's timeline." See Donald J. Trump, President of the United States et al. Petitioners v Knight First Amendment Institute at Columbia University et al. Petition for a writ of Certiorari to the United States Court of Appeals for the Second Circuit (In the Supreme Court of the United States) at p. 26.

their presidentially impugned views on a public platform does not cure the constitutional breach.[53]

The current author thus respectfully contests Justice Thomas's view that "Because unbridled control of the account resided in the hands of a private party,[54] First Amendment doctrine *may* not have applied to respondents' complaint of stifled speech (emphasis added)."[55] It is here contended that a private company cannot be held responsible for (on the view here) an unconstitutional State action (then President Trump's blocking of selected political dissenters from @realDonaldTrump) in violation of their First Amendment rights. Nor can the ability of Twitter to remove access from their platform for speech that allegedly violates their rules[56] be a vehicle for *deflecting* from the President's duty to protect the First Amendment rights of all Americans who exercise those rights in a lawful manner. The decision of then President Trump to block selected users (certain political dissenters) from @realDonaldTrump was made by the then President and is one that was independent of Twitter's rules and the company's discontinuing of accounts whose users purportedly promoted or condoned violence via specific speech on those accounts. The blocking decision by Trump in respect of @realDonaldTrump is one for which the President is, on the analysis here, accountable (putting aside for the moment the issue of alleged mootness discussed here in a later section).

On the view here, blocking some from the @realDonaldTrump account did more than simply "ignoring those persons while listening to others."[57] Since the account was being used as a public forum, President Trump's blocking some dissenters, it is here contended, sent a message to the rest of the public as to (i) what was deemed by the government to be "acceptable speech" in a public forum concerning the administration's decisions and (ii) a message about the President's *willingness* (setting aside for the moment the constitutionality issue) to shut

53 Donald J. Trump, President of the United States et al. Petitioners v Knight First Amendment Institute at Columbia University et al. Petition for a writ of Certiorari to the United States Court of Appeals for the Second Circuit (In the Supreme Court of the United States) at Appendix A: Appeals Court for the Second Circuit Judgement pp. 20a–21a.

54 Twitter (owned by a private entity), it will be recalled, ultimately blocked President Trump permanently from Twitter.

55 In the Supreme Court of the United States, Joseph R. Biden Jr., President of the United States et al. v Knight First Amendment Institute at Columbia University et al. On Petition for Writ of Certiorari to the United States Court of Appeals for the Second Circuit (Decided April 5, 2021), Justice Thomas's concurring opinion at p. 5.

56 Though, in principle, Twitter has "unbridled" control of its platform (as Justice Thomas suggests), in practice the company has been criticized for not exercising enough control where its rules have been allegedly violated. This since Twitter discontinues accounts, it would appear, sparingly given the enormity of the magnitude of the overall operation and reach of the platform.

57 Contrast the President's position. See Donald J. Trump, President of the United States et al. Petitioners v Knight First Amendment Institute at Columbia University et al. Petition for a writ of Certiorari to the United States Court of Appeals for the Second Circuit (In the Supreme Court of the United States) at p. 26.

down lawfully expressed dissenting views that challenged his administration in a manner he found unacceptable when voiced in a public platform where he had the ability to suppress/exclude that speech on that particular public platform. Mr. Trump as President did so on Twitter with @realDonaldTrump, though the courts found the blocking of certain users on that account unconstitutional (and the case was pending before the United States Supreme Court when the decision below was vacated on the grounds of alleged mootness). He did so also, for instance, in revoking Jim Acosta's hard press pass (and threatening he might do so with respect to certain other White House reporters as well).[58] Acosta's press pass, as discussed, was restored after a District Court ruled the revocation of the hard press pass had been implemented without the due process protections that attach to the First Amendment liberty interest implicated in the situation.

## The Mootness and Vacatur Issues in the Trump Twitter Case

In January 2021, counsel for Donald J. Trump, then President of the United States filed a supplemental brief to the United States Supreme Court (USSC) in the government's application for certiorari regarding the judgement of the Appeals Court in the Twitter case. That Appeals Court judgement held that then President Trump's blocking of certain Twitter accounts of particular users from the @realDonaldTrump social media platform based on their political views was discriminatory and a violation of their First Amendment rights. The President argued that the case was worthy of review by the USSC, but it would be moot once Mr. Biden became President on January 20, 2021. Furthermore, Mr. Biden would have no control over the @realDonaldTrump account and would not be able to block or unblock any user account from interacting with @realDonaldTrump. President Trump on that rationale petitioned the USSC to grant certiorari, consider the case moot and vacate the Appeals Court judgement. The petitioners highlighted the fact that:

> After the inauguration . . . Mr. Trump will no longer be a party to this case, because respondents sued him only in his official capacity. In an official-capacity suit, the relief obtained by respondents "is only nominally against the official and in fact is against the official's office," meaning that when President Trump "leave[s] office, [his] successor] automatically assume[s] [his] role in the litigation.[59]

58 In the United States District Court for the District of Columbia Cable News Network Inc. et al. (Plaintiffs) v. Donald J. Trump et al. (Defendants) Transcript of a Motions Hearing Held Before the Honorable Timothy J. Kelly, United States District Judge (Heard November 16, 2018) at p. 4.

59 Supplemental Brief of the Petitioners in Donald J. Trump, President of the United States et al. Petitioners v Knight First Amendment Institute at Columbia University et al. Petition for a writ of Certiorari to the United States Court of Appeals for the Second Circuit (In the Supreme Court of the United States) at p. 3.

President Trump further argued in the Petitioner's supplemental brief to the Supreme Court of the United States that Mr. Trump did not block certain user accounts from @realDonaldTrump by exercising his authority under federal law as then President. This President Trump contended is evidenced by the fact that

> If he had, then President Biden would have that same power extended to him under federal law upon his inauguration. That President Biden will be powerless to control the @realDonaldTrump account thus confirms the error in the opinion below, which should not be allowed to stand without this Court's review.[60]

The current author, however, concurs with the Appeals Court in this case that the fact that the @realDonaldTrump account was being used as a government account by the President to make official statements about governance as President meant that the blocking was rendered a government (State) action. This since then U.S. President Trump did nothing to indicate (assuming that was even possible given the manner of the President's use of the account for governmental purposes) that he had shed his official status as U.S. President when (i) managing the interactive public forum on the account and (ii) selectively exercising Twitter's blocking function against users with dissenting political views to which he strenuously objected.

The Respondents argued in their reply supplemental brief that (i) the Appeals Court ruling would, as the Petitioners acknowledged, *not* disadvantage Mr. Trump or Mr. Scavino going forward when the new administration was installed and hence vacatur was unnecessary to prevent an unfairness that was *not* going to occur (i.e. former President Trump and Mr. Scavino would no longer be managing the @realDonaldTrump Twitter account in an official capacity, and as private citizens post January 20, 2021, neither of them would thus be subject to the First Amendment constraints on government officials);[61](ii) vacatur was precluded in any case by the fact that Donald J. Trump et al. were themselves responsible for rendering the case moot in the first instance ((i) by Donald J. Trump's speech to the crowd at the ellipse in Washington, D.C. January 6, 2021, which triggered Twitter's removing him from the Twitter service for 12 days while his further tweets on January 8, 2021, caused his permanent removal from Twitter. (This since Twitter deemed these tweets (correctly or incorrectly)

60 Supplemental Brief of the Petitioners in Donald J. Trump, President of the United States et al. Petitioners v Knight First Amendment Institute at Columbia University et al. Petition for a writ of Certiorari to the United States Court of Appeals for the Second Circuit (In the Supreme Court of the United States) at p. 5.

61 Supplemental Brief of Respondents (in reply) in Donald J. Trump, President of the United States et al. Petitioners v Knight First Amendment Institute at Columbia University et al. Petition for a writ of Certiorari to the United States Court of Appeals for the Second Circuit (In the Supreme Court of the United States) at p. 7.

to be a violation of their policies on Civic Integrity and Violent Threats[62]) and (ii) by losing the 2020 election such that Trump was no longer the petitioner for certiorari as this role passed to the next holder of the Office of the Presidency, Joseph Biden Jr.)[63]

It is here argued that the case should be considered moot but that vacatur is here inappropriate. Though this issue will not recur with former President Trump in the future with respect to the Twitter platform at least (since he has been permanently banned from it), the (on the view here) constitutionally sound Appeals Court ruling in the case remains relevant and should stand. This as the lower court ruling serves as guidance as to what is an impermissible manner of use of a registered personal social media account by any U.S. government official where that particular manner of use on the Court's view adversely affects the public's right to free speech under the First Amendment.

> Here, the public interest in preventing impermissible viewpoint discrimination in *government-operated* social media accounts weighs heavily in favor of keeping the Second Circuit's judgment in place. As the Court has recognized, social media platforms like Twitter offer "perhaps the most powerful mechanisms available to a private citizen to make his or her voice heard," in part because these platforms permit citizens to "engage with [their elected representatives] in a direct manner (emphasis added)."[64]

On the view of the lower courts then in Trump's Twitter case, a social media account being registered to a person in his or her private capacity is not a shield against that person, who later becomes a government official, being held accountable in some form where there are violations of the First Amendment rights of private citizens. The latter alleged violations arose through the particularities of the management and use of that specific account operated as a government account (i.e. the indicia of an account being operated as a government account include using it to make official government statements and to host an interactive open public forum for discussion of the administration's governance).

62 Supplemental Brief of Respondents (in reply) in Donald J. Trump, President of the United States et al. Petitioners v Knight First Amendment Institute at Columbia University et al. Petition for a writ of Certiorari to the United States Court of Appeals for the Second Circuit (In the Supreme Court of the United States) at pp. 4–5.

63 Supplemental Brief of Respondents (in reply) in Donald J. Trump, President of the United States et al. Petitioners v Knight First Amendment Institute at Columbia University et al. Petition for a writ of Certiorari to the United States Court of Appeals for the Second Circuit (In the Supreme Court of the United States) at pp. 6–7.

64 Supplemental Brief of Respondents (in reply) in Donald J. Trump, President of the United States et al. Petitioners v Knight First Amendment Institute at Columbia University et al. Petition for a writ of Certiorari to the United States Court of Appeals for the Second Circuit (In the Supreme Court of the United States) at p. 8.

It is here respectfully contended that the Supreme Court of the United States *erred in vacating* the ruling of the Appeals Court for the Second Circuit[65] in the Trump Twitter case. This as doing so was, on the analysis here, contrary to the U.S. public interest. This author finds it instructive that the USSC did *not* detail how the particular facts of the Trump Twitter case as to what precipitated mootness (Trump's own actions) still allowed for *vacatur* but simply cryptically stated:

> The petition for a writ of certiorari is granted. The judgment is vacated, and the case is remanded to the United States Court of Appeals for the Second Circuit with instructions to dismiss the case as moot. See United States v. Munsingwear, Inc., 340 U. S. 36 (1950).[66]

The vagueness of the ruling is reflected in the following commentary on the case:

> The Supreme Court vacated the decision in a one-sentence opinion in April 2021 and remanded the case to the appeals court with instructions to dismiss the case as moot, *presumably* on the grounds that Trump was no longer president and that Twitter's owners had, in the wake of attacks on the U.S. Capitol, banned Trump from making further posts (emphasis added).[67]

That the Supreme Court struggled with the issue is reflected perhaps in the fact that only "After considering the case at 11 consecutive conferences" did the court finally "sen[d] the case back to the 2nd Circuit with instructions to dismiss it as moot."[68]

As only Justice Thomas provided any elaboration as to the court's ruling—this through his concurrence with the majority opinion—we will consider his analysis. Justice Thomas stated:

> Respondents have a point, for example, that some aspects of Mr. Trump's account resemble a constitutionally protected public forum.[69] *But it seems*

65 Knight First Amendment Institute at Columbia University, Rebecca Buckwalter, Philip Cohen, Holly Figueroa, Eugene Gu, Brandon Neely, Joseph Papp, and Nicholas Pappas (Plaintiffs) v Donald J. Trump, President of the United States and Daniel Scavino, White House Director of Social Media and Assistant to the President (Defendants) and Sarah Huckabee Sanders (Defendants). In the United States Court of Appeals for the Second Circuit (Decided July 9, 2019).

66 In the Supreme Court of the United States, Joseph R. Biden Jr., President of the United States et al. v Knight First Amendment Institute at Columbia University et al. On Petition for Writ of Certiorari to the United States Court of Appeals for the Second Circuit decided (April 5, 2021).

67 The First Amendment Encyclopedia *Biden v. Knight First Amendment Institute at Columbia University* (2021) (authored by Vile, J.R.).

68 SCOTUSblog Justices throw out Trump Twitter case (by Howe, A, April 5, 2021).

69 A designated public forum is "property that the State has opened for expressive activity by part or all of the public." Supreme Court of The United States, Joseph R. Biden Jr. et al. v Knight First Amendment Institute at Columbia University et al. (Decided April 5, 2021)

> ***rather odd to say that something is a government forum when a private company has unrestricted authority to do away with it.*** Mr. Trump blocked several people from interacting with his messages. Twitter barred Mr. Trump not only from interacting with a few users, but removed him from the entire platform, thus barring all Twitter users from interacting with his messages. Under its terms of service, Twitter can remove any person from the platform—including the President of the United States—"at any time for any or no reason." Twitter Inc., User Agreement (effective June 18, 2020) (emphasis added).[70]

In fact, on the view of the current author, the Trump Twitter case unmasks an improper shield for government violations of First Amendment rights, namely as afforded when a personal social media account is used to communicate government speech and, at the same time, to selectively suppress certain dissenting voices raised in response to that government speech. It is, it is here argued, not the case then that a "government forum" exists only when the interactive public platform in respect of a social media account is registered to a government official in his or her official capacity. It is, on the analysis here, the manner of use of a social media account that is registered to a government official in his or her personal capacity that determines whether in fact it is a government forum or not.

On the respectful view here, Justice Thomas's concurring opinion *distracts* from the central issue of the Trump case when he states:

> Today's digital platforms provide avenues for historically unprecedented amounts of speech, including speech by government actors. Also unprecedented, however, is the concentrated *control of so much speech* in the hands of a few private parties (emphasis added).[71]

The Trump Twitter case (on the view here) concerns at its core government regulation of dissenting voices in violation of the First Amendment. Then President Trump's blocking of the accounts of certain users who expressed dissenting political opinions to those reflected in the decisions and policies of his administration could have in the long run (had he won re-election and not been banned permanently from Twitter) served to significantly chill public dissent generally and thus not only on the @realDonaldTrump Twitter platform. The latter inasmuch as the blocking of certain users by then President Trump implicitly conveyed a message from the government

---

Concurring Opinion of Justice Thomas at p. 3. Here Donald J. Trump as President after his inauguration opened up the interactive public forum component of @realDonald Trump to all of the public before choosing in 2017 to block certain accounts.

70 Supreme Court of The United States, Joseph R. Biden Jr. et al. v. Knight First Amendment Institute at Columbia University et al. (Decided April 5, 2021) Concurring Opinion of Justice Thomas at p. 2.

71 Supreme Court of The United States, Joseph R. Biden Jr. et al. v. Knight First Amendment Institute at Columbia University et al. (Decided April 5, 2021) Concurring Opinion of Justice Thomas at p. 2.

about government-preferred speech and that there could be possible consequences for speaking out against the administration—starting with blocked access to @realDonald Trump and possibly progressing to other measures. When Twitter Inc. removes tweets or an account from its service for alleged violation of certain of its policies, there is no doubt amongst the public that it is doing so as a private actor. Hence, there is unlikely to be a chilling effect on the free expression through other avenues of those political/social views Twitter found violated its policies.

There may indeed be a legitimate issue of concern about the "concentrated control of so much speech in the hands of a few private parties"[72] (i.e. those few private parties being those that own major social media platforms such as Twitter). However, that concern is quite different from the matter central to the Trump Twitter case, namely the alleged undermining of First Amendment rights. This through potential unfettered government suppression of speech on certain platforms, that is as when a government official blocks political dissenters on a social media account registered to him or her in his or her private capacity but one being used as a government account. The latter risks the chilling of dissenting political voices more generally, hence seriously eroding First Amendment rights and undermining the democracy itself. On the view here, the Appeals Court Second Circuit ruling in the Trump Twitter case spoke to the latter issue (government content-based suppression of politically dissenting speech on social media platforms), and it was in the public interest to have let it stand even though the case was moot.[73] Technically, this would have been legally supportable also in that Trump himself was responsible for the case becoming moot.

## References

### *Materials*

The First Amendment Encyclopedia. *Biden v. Knight First Amendment Institute at Columbia University* (2021) (authored by Vile, J.R.) https://mtsu.edu/first-amendment/article/1907/biden-v-knight-first-amendment-institute-at-columbia-university (accessed April 30, 2021).

First Amendment Watch at New York University "What Rights Do Reporters Have When Covering Official Press Briefings?" https://firstamendmentwatch.org/deep-dive/reporters-persona-non-grata-at-white-house/ (accessed April 27, 2021).

Fritze, J. and Wolf, R. Supreme Court Dismisses as Moot Case Questioning Donald Trump's Blocking of Critics on Twitter. *USA Today* (April 5, 2021) www.msn.com/en-us/news/politics/supreme-court-dismisses-as-moot-case-questioning-donald-trump-s-blocking-of-critics-on-twitter/ar-BB1fk0Z1 (accessed April 23, 2021).

72 Supreme Court of The United States, Joseph R. Biden Jr. et al. v. Knight First Amendment Institute at Columbia University et al. (Decided April 5, 2021) Concurring Opinion of Justice Thomas at p. 2.

73 The case was rendered moot arguably due in any case to Trump's own actions leading to his being permanently banned from Twitter even before his term of office as President of the United States had expired.

Knight Institute at Columbia University, Knight Institute v Trump: A Lawsuit Challenging President Trump's Blocking of Critics on Twitter https://knightcolumbia.org/cases/knight-institute-v-trump (accessed April 24, 2021).

SCOTUSblog Justices Throw Out Trump Twitter Case (by Howe, A, April 5, 2021) www.scotusblog.com/2021/04/justices-throw-out-trump-twitter-case/ (accessed April 30, 2021).

Shepardson D. No Action Yet on Trump Social Media Liability Proposal. *Insurance Journal* (online) (October 8, 2020) www.insurancejournal.com/news/national/2020/10/08/585838.htm (accessed April 26, 2021).

Twitter Inc. *Permanent Suspension of @realDonald Trump* (January 8, 2021) https://blog.twitter.com/en_us/topics/company/2020/suspension.html (accessed April 24, 2021).

United Nations Economic and Social Council E/CN.4/2006/91 Promotion and Protection of Human Rights: Study on the right to the truth. Report of the Office of the United Nations High Commissioner for Human Rights (February 8, 2006) https://digitallibrary.un.org/record/567521 (accessed April 26, 2021).

Wheeler, L. Judge Orders White House to Reinstate Acosta's Press Credentials. *The Hill* (November 16, 2018) https://thehill.com/regulation/court-battles/416935-judge-rules-against-white-house-in-cnn-dispute (accessed April 27, 2021).

### *Cases*

Donald J. Trump, President of the United States et al. Petitioners v Knight First Amendment Institute at Columbia University et al. Petition for a Writ of Certiorari to the United States Supreme Court www.supremecourt.gov/DocketPDF/20/20-197/150726/20200820102824291_Knight%20First%20Amendment%20Inst.pdf (accessed April 25, 2021).

In the Supreme Court of the United States, Joseph R. Biden Jr., President of the United States et al. v Knight First Amendment Institute at Columbia University et al. on Petition for Writ of Certiorari to the United States Court of Appeals for the Second Circuit (Decided April 5, 2021) www.supremecourt.gov/opinions/20pdf/20-197_5ie6.pdf (accessed April 30, 2021).

In the United States District Court for the District of Columbia, Cable News Network Inc. et al. (Plaintiffs) v Donald J. Trump et al. (Defendants) Transcript of a Motions Hearing Held before the Honorable Timothy J. Kelly, United States District Judge (heard November 16, 2018) https://www.courtlistener.com/docket/8169022/cable-news-network-inc-v-trump (accessed April 27, 2021).

Knight First Amendment Institute at Columbia University, Rebecca Buckwalter, Philip Cohen, Holly Figueroa, Eugene Gu, Brandon Neely, Joseph Papp, and Nicholas Pappas (Plaintiffs) v Donald J. Trump, President of the United States and Daniel Scavino, White House Director of Social Media and Assistant to the President (Defendants) and Sarah Huckabee Sanders (Defendant) in the United States Court of Appeals for the Second Circuit (Decided July 9, 2019) https://casetext.com/case/knight-first-amendment-inst-at-columbia-univ-v-trump-1 (accessed April 23, 2021).

Knight Institute v Trump (filed July 11, 2017) https://knightcolumbia.org/cases/knight-institute-v-trump (accessed May 10, 2021) See In the United States District Court for the Southern District of New York Knight First Amendment Institute at

Columbia University, Rebecca Buckwalter, Philip Cohen, Holly Figueroa, Eugene Gu, Brandon Neely, Joseph Papp, and Nicholas Pappas (Plaintiffs) v Donald J. Trump, President of the United States, Sean M. Spicer, Whitehouse Press Secretary and Daniel Scavino, White House Director of Social Media and Assistant to the President (Defendants) Complaint for Declaratory and Injunctive Relief.

Supplemental Brief of Petitioners Trump, Donald J., President for the United States, et al. in Donald J. Trump, President of the United States et al. Petitioners v Knight First Amendment Institute at Columbia University et al. Petition for a Writ of Certiorari www.scotusblog.com/case-files/cases/biden-v-knight-first-amendment-institute/ (April 30, 2021).

Supplemental Brief of Respondents in Donald J. Trump, President of the United States et al. Petitioners v Knight First Amendment Institute at Columbia University et al. Petition for a Writ of Certiorari www.scotusblog.com/case-files/cases/biden-v-knight-first-amendment-institute/ (April 30, 2021).

# 3 The First Amendment Defence, Alleged "Political Speech" and Disinformation Campaigns

## Case 1: Smartmatic et al. v. Fox Corporation, Fox News Network LLC et al. and Case 2: U.S. Dominion Inc., Dominion Voting Systems Inc., and Dominion Voting Systems Corporation v. Fox News Network LLC

The cases addressed in this chapter involve the allegation that Fox News and certain of its personalities as well as invited guests on its broadcast shows spread highly damaging defamatory "fake news" targeting the Smartmatic and Dominion election technology corporations. It is to be noted that:

> the term "fake news" has become highly political and is often used as a buzzword not only used to describe fabricated information but to undermine the credibility of news organizations or argue against commentary that disagrees with our own opinion.[1]

For our purposes here, we will define "fake news" as intentionally fabricated items knowingly and intentionally or recklessly promulgated as informational verified news. This though the communicator has *not* with due diligence investigated and verified the information as correct and/or is well aware that the so-called news item is (i) grounded on verifiably *false* alleged facts and/or connotations and/or misleading or incorrect assumptions as well as in some instances (ii) false conspiracy theories and claims. We are referring here then to material which is presented as verified news rather than as commentary and opinion and which is represented by the communicator as true when in fact it is false and the broadcast personality either (i) was aware that the item was factually false and/or grossly misleading at the time he or she communicated it to the audience and/or (ii) showed a wilful and reckless disregard for the truth by not duly investigating whether the material was true and not misleading. "Fake news" for our purposes here then is:

> fabricated information that mimics news media content in form but not in organizational process or intent. Fake news outlets, in turn, lack the news

1 Molina, M.D., Sundar, S.S. and Le, D. "Fake News" Is Not Simply False Information: A Concept Explication and Taxonomy of Online Content. *American Behavioral Scientist*, Vol. 65, Issue 2 (2021), 180–212 at p. 184.

DOI: 10.4324/9781003153764-3

> media's editorial norms and processes for ensuring the accuracy and credibility of the information. Fake news overlaps with other information disorders, such as misinformation (false and misleading information) and disinformation (false information that is purposely spread to deceive people).[2]

It is alleged fake news in the context of a purported disinformation campaign that is the broader context for our discussion here of the Dominion and Smartmatic defamation lawsuits against Fox News et al.

Smartmatic alleged that each of the Defendants acted with "actual malice and ill-will toward Smartmatic" in that purportedly "Each of the Defendants knew that the statements and implications that they made about Smartmatic were false and/or they acted with reckless disregard for whether their statements and implications were true."[3] Smartmatic argued that:

> These statements and implications were defamatory because they exposed Smartmatic to public hate, contempt, ridicule, and disgrace, and because they induced an evil and unsavory opinion of Smartmatic and its business into the minds of a substantial number of the community. These statements and implications were defamatory per se since they charged Smartmatic with a serious crime and were of a nature tending to injure Smartmatic in its trade, business, and profession.[4]

The narrative (a false one according to Smartmatic) that the Defendants propagated was that "Smartmatic fixed, rigged, and stole the 2020 U.S. election for Joe Biden and Kamala Harris."[5] Essentially, Smartmatic maintains that the Defendants knew they were making up a false story that Smartmatic had allegedly stolen the 2020 Presidential election from the rightful winner. This since the Defendants knew that neither they nor their so-called sources had any evidence whatsoever of the claims they were repeatedly and incessantly communicating to the public using various media. Further, according to Smartmatic,

> Defendants possessed or had access to a significant volume of information that contradicted the story they told about Smartmatic. Defendants either

2 The American Association for the Advancement of Science. The Science of Fake News. *Insights Policy Forum*, Vol. 359, Issue 6380 (March 9, 2018), 1094–1097 at p. 1094.

3 Supreme Court of the State of New York, Smartmatic U.S.A. Corp, Smartmatic International Holding B.V., and S.G.O. Corporation Limited v. Fox Corporation, Fox News Network LLC, Lou Dobbs, Maria Bartiromo, Jeanine Pirro, Rudolph Giuliani and Sidney Powell Summons (February 4, 2021) at p. 132.

4 Supreme Court of the State of New York, Smartmatic U.S.A. Corp, Smartmatic International Holding B.V., and S.G.O. Corporation Limited v. Fox Corporation, Fox News Network LLC, Lou Dobbs, Maria Bartiromo, Jeanine Pirro, Rudolph Giuliani and Sidney Powell Summons (February 4, 2021) at p. 240 Point 527–528.

5 Supreme Court of the State of New York, Smartmatic U.S.A. Corp, Smartmatic International Holding B.V., and S.G.O. Corporation Limited v. Fox Corporation Summons (February 4, 2021) at p. 132.

> reviewed this information (and therefore knew their statements and implications were false) or purposefully avoided reviewing this information because they did not want to know the truth.[6]

Smartmatic argued that one overwhelming fact (according to Smartmatic), among other facts, undermines the narrative that the Smartmatic Corporation was a co-conspirator in allegedly stealing the 2020 election for Biden (the Defendants thus presupposing in the first instance that the 2020 Presidential election was stolen). That fact is that Smartmatic contends it played a relatively very small part in the 2020 Presidential election and hence, practically speaking, it was not possible that Smartmatic stole the 2020 election from former President Trump:

> Smartmatic's only role in the 2020 U.S. election was as a provider of election technology and software to Los Angeles County. This fact was known to Defendants or readily ascertainable, and it puts the lie to nearly everything they said.[7]

If that claim is correct, then Smartmatic, by implication, could not, for instance, have been instrumental in Biden winning close races in swing States during the 2020 Presidential election.

Dominion likewise accused Fox News Network of "actual malice" in promulgating what Dominion holds is a completely false defamatory story that includes, according to Dominion, the "fictitious" claims that:

> (1) Dominion committed election fraud by rigging the 2020 Presidential Election; (2) Dominion's software and algorithms manipulated vote counts in the 2020 Presidential Election; (3) Dominion is owned by a company founded in Venezuela to rig elections for the dictator Hugo Chávez; and (4) Dominion paid kickbacks to government officials who used its machines.[8]

Dominion in part argued further that:

> Fox recklessly disregarded the truth. Indeed, Fox knew these statements about Dominion were lies. Specifically, Fox knew the vote tallies from Dominion machines could easily be confirmed by independent audits and

6 *Id. supra* Supreme Court of the State of New York, Smartmatic U.S.A. Corp et al. v. Fox Corporation et al., Summons (February 4, 2021) at p. 133.

7 *Id. supra* Supreme Court of the State of New York, Smartmatic U.S.A. Corp et al. v. Fox Corporation, Fox News Network LLC, Lou Dobbs, Maria Bartiromo, Jeanine Pirro, Rudolph Giuliani and Sidney Powell, Summons (February 4, 2021) at p. 133.

8 In the Superior Court of the State of Delaware, U.S. Dominion Inc., Dominion Voting Systems Inc., and Dominion Voting Systems Corporation v. Fox News Network LLC Complaint, Jury Trial demanded (March 26, 2021) at p. 2, point 2.

hand recounts of paper ballots, as has been done repeatedly since the election.[9]

These lies transformed Dominion into a household name. As a result of Fox's orchestrated defamatory campaign, Dominion's employees, from its software engineers to its founder and Chief Executive Officer, have been repeatedly harassed. Some have even received death threats. And of course, Dominion's business has suffered enormous and irreparable economic harm.[10]

The truth matters. Lies have consequences. Fox sold a false story of election fraud in order to serve its own commercial purposes, severely injuring Dominion in the process. If this case does not rise to the level of defamation by a broadcaster, then nothing does.[11]

Dominion advanced as the alleged factual basis for its defamation claim the following: (i) Fox lost viewers due to accurately reporting the results of the 2020 Presidential election and (ii) thereafter, according to Dominion, began to spread a false narrative about Dominion consistent with that spearheaded by former President Trump. This in an effort purportedly to woo back viewers.[12] That false narrative, Dominion contended, was defamatory per se:

> Fox's statements are defamatory per se, as they impute serious criminal conduct to Dominion and also malign Dominion in the conduct of its business or trade. Fox's statements have exposed Dominion to the most extreme hatred and contempt. Fox . . . has accused Dominion of fraud, election-rigging, conspiracy, and bribery, which are serious crimes.[13]

A core issue in both the Dominion and Smartmatic defamation lawsuits is whether—assuming for the sake of argument Fox News et al. did advance false claims about these companies purportedly stealing the 2020 Presidential election from former President Trump—"Fox had no applicable privilege or legal

9 In the Superior Court of the State of Delaware, U.S. Dominion Inc., Dominion Voting Systems Inc., and Dominion Voting Systems Corporation v. Fox News Network LLC Complaint, Jury Trial demanded (March 26, 2021) at p. 2, point 3.

10 In the Superior Court of the State of Delaware, U.S. Dominion Inc., Dominion Voting Systems Inc., and Dominion Voting Systems Corporation v. Fox News Network LLC Complaint, Jury Trial demanded (March 26, 2021) at p. 4, point 6.

11 In the Superior Court of the State of Delaware, U.S. Dominion Inc., Dominion Voting Systems Inc., and Dominion Voting Systems Corporation v. Fox News Network LLC Complaint, Jury Trial demanded (March 26, 2021) at p. 4, point 7.

12 In the Superior Court of the State of Delaware, U.S. Dominion Inc., Dominion Voting Systems Inc., and Dominion Voting Systems Corporation v. Fox News Network LLC Complaint, Jury Trial demanded (March 26, 2021) at pp. 23–32.

13 In the Superior Court of the State of Delaware, U.S. Dominion Inc., Dominion Voting Systems Inc., and Dominion Voting Systems Corporation v. Fox News Network LLC Complaint, Jury Trial demanded (March 26, 2021) at pp. 130–131, point 191.

authorization to make these false and defamatory statements, or if it did, it abused it."[14]

Fox News et al. in part argued in reply to Dominion and Smartmatic that "Plaintiffs' defamation lawsuit against Fox News threatens to stifle the media's free-speech right to inform the public about newsworthy allegations of paramount public concern."[15] The Defendants characterized the defamation lawsuit brought by Smartmatic as "a First-Amendment denying request"[16] and maintained that:

> Smartmatic strains to make this lawsuit seem like a garden-variety defamation suit rather than a glaring threat to core First Amendment freedoms. But there is no escaping the reality that it seeks to impose massive liability on Fox for doing exactly what the First Amendment protects in the context where the First Amendment matters most . . . it was the President's allegations, not the press coverage of them, that put Smartmatic in the spotlight.[17]

## Commentary

### *The First Amendment Issue in the Smartmatic and Dominion Defamation Cases*

We for our limited purposes here are not concerned with determining the truth or falsity of the competing factual claims of the parties in the Smartmatic and Dominion Corporation defamation cases against Fox News et al. Rather, we will focus on considering whether the First Amendment protects the said Defendants in their promulgating the alleged defamatory speech to millions of media consumers in the United States and internationally. The plaintiffs in these aforementioned defamation cases must show, it is here contended, that (i) the First Amendment does *not* protect against the speech that was

14 In the Superior Court of the State of Delaware, U.S. Dominion Inc., Dominion Voting Systems Inc., and Dominion Voting Systems Corporation v. Fox News Network LLC Complaint, Jury Trial demanded (March 26, 2021) at p. 130, point 187.

15 In the Superior Court of the State of Delaware, U.S. Dominion Inc., Dominion Voting Systems Inc., and Dominion Voting Systems Corporation v. Fox News Network LLC Defendants Brief in Support of Rule 12(b)(6) Motion to Dismiss for Failure to State a Claim, Preliminary Statement at p. 1.

16 Supreme Court of the State of New York, Smartmatic U.S.A. Corp, Smartmatic International Holding B.V., and S.G.O. Corporation Limited v. Fox Corporation, Fox News Network LLC, Lou Dobbs, Maria Bartiromo, Jeanine Pirro, Rudolph Giuliani and Sidney Powell. Reply Memorandum of Law in Further Support of Fox Defendants' Motion to Dismiss Pursuant to the First Amendment and CPLR paras 3211(a)(1), (a)(7) and (g) At p. 7.

17 Supreme Court of the State of New York, Smartmatic U.S.A. Corp, Smartmatic International Holding B.V., and S.G.O. Corporation Limited v. Fox Corporation, Fox News Network LLC, Lou Dobbs, Maria Bartiromo, Jeanine Pirro, Rudolph Giuliani and Sidney Powell. Reply Memorandum of Law in Further Support of Fox Defendants' Motion to Dismiss Pursuant to the First Amendment and CPLR paras 3211(a)(1), (a)(7) and (g) at p. 7.

promulgated via the impugned Fox News television broadcasts and on various other media platforms the Fox Corporation is involved with and by certain of their guests including some of former President Trump's personal lawyers; that (ii) Fox News acted with "actual malice" such that its speech in this case did not meet the standard of neutral balanced reporting on a controversy that involved arguably corporations that were public figures[18] due to their involvement in a globally scrutinized, highly politically heated U.S. Presidential election and that (iii) many of the so-called reasonable consumers of the impugned Fox entity news broadcasts would be foreseeably easily susceptible to the purported disinformation campaign that Fox News and Fox Corporation allegedly waged against Smartmatic and Dominion. The latter given the purported manipulative tactics and depth of penetration of the alleged disinformation campaign waged by the Defendants.

The question arises whether these impugned election technology corporations (Dominion and Smartmatic) could prove their defamation case if they can show that Fox News Network and certain of its personalities (in their capacities as Fox personalities on air and on other media platforms) as well as certain of former President Trump's personal lawyers engaged in a systematic wide-ranging "disinformation campaign" against the Smartmatic and Dominion Corporations. We will not attempt to determine whether such a disinformation campaign was in fact waged against Smartmatic and Dominion by Fox News Network but rather consider the legal implications for the aforementioned defamation suits if this was in fact the case. It is argued here that if a disinformation campaign can be proven, then *ipso facto the First Amendment protection does not apply.* This given the fact that disinformation campaigns are much more widespread, manipulative, impenetrable and insidious for the consumer than a simple collection of false statements. This makes it extremely difficult, if not impossible, for multitudes of even reasonable consumers of that disinformation to identify it as such, that is to discern that the communications are actually "fake news" (as defined here previously). The end result of successful disinformation campaigns is then that the targeted victim consumers are not able to form an independent and accurately *informed* opinion on a matter, especially one of public concern, thus itself undermining their First Amendment right.

## *On the Issue of Alleged "Actual Malice" of the Defendants in the Smartmatic and Dominion Defamation Cases*

"Actual malice" is proven by clear and convincing evidence that the communicator of the defamation knew that what was conveyed was false and/or by proof that the communicator of the defamation had a reckless disregard for the truth. *Actual malice is arguably a feature of many if not all disinformation campaigns.*

18 Whether or not Dominion and Smartmatic were in fact public figures legally given their involvement in the 2020 U.S. Presidential election is a contested point in the cases here discussed.

This in that such broad campaigns (including the repeated spreading of "fake news") represent a concerted intentional effort to manipulate the consumer of the communications using propaganda and other psychological techniques that are knowingly underhanded and difficult for even a reasonable person to resist without the necessary support to gain the skills in doing so. Countervailing communications relating to fact-checks, social science research reveals, are *not* especially effective in overcoming the psychological manipulation involved that has led multitudes of average consumers to internalize as true and endorse the disinformation and often also to spread it further.[19] When inundated with a disinformation campaign, the reasonable consumer/audience can no longer be assumed to be adequately discerning about the "information" presented. That is even multitudes of so-called reasonable persons are as likely as not to be susceptible to the disinformation campaign (i.e. many in the audience may be unable to recognize the disinformation as self-interested opinion or commentary rather than fact even when the communications may include some oblique references/disclaimers to that effect).

The resistance of certain segments of consumers to fact-checking news stories that effectively dispel the disinformation "fake news" may in part relate to the creation of large particular communities who are consistently exposed to a steady media diet of misinformation and disinformation conveying the same i.e. political themes. That particular audience's "buy in" to fake news:

> may reflect broader tendencies in *collective cognition*. . . . People tend to align their belief with the values of *their* community (emphasis added).[20]

Furthermore,

> mediation of much fake news via social media might accentuate its effect because of the implicit endorsement that comes with sharing. Beyond electoral impacts, what we know about the effects of media more generally suggests many potential pathways of influence, from increasing cynicism and apathy to encouraging extremism.[21]

The contention is advanced here, furthermore, that when a defamation suit involves victims actually harmed by a systematic, widespread *disinformation campaign*, the victims' failure for whatever reason to succeed in such a suit though the suit had merit will itself do much to further bolster the disinformation campaign.

19 The American Association for the Advancement of Science. The Science of Fake News. *Insights Policy Forum*, Vol. 359, Issue 6380 (March 9, 2018), 1094–1097 at 1095.
20 The American Association for the Advancement of Science. The Science of Fake News. *Insights Policy Forum*, Vol. 359, Issue 6380 (March 9, 2018), 1094–1097 at 1095.
21 The American Association for the Advancement of Science. The Science of Fake News. *Insights Policy Forum*, Vol. 359, Issue 6380 (March 9, 2018), 1094–1097 at 1095.

### *Defamation in the Context of a Disinformation Campaign and the "Reasonable Person" Standard*

The question arises whether a systematic broad-ranging disinformation campaign that defames the targeted victims is different from run-of-the-mill defamation through false and/or misleading statements. The current author proffers no assessment on whether the Dominion and Smartmatic defamation lawsuits have merit since it is beyond the scope of this work to investigate the truth or falsity of the various factual claims made by the plaintiffs. What is a central focus of discussion that remains here is, however, the arguably unique defence that some of the Defendants in these cases have raised. That purported defence is that even if the challenged statements were in fact false and/or grossly misleading just as the corporate plaintiffs allege, this would be of no import. *This since purportedly no "reasonable person" would have believed the challenged statements promulgated to be facts or hence to possibly be factually true.* Let us consider then (in the context of the next case) the challenge for the Court in deciding whether the "reasonable person" standard is still workable as a defence in a case involving a purported *defamatory disinformation campaign* such that the impugned defamatory statements are still protected by the First Amendment.

## Case 3: U.S. Dominion Inc., Dominion Voting Systems Inc., Dominion Voting Systems Corporation v. Sidney Powell, Sidney Powell P.C. and Defending the Republic Inc.

Sidney Powell (one of Trump's personal lawyers) raised a number of jurisdictional arguments in her defence, but we will concentrate here only on her defence as to the substantive defamation claims in the Dominion lawsuit. Powell is one of the Defendants who allegedly defamed the Dominion company and did so purportedly knowingly, intentionally and with actual malice. Powell argued, among other things, that the plaintiffs allegedly failed to state a claim.

Powell in her motion to dismiss relies heavily on the notion that her impugned speech was protected by the First Amendment. This in that it concerned a high-profile public affairs topic, namely the doubts among some about the integrity of the 2020 U.S. Presidential election and the role of Dominion in that election. In attempting to bolster this argument, Sidney Powell cites the United States Supreme Court in her motion to dismiss as follows "speech concerning public affairs is more than self-expression; it is the essence of self-government."[22] She then highlights that the U.S. courts for that reason have held that political speech

22 Garrison v. Louisiana 379 US, 64 74–75 (1964) Cited in U.S. Dominion Inc., Dominion Voting Systems Inc., Dominion Voting Systems Corporation v. Sidney Powell, Sidney Powell P.C. and Defending the Republic Inc. Defendants' Motion to Dismiss (March 3, 2021) at p. 21 (In the United States District Court for the District of Columbia, Civil Action No. 1.21- cv -00040-CJN).

"is entitled to the fullest possible measure of constitutional protection."[23] We will address here shortly whether, on the analysis here, Powell's speech at issue was in fact protected political speech.

Powell also points to cases which establish that for a defamation claim to be actionable, it must reference challenged statements that make a factual claim(s) or have a factual connotation(s) that can be demonstrably proven to be false.[24] Hence, mere opinion or commentary on matters of public concern/ public affairs without allegations or connotations of fact will not suffice to meet the standard for an actionable defamation claim.[25] Rather, "reasonable people" listening or reading the statement (i) must be inclined to consider the impugned statement as a statement of fact or connotation of fact and not one of opinion and (ii) that allegation of fact or connotation of fact must be provably false. Whether the challenged statements are to be considered statements of alleged fact that are provably true or false and—based on their phrasing, context and the specific and broader circumstances in which they occurred—statements likely to be understood by "reasonable persons" as such rather than as opinion/commentary is, Powell contends, and this author concurs, a "matter of law."[26]

Powell, furthermore, highlights cases in which the defamation claim at issue was defeated on the grounds that it was *self-evident* "rhetorical hyperbole" and/ or its alleged factual basis was revealed to the audience at the time the purported defamatory statement was communicated.[27] She then goes on to cite the court's reasoning that when the factual basis for the impugned statements are revealed, the defamation claim does not meet the actionable standard. This since "it is clear

23 Members of City Council of Los Angeles v Taxpayers for Vincent, 466 US 789, 816 (1984) Cited in U.S. Dominion Inc., Dominion Voting Systems Inc., Dominion Voting Systems Corporation v. Sidney Powell, Sidney Powell P.C. and Defending the Republic Inc. Defendants' Motion to Dismiss (March 3, 2021) at p. 21 (In the United States District Court for the District of Columbia, Civil Action No. 1.21- cv -00040-CJN).

24 In the United States District Court for the District of Columbia, Civil Action No. 1.21- cv -00040-CJN, U.S. Dominion Inc., Dominion Voting Systems Inc., Dominion Voting Systems Corporation v. Sidney Powell, Sidney Powell P.C. and Defending the Republic Inc. Defendants' Motion to Dismiss (March 3, 2021) at p. 21 (referring to Keohane v Stewart 882 P. 2d, 1293. 1299 (Colo. (1994)).

25 In the United States District Court for the District of Columbia, Civil Action No. 1.21- cv -00040-CJN, U.S. Dominion Inc., Dominion Voting Systems Inc., Dominion Voting Systems Corporation v. Sidney Powell, Sidney Powell P.C. and Defending the Republic Inc. Defendants' Motion to Dismiss (March 3, 2021) at p. 21.

26 In the United States District Court for the District of Columbia, Civil Action No. 1.21- cv -00040-CJN, U.S. Dominion Inc., Dominion Voting Systems Inc., Dominion Voting Systems Corporation v. Sidney Powell, Sidney Powell P.C. and Defending the Republic Inc. Defendants' Motion to Dismiss (March 3, 2021) at p. 27.

27 In the United States District Court for the District of Columbia, Civil Action No. 1.21- cv -00040-CJN, U.S. Dominion Inc., Dominion Voting Systems Inc., Dominion Voting Systems Corporation v. Sidney Powell, Sidney Powell P.C. and Defending the Republic Inc. Defendants' Motion to Dismiss (March 3, 2021) at p. 22.

that the challenged statements represent his own interpretation of these facts"[28] and this "leaves the reader free to draw his own conclusions."[29] In her motion to dismiss, Powell thus argues, among other things, that (i) she was engaged in constitutionally protected "political speech" when discussing Dominion's involvement in the U.S. 2020 Presidential election as (according to her) that of participating in contributing to an alleged steal of the election for Biden; and (ii) that her speech in that regard was not unexpectedly infused with hyperbolic rhetoric and opinion commentary that no "reasonable person" would have taken as statements or connotations of fact that were amenable to being shown to be demonstrably true or false.

Powell, in addition, relies on the notion that "the states are free to provide greater protections to individual liberties—including free speech—than those provided by the First Amendment"[30] and contended that the plaintiffs in this case must prove actual malice. Another argument Powell raised in her defence was that (i) the challenged statements she made were part of pending and ongoing litigation and therefore protected speech under the "right to petition" which is itself a protected First Amendment right and that (ii) her public disclosures at certain press conferences or news releases regarding that litigation were relevant to matters of public concern and in the public interest and hence protected speech.[31] In regard to the latter point, Powell's motion for dismissal in part states:

> It would make no sense and serve no public purpose, to give immunity for statements made during the course of litigation—which are themselves public—but burden lawyers with the threat of billion-dollar defamation verdicts when the same allegations are made at press conferences and news releases announcing the case.[32]

28 Referring to the communicator's own interpretation of the facts alleged in the purported defamatory statements.

29 Bauman v. Butowsky 377 F. Supp 3d 1, 11 at n.7 Cited in U.S. Dominion Inc., Dominion Voting Systems Inc., Dominion Voting Systems Corporation v. Sidney Powell, Sidney Powell P.C. and Defending the Republic Inc. Defendants' Motion to Dismiss (March 3, 2021) at p. 22 (In the United States District Court for the District of Columbia, Civil Action No. 1.21- cv -00040-CJN).

30 U.S. Dominion Inc., Dominion Voting Systems Inc., Dominion Voting Systems Corporation v. Sidney Powell, Sidney Powell P.C. and Defending the Republic Inc. Defendants' Motion to Dismiss (March 3, 2021) at p. 23 (In the United States District Court for the District of Columbia, Civil Action No. 1.21- cv -00040-CJN).

31 U.S. Dominion Inc., Dominion Voting Systems Inc., Dominion Voting Systems Corporation v. Sidney Powell, Sidney Powell P.C. and Defending the Republic Inc. Defendants' Motion to Dismiss (March 3, 2021) at p. 23 (In the United States District Court for the District of Columbia, Civil Action No. 1.21- cv -00040-CJN) at pp. 34–35.

32 U.S. Dominion Inc., Dominion Voting Systems Inc., Dominion Voting Systems Corporation v. Sidney Powell, Sidney Powell P.C. and Defending the Republic Inc. Defendants' Motion to Dismiss (March 3, 2021) at p. 23 (In the United States District Court for the District of Columbia, Civil Action No. 1.21- cv -00040-CJN) at p. 35.

Sidney Powell argued in essence then that (i) her claims about Dominion are not actionable defamation as they are protected hyperbolic rhetoric and political opinion/commentary that no reasonable person would regard as demonstrably provable factual claims;[33] (ii) that "the challenged statements relate to matters of public concern" pertaining to the integrity of the 2020 U.S. Presidential election and the reliability and accuracy of the electoral technology and software used to count the electoral college votes and as such deserve a high level of First Amendment protection;[34] and that (iii) "Dominion is a public figure" and hence is required to prove "actual malice" in Sidney Powell's making of the challenged statements (that is the plaintiff must prove the statement was made "with knowledge it was false or with reckless disregard that it was false").[35] We will focus here next for our limited purposes mostly on Powell's contention that her impugned claims about Dominion are protected under the First Amendment as "political speech" and therefore not actionable.

Powell argues based on case law that determining whether a statement is protected involves assessing (i) whether it is a statement that can be proven to be true or false and (ii) whether "reasonable people" would "conclude that the statement is one of fact, in light of its phrasing, context and the circumstances of its publication."[36] Powell argues in her defence that even if each and every one of her impugned statements could be proven true or false, "no reasonable person would conclude that the statements were truly statements of fact."[37] Powell, in defending her alleged defamatory communications to the public about Dominion, however, gives no reason as to why she assumes that "no reasonable person would conclude that the statements [she made about Dominion] were truly statements of fact." *If* her statements were part of a broader alleged disinformation campaign about the 2020 election being stolen, the political and social

33 U.S. Dominion Inc., Dominion Voting Systems Inc., Dominion Voting Systems Corporation v. Sidney Powell, Sidney Powell P.C. and Defending the Republic Inc. Defendants' Motion to Dismiss (March 3, 2021) at p. 23 (In the United States District Court for the District of Columbia, Civil Action No. 1.21- cv -00040-CJN) at p. 27.

34 U.S. Dominion Inc., Dominion Voting Systems Inc., Dominion Voting Systems Corporation v. Sidney Powell, Sidney Powell P.C. and Defending the Republic Inc. Defendants' Motion to Dismiss (March 3, 2021) at p. 24 (In the United States District Court for the District of Columbia, Civil Action No. 1.21- cv -00040-CJN).

35 U.S. Dominion Inc., Dominion Voting Systems Inc., Dominion Voting Systems Corporation v. Sidney Powell, Sidney Powell P.C. and Defending the Republic Inc. Defendants' Motion to Dismiss ((March 3, 2021) at p. 25 (In the United States District Court for the District of Columbia, Civil Action No. 1.21- cv -00040-CJN).

36 U.S. Dominion Inc., Dominion Voting Systems Inc., Dominion Voting Systems Corporation v. Sidney Powell, Sidney Powell P.C. and Defending the Republic Inc. Defendants' Motion to Dismiss (March 3, 2021) at p. 27 (In the United States District Court for the District of Columbia, Civil Action No. 1.21- cv -00040-CJN).

37 U.S. Dominion Inc., Dominion Voting Systems Inc., Dominion Voting Systems Corporation v. Sidney Powell, Sidney Powell P.C. and Defending the Republic Inc. Defendants' Motion to Dismiss (March 3, 2021) at pp. 27–28 (In the United States District Court for the District of Columbia, Civil Action No. 1.21- cv -00040-CJN).

science evidence is that disinformation campaigns involving hyperbolic rhetoric are highly persuasive. This is the case even for persons who, in other contexts, may be more discerning and reasonable in their judgements. Nor did Powell explain why she would assume—as she implies—that reasonable people would yet be convinced by her allegations of Dominion's role in a purported steal of the 2020 U.S. Presidential election if she were perceived as merely expressing a personal opinion rather than making allegations of fact.

It is to be emphasized that there is no assertion or conclusion made by the current author one way or the other on either the merits of Powell's defence, the truth or falsity of her challenged statements or on whether Powell's statements were or were not a part of a political disinformation campaign. This in that the author's personal opinion on those matters as relates to the particular fact pattern in Powell's case are not particularly relevant to the main point for discussion here. That point of central interest for this author's purpose is only (i) Powell's reliance on a defence that does *not* claim the alleged substantive factual truth of the challenged statements she made and (ii) reflects instead a contrary tact in setting out the argument that no "reasonable person" would take the challenged statements she made to be "truly statements of fact."[38]

Interestingly *outside of court*, and since filing her motion to dismiss in the Dominion case, Powell asserted forcefully that she *does* actually continue to believe the challenged election fraud claims she made and stands by the alleged truth of her challenged claims about Dominion saying "Oh, no, I am not backtracking a bit."[39] This notwithstanding that in her motion to dismiss, as discussed, Powell contended that no "reasonable person" would take her impugned claims regarding the Presidential election being stolen and Dominion's alleged role in the purported steal of the 2020 U.S. Presidential election as true statements of fact. It is unclear then upon what basis Powell rests her faith in the fidelity of her communications regarding Dominion.

Respectfully, and without reaching any conclusion on the issue of plaintiff's allegation of "actual malice" on Powell's part, on the author's current analysis, Powell's defence is contradictory. This in that, on the one hand, Powell argues in her motion to dismiss the Dominion suit that no "reasonable person" would have taken her impugned so-called political speech about Dominion to be "truly statements of fact."[40] On the other hand, in the same court filing, Powell argues

38 U.S. Dominion Inc., Dominion Voting Systems Inc., Dominion Voting Systems Corporation v. Sidney Powell, Sidney Powell P.C. and Defending the Republic Inc. Defendants' Motion to Dismiss (March 3, 2021) at pp. 27–28 (In the United States District Court for the District of Columbia, Civil Action No. 1.21- cv -00040-CJN).

39 Sidney Powell cited in Durkee, A. *Forbes Business* online "Sidney Powell's Admission in Dominion Case Could Haunt Her in Michigan as State AG makes New Move for Sanctions" (April 7, 2021).

40 U.S. Dominion Inc., Dominion Voting Systems Inc., Dominion Voting Systems Corporation v. Sidney Powell, Sidney Powell P.C. and Defending the Republic Inc. Defendants' Motion to Dismiss (March 3, 2021) at pp. 27–28 (In the United States District Court for the District of Columbia, Civil Action No. 1.21- cv -00040-CJN).

(likely in an effort to defend against the "actual malice" claim) that "she believed the challenged allegations" about Dominion when she made them and "she believes them now."[41] Presumably, she regards herself and wishes to be perceived as a reasonable person. This implicates and gives rise most likely then, since Powell is an attorney, to the audience perception of Powell communicating an allegedly factually grounded belief of hers as to Dominion's purported nefarious role in the 2020 U.S. Presidential election. This is especially likely to have been the case given that Powell advanced her alleged defamatory claims about Dominion as a legal representative of Trump and, as a lawyer then, someone expected to be bound by the profession's ethical conduct rules. In the latter regard, counsel for Powell in the Dominion lawsuit stated: "Furthermore, it is clear that Powell's statements *were made as an attorney-advocate* for her preferred candidate and in support of her legal and political positions (emphasis added)."[42]

Further, on the view here, there seems to be a plausible argument that Powell's damaging allegations about Dominion were articulated as *factual claims* that could be demonstrably shown to be either true or false. For instance, Powell charged that

> Democrats were trying to "steal the vote" from Trump and that "they ha[d] developed a computer system to alter votes electronically". . . . *She claimed that she had evidence* that the election result was the "greatest crime of the century if not the life of the world (emphasis added)."[43]

The reference to alleged evidence of her claims, on the analysis here, implied that Powell had thoroughly vetted the claims against Dominion. Indeed, the allegation that Dominion machines altered votes was independently investigated by certain States after-the-fact and no corroborating evidence was evinced.

Furthermore, Powell's counsel in the motion to dismiss conceded that "it is clear that Powell was describing *the facts* on which she based the lawsuits she filed in support of President Trump (emphasis added)."[44] Filing such potentially defamatory claims requires that counsel will have first exercised due diligence

41 U.S. Dominion Inc., Dominion Voting Systems Inc., Dominion Voting Systems Corporation v. Sidney Powell, Sidney Powell P.C. and Defending the Republic Inc. Defendants' Motion to Dismiss (March 3, 2021) at p. 37 (In the United States District Court for the District of Columbia, Civil Action No. 1.21- cv -00040-CJN).

42 U.S. Dominion Inc., Dominion Voting Systems Inc., Dominion Voting Systems Corporation v. Sidney Powell, Sidney Powell P.C. and Defending the Republic Inc. Defendants' Motion to Dismiss (March 3, 2021) at p. 37 (In the United States District Court for the District of Columbia, Civil Action No. 1.21- cv -00040-CJN) at p. 29.

43 U.S. Dominion Inc., Dominion Voting Systems Inc., Dominion Voting Systems Corporation v. Sidney Powell, Sidney Powell P.C. and Defending the Republic Inc. Defendants' Motion to Dismiss (March 3, 2021) at p. 37 (In the United States District Court for the District of Columbia, Civil Action No. 1.21- cv -00040-CJN) at pp. 31–32 citing the Plaintiffs' complaint.

44 U.S. Dominion Inc., Dominion Voting Systems Inc., Dominion Voting Systems Corporation v. Sidney Powell, Sidney Powell P.C. and Defending the Republic Inc. Defendants'

in vetting them which necessitates verifying the purported facts underlying the claims to the reasonable degree possible in the circumstance. It is no answer (on the view here) to simply contend, as did Powell in defending against the Dominion suit, that "reasonable people would not accept such statements as fact but view them only as claims that await testing by the courts through the adversary process."[45] Great numbers of reasonable people may commonly in fact have taken Powell's allegations about Dominion as demonstrably true factual claims. This where they relied on the duty of trust owed to the public to tell the truth about factual claims (i) by the holder of the Office of the President and (ii) by his legal representatives in communicating the President's legal positions to the public. Put somewhat differently, the consumer of Powell's impugned communications about Dominion may oftentimes assume no lawyer would be making these potentially defamatory claims to the courts unless they were factual and hence not view them as unsubstantiated claims to be tested through litigation. Furthermore, if and where claims are part of a well-tuned prolonged disinformation campaign—and this author makes no assertion in that regard insofar as Powell's claims are concerned—it is here argued that the consumer often is unable to distinguish substantiated claims from factually unfounded hyperbolic politically charged claims.

Powell's defence on the "actual malice" involved arguing that no facts were adduced or alleged by the plaintiffs that Powell "in fact entertained serious doubts as to the truth of her publication" concerning Dominion.[46] The defence proposition being advanced then in the latter regard is that Powell did not (i) knowingly or (ii) recklessly without regard for the truth spread falsehoods about Dominion. However, if the latter defence on "actual malice" succeeds arguably, the defence on Powell's speech being purely protected "political speech" that no "reasonable person" could consider as assertions of demonstrably true facts fails. By Powell's own account, as argued in her motion to dismiss, no reasonable person would consider her hyperbolic statements/claims about Dominion to equate to demonstrably true fact. If the latter is the case, then it is unclear why Powell, as presumably a reasonable person, would not indeed have "entertained serious doubts as to the truth of her publication" concerning Dominion. Powell, after all, states that the Plaintiff's characterizations of her impugned statements as "wild accusations," "outlandish claims," "inherently improbable" and "even impossible" serve to "further support Defendants' position that reasonable people would not

---

Motion to Dismiss (March 3, 2021) at p. 37 (In the United States District Court for the District of Columbia, Civil Action No. 1.21- cv -00040-CJN) at p. 32.

45 U.S. Dominion Inc., Dominion Voting Systems Inc., Dominion Voting Systems Corporation v. Sidney Powell, Sidney Powell P.C. and Defending the Republic Inc. Defendants' Motion to Dismiss (March 3, 2021) at p. 37 (In the United States District Court for the District of Columbia, Civil Action No. 1.21- cv -00040-CJN) at p. 32.

46 U.S. Dominion Inc., Dominion Voting Systems Inc., Dominion Voting Systems Corporation v. Sidney Powell, Sidney Powell P.C. and Defending the Republic Inc. Defendants' Motion to Dismiss (March 3, 2021) at p. 37 (In the United States District Court for the District of Columbia, Civil Action No. 1.21- cv -00040-CJN).

accept such statements as fact."[47] Given the foregoing alleged substantive *contradiction* in Powell's defence arguments; on the view here, arguably, there was no effective defence that was in fact mounted to Dominion's claims. This conclusion, however, does not speak to the issue of whether a proper defence potentially was available.

Powell's counsel argued in the motion to dismiss also that (i) Powell revealed the alleged facts upon which she filed lawsuits claiming that the 2020 election was stolen from former President Trump[48] and that (ii) hence the consumer of those related claims about Dominion would understand that she was simply proffering her own opinions and interpretations regarding those underlying facts.[49] It is here contended, however, that whether Powell revealed objective alleged "underlying facts" upon which she based her impugned challenged opinions/interpretations or whether those statements of so-called underlying facts were in themselves also—given the phrasing used, and context and broader circumstances in which that information was conveyed—actually opinion is again a matter to be determined by the Courts as a "matter of law."

A key question is whether the Powell defence of "no reasonable person would believe her challenged statements to be statements of true facts" is actually a viable defence especially if the purported defamatory statements are allegedly embedded in the broader context of a wide-ranging purposeful and knowing disinformation campaign. It is argued by the current author that in any legal case the defence of (i) no "reasonable person" would take the challenged statements to be statements of fact or accurate statements of fact and (ii) the underlying actual facts were disclosed both crumble *if and when* the impugned alleged defamatory statements occur in the context of a massive disinformation campaign of which those challenged statements are a part and a reiteration of selected main theme(s) of the disinformation campaign. Bombarded with "fake news" and overwhelmed by a disinformation campaign, the so-called reasonable person may all too frequently become unreasonable and less and less able and/or willing to adequately reason, discern and access factual information.

47 U.S. Dominion Inc., Dominion Voting Systems Inc., Dominion Voting Systems Corporation v. Sidney Powell, Sidney Powell P.C. and Defending the Republic Inc. Defendants' Motion to Dismiss (March 3, 2021) at p. 32 (In the United States District Court for the District of Columbia, Civil Action No. 1.21- cv -00040-CJN).

48 "Powell alleged 'Democrats were trying to steal the vote from Trump' and had 'developed a computer system to alter the votes electronically.'" U.S. Dominion Inc., Dominion Voting Systems Inc., Dominion Voting Systems Corporation v. Sidney Powell, Sidney Powell P.C. and Defending the Republic Inc. Defendants' Motion to Dismiss (March 3, 2021) at p. 31 (In the United States District Court for the District of Columbia, Civil Action No. 1.21- cv -00040-CJN).

49 U.S. Dominion Inc., Dominion Voting Systems Inc., Dominion Voting Systems Corporation v. Sidney Powell, Sidney Powell P.C. and Defending the Republic Inc. Defendants' Motion to Dismiss (March 3, 2021) at pp. 32–33 (In the United States District Court for the District of Columbia, Civil Action No. 1.21- cv -00040-CJN) Citing the Dominion complaint at para 52.

It is here argued that the First Amendment free expression rights of the audience are subverted when the impugned purportedly defamatory statements are embedded in a concerted broad-ranging intentional campaign of disinformation. After all free speech rights incorporate, as the opposite side of the coin of free expression and thought, the right also to access reliable, accurate information upon which to form cogent independent thoughts, opinions and conclusions that can guide one's conduct hopefully in the interest of self and community consistent with democratic values. The social science research appears to indicate that the manipulative tactics that are so central to a concerted intense, repetitive broad disinformation campaign (including the communication of politically charged "fake news") are quite effective in rendering the cognitive and emotional bent of great numbers of consumers relatively impervious to fact-checking stories:

> people tend to remember information, or how they feel about it, while forgetting the context in which they encountered it. Moreover, they are more likely to accept familiar information as true. There is therefore a risk that repeating false information, even in a fact-checking context, may increase individual's likelihood of accepting it as true. The evidence on the effectiveness of claim repetition in fact checking is mixed.[50]

The problem of blind acceptance of "fake news" would likely, furthermore, be exacerbated where the defamatory information is communicated by persons in power or their agents whom the audience respects and has come to depend on for what they are being told is an accurate factually grounded perspective on matters of public concern.[51] As discussed, the mere disclosure (should that occur) of the actual basis for the impugned alleged defamatory factual claim and/or the hyperbolic rhetorical context is often *not* a sufficient cue to allow the person targeted for a disinformation campaign to adequately assess the claim and come to a truly independent conclusion as to its truth or falsity. It is argued here then that the "reasonable person standard" is not in fact adequate as so many persons are unable to resist the manipulative tactics of fake news occurring in the context of a massive disinformation campaign which inundates them repeatedly with falsehoods. This author's respectful conclusion is then that fake news *when embedded in a broad disinformation campaign* is *not* protected by the First Amendment. This since fake news in the aforementioned particular circumstance/context is part of a knowing, intentional and concerted effort to overwhelm and disarm the consumer psychologically such that the targeted victims are thwarted from exercising their competence to think independently and critically to the same extent that they were able to do so prior to being exposed to that disinformation

50 The American Association for the Advancement of Science. The Science of Fake News. *Insights Policy Forum*, Vol. 359, Issue 6380 (March 9, 2018), 1094–1097 at p. 1095.

51 Disinformation campaigns typically are carried out by numbers of persons, some who may be named as Defendants in defamation suits and others unknown but yet key to the disinformation effort.

campaign. Respectfully, it is here contended that to the extent that the courts do not consider whether the particular "fake news" claims challenged as defamatory unprotected speech are part of a *larger disinformation context* on the same and related topics, the legal analysis is incomplete and inadequate. Powell herself cites case law in her motion to dismiss the Dominion defamation suit against her which cases reference the courts' emphasis on the fact that both the specific and broader context of the challenged speech must be considered in a defamation case, especially one involving political speech.[52] It is here contended that whether the impugned statements occurred as part of a larger disinformation campaign is a highly relevant aspect of the broader context of the challenged speech and the circumstances of its publication. From that perspective then, the courts would be well-advised to set a judicial test for what constitutes a disinformation campaign when assessing whether specific challenged political and other statements are defamatory and are part of a larger orchestrated intentional and knowing disinformation campaign.

In a case in which the allegedly defamatory statements are proven to be embedded in a broad purposeful disinformation campaign, the current author argues that reliance on the "reasonable person standard" is itself in fact unreasonable. This given that many so-called otherwise reasonable persons are susceptible to the psychological manipulative tactics involved in an intensive disinformation campaign and cannot distinguish hyperbolic rhetoric from demonstrable fact in that context. Further, it is here argued that the impugned statements being knowingly and intentionally advanced as part of a broader disinformation campaign should be considered proof *ipso facto* of "actual malice." It is here contended then that the courts, when considering fake political news that is purposefully and knowingly embedded in a broader disinformation campaign and asserting false facts, can no longer properly consider it as but non-defamatory, hyperbolic political opinion or rhetoric. This since many multitudes of consumers have shown themselves to be vulnerable to accepting fake news when embedded in a disinformation campaign.[53] Hence that "courts shelter even outrageous political speech" on the assumption that "the ordinary reader or listener, will in the context of political debate, assume that vituperation is some form of political opinion

52 U.S. Dominion Inc., Dominion Voting Systems Inc., Dominion Voting Systems Corporation v. Sidney Powell, Sidney Powell P.C. and Defending the Republic Inc. Defendants' Motion to Dismiss (March 3, 2021) at p. 28 (In the United States District Court for the District of Columbia, Civil Action No. 1.21- cv -00040-CJN).

53 Many for instance believe the "fake news" false conspiracy theory that unnamed "unindicted co-conspirators" in the January 6, 2021, attempt to overrun the U.S. Capitol to stop certification of the electoral college wins in the 2020 U.S. Presidential election are FBI agents who organized and fomented the attempted takeover of the Capitol building and presumably taking of congressional persons hostage. The latter is part of a disinformation campaign that includes rewriting history to suggest that the January 6, 2021, events at the Capitol were all peaceful and factually speaking in lawful constitutional defence of democratic values. In fact, legally FBI undercover working for the government cannot in any case be labelled as "unindicted co-conspirators."

neither demonstrably true nor demonstrably false"[54] is, it is here contended, *not* in some contexts a legally supportable approach, that is as when the challenged statements occur as part of a larger intense prolonged disinformation campaign.

Thus, on the view here, statements that repeat core messages of a broader disinformation campaign in a political context cannot be considered protected non-defamatory "political speech." Without deciding for our limited purposes whether Powell's challenged speech was mere "political speech," nevertheless recall that Powell argued in her motion to dismiss that her speech was protected and non-actionable "political speech" and as such "lies at the core of First Amendment protection" since "such speech must be uninhibited, robust and wide-open."[55] The current author concurs that actual "political speech" in a democracy is strongly protected by the First Amendment in that it is intended to stimulate free and open debate and independent thinking. However, the current author makes the point that, in contrast, statements that perpetuate disinformation message(s) create rigid mindsets for many consumers vulnerable to the intense and varied psychological manipulation tactics used in disinformation campaigns. This then renders those media consumers unable to engage politically as truly free and independently minded members of a polity in a democracy. In sum, messages that form part of a disinformation campaign where this occurs (and again this author makes no claims as to whether it did occur in relation to the speech challenged in the Dominion and Smartmatic lawsuits), on the view here, *cannot* properly in law be considered protected "political speech" in the sense intended when covered by the First Amendment even though the content may pertain to political matters of public concern.

## The Rudolph W. Giuliani–Trump Saga

Dominion also sued Rudolph W. Giuliani, personal lawyer to former President Trump, for defamation. According to the Dominion complaint, during a court hearing regarding a challenge to the 2020 U.S. Presidential vote outcome in Pennsylvania, Giuliani stated that "the Trump campaign 'doesn't plead fraud' and that 'this is not a fraud case.'"[56] Dominion further alleged the following regarding Giuliani's alleged conduct:

54 Adelson 973 F. Supp 2d at 489–491. Cited in in U.S. Dominion Inc., Dominion Voting Systems Inc., Dominion Voting Systems Corporation v. Sidney Powell, Sidney Powell P.C. and Defending the Republic Inc. Defendants' Motion to Dismiss (March 3, 2021) at p. 28 (In the United States District Court for the District of Columbia, Civil Action No. 1.21- cv -00040-CJN).

55 U.S. Dominion Inc., Dominion Voting Systems Inc., Dominion Voting Systems Corporation v. Sidney Powell, Sidney Powell P.C. and Defending the Republic Inc. Defendants' Motion to Dismiss (March 3, 2021) at p. 33 (In the United States District Court for the District of Columbia, Civil Action No. 1.21- cv -00040-CJN).

56 Giuliani cited in U.S. Dominion Inc., Dominion Voting Systems Inc., Dominion Voting Systems Corporation v. Rudolph W. Giuliani United States District Court for the District of Columbia (January 25, 2021) at p. 1.

> Although he was unwilling to make false election fraud claims about Dominion and its voting machines in a court of law because he knew those allegations are false, he and his allies manufactured and disseminated the "Big Lie," which foreseeably went viral and deceived millions of people into believing that Dominion had stolen their votes and fixed the election.[57]

Giuliani denied the defamation claims and also rejected the claim that he had engaged in any malicious conduct against Dominion.[58] Giuliani argued that the plaintiffs "have not sufficiently pleaded subject matter jurisdiction, have failed to state a claim and have failed to properly and adequately plead special damages."[59] Some of the latter are fairly technical arguments concerning, for instance, Dominion as a single corporation versus a family of corporations and the required nature of the pleadings when a corporation or family of corporations is the plaintiff(s).

Giuliani did not appear at a court hearing June 24, 2021, in the Dominion defamation suit against him, though his lawyer representing him in the 1.3 billon dollar suit was present. Just hours before, a New York five-panel Appeals Court had temporarily suspended Giuliani's New York law licence. Giuliani responded to the temporary suspension of his law licence in an interview with news media, lamenting that the judgement was rendered without his having had a full hearing (Giuliani may request such a formal full disciplinary hearing within 20 days of the court order that issued the temporary suspension decision regarding his New York law licence). Giuliani in an interview with the press subsequent to the law licence temporary suspension stated that everything he said that was challenged was supported by affidavits.[60] He alleged the judges "listened to false allegations made by Democrats. The same thing they did to President Trump."[61] It is to that ruling temporarily suspending Giuliani's New York law licence that we turn now. We will consider what, if any, relevance the ruling has for our analysis here regard-

57 U.S. Dominion Inc., Dominion Voting Systems Inc., Dominion Voting Systems Corporation v. Rudolph W. Giuliani United States District Court for the District of Columbia (January 25, 2021) at p. 1.
58 Dominion Inc., Dominion Voting Systems Inc., Dominion Voting Systems Corporation v. Rudolph W. Giuliani, United States District Court for the District of Columbia, Civil Action No. 1:21-cv-00213-CJN Defendant's Motion to Dismiss Plaintiffs' Original Complaint (April 7, 2021).
59 Dominion Inc., Dominion Voting Systems Inc., Dominion Voting Systems Corporation v. Rudolph W. Giuliani, United States District Court for the District of Columbia, Civil Action No. 1:21-cv-00213-CJN Defendant's Motion to Dismiss Plaintiffs' Original Complaint (April 7, 2021) at pp. 1–2.
60 CNBC Rudy Giuliani skips Dominion, Powell, MyPillow-Lindell defamation case hearing after his law license gets revoked in NY Published June 24, 2021 (Kevin Breuninger) www.cnbc.com/2021/06/24/rudy-giuliani-skips-dominion-powell-mypillow-lindell-hearing.html
61 CNBC Rudy Giuliani skips Dominion, Powell, MyPillow-Lindell defamation case hearing after his law license gets revoked in NY Published June 24, 2021 (Kevin Breuninger) www.cnbc.com/2021/06/24/rudy-giuliani-skips-dominion-powell-mypillow-lindell-hearing.html

ing a First Amendment defence in a case such as Dominion's involving allegations of defamation as part of a purported larger concerted well-orchestrated disinformation campaign.

The Giuliani law licence hearing was held by the Supreme Court of the State of New York, Appellate Division, First Judicial Department in response to a request from the Attorney Grievance Committee (AGC) for the First Judicial Department for an order immediately suspending Giuliani from the practice of law due to the alleged violation of particular professional rules of conduct. The Supreme Court of the State of New York, Appellate Division concluded that:

> there is incontrovertible evidence that respondent communicated demonstrably false and misleading statements to courts, lawmakers and the public at large in his capacity as lawyer for former President Donald J. Trump and the campaign in connection with Trump's failed effort at re-election in 2020. *These false statements were made to improperly bolster respondent's narrative that due to widespread voter fraud, victory in the 2020 United States presidential election was stolen from his client.* We conclude that respondent's conduct immediately threatens the public interest and warrants interim suspension from the practice of law, pending further proceedings before the Attorney Grievance Committee (emphasis added).[62]

It is to be emphasized that the court explained that

> The ultimate purpose of any disciplinary proceeding . . . is not to impose punishment for breaches of the Rules of Conduct, but rather "to protect the public in its reliance upon the integrity and responsibility of the legal profession."[63]

Speaking here now in a general sense and not in reference to the Giuliani case since Giuliani has not yet been heard at the time of writing in a full disciplinary hearing, the aforementioned point highlighted by the Court underscores the risk to a pillar of democracy, namely the independent judiciary, when the judicial process is politicized as for instance being used as a potential vehicle for legitimizing and communicating disinformation.

The Supreme Court of the State of New York, Appellate Division, First Judicial Department then went on to particularize its findings (based on what it

62 Supreme Court of the State of New York, Appellate Division, First Judicial Department, In the Matter of Rudolph W. Giuliani, Admitted as attorney and counselor-at law: Attorney Grievance Committee for the First Judicial Department (Petitioner) and Rudolph W. Giuliani (Respondent) at p. 2.

63 Supreme Court of the State of New York, Appellate Division, First Judicial Department, In the Matter of Rudolph W. Giuliani, Admitted as attorney and counselor-at law: Attorney Grievance Committee for the First Judicial Department (Petitioner) and Rudolph W. Giuliani (Respondent) at p. 2.

considered incontrovertible evidence) regarding which professional rules of attorney conduct it held were violated by Giuliani and under what circumstances. In regard to the Dominion election technology corporation, the Court stated that:

> Respondent made extensive and wide-ranging claims about Dominion Voting Systems Inc.'s voting machines manipulating the vote tallies to support his narrative that votes were incorrectly reported. Georgia, however, had completed a hand count of all ballots cast in the presidential audit. The hand audit . . . confirmed the results of the election with a zero percent risk limit. Respondent's statement that the vote count was inaccurate, without referencing the hand audits, was misleading. . . . We understand that Dominion has sued respondent for defamation in connection with his claims about their voting machines. . . . Consequently, we do not reach the issue of whether respondent's claims about the Dominion voting machines were false, nor do we need to. In view of the hand counts conducted in Georgia, we find that respondent's statements about the results of the Georgia election count are false.[64]
>
> The Court found the misleading or false statements about the Georgia vote were made to the Georgia Legislature's Senate Judiciary Committee, December 3, 2020 and on specified dates on certain media platforms.[65]

Especially relevant to our discussion is the fact that the court mentioned that Giuliani in his affidavit to the court considering the AGC petition

> raises an overarching argument that the AGC's investigation into his conduct violates his First Amendment right of free speech. He does not attack the constitutionality of the particular disciplinary rules; he seemingly claims that they are unconstitutional as applied to him.[66]

The court rejected the argument stating:

> We reject respondent's argument. This disciplinary proceeding concerns the professional restrictions imposed on respondent as an attorney to not

64 Supreme Court of the State of New York, Appellate Division, First Judicial Department, In the Matter of Rudolph W. Giuliani, Admitted as attorney and counselor-at law: Attorney Grievance Committee for the First Judicial Department (Petitioner) and Rudolph W. Giuliani (Respondent) at pp. 16–17.

65 Supreme Court of the State of New York, Appellate Division, First Judicial Department, In the Matter of Rudolph W. Giuliani, Admitted as attorney and counselor-at law: Attorney Grievance Committee for the First Judicial Department (Petitioner) and Rudolph W. Giuliani (Respondent) at p. 17.

66 Supreme Court of the State of New York, Appellate Division, First Judicial Department, In the Matter of Rudolph W. Giuliani, Admitted as attorney and counselor-at law: Attorney Grievance Committee for the First Judicial Department (Petitioner) and Rudolph W. Giuliani (Respondent) at p. 6.

> knowingly misrepresent facts and make false statements in connection with his representation of a client. . . . As officers of the court, attorneys are "an intimate and trusted and essential part of the machinery of justice." . . . In other words, they are perceived by the public to be in a position of knowledge, and therefore, "a crucial source of information and opinion." . . . While there are limits on the extent to which a lawyer's right of free speech may be circumscribed, these limits are not implicated by the circumstances of the knowing misconduct that this Court relies upon in granting temporary suspension in this case.[67]

It appears to the current author that the Supreme Court of the State of New York, Appellate Division[68] in essence held that Giuliani made misleading and false statements that were ***part of a Trump campaign disinformation campaign*** regarding the 2020 U.S. Presidential election being stolen. Rather than use the words "disinformation campaign," the court referred to Giuliani's impugned statements as being part of the Trump stolen 2020 U.S. Presidential election "narrative" which Giuliani, according to the court, attempted to bolster.[69] This, according to the court, by "his . . . persistent and pervasive dissemination of these false statements in the media."[70] Without here asserting a conclusion about the legal merits of the Giuliani law licence immediate temporary suspension (since no full disciplinary hearing has yet been held at the time of writing), this author contends that the court's situating what it found to be Giuliani's misleading and false statements about the 2020 U.S. Presidential election directly into the context of a larger "disinformation campaign" had significant legal implications. It served to (i) highlight the court's perception of a heightened risk to the public interest in the situation (in the court's estimation, the public's ultimate faith in the justice system was potentially in jeopardy given Giuliani's court-impugned conduct and the likelihood of that conduct continuing) and therefore to (ii) provide a rationale for the unusual step of immediately temporarily stripping Giuliani of his New York bar licence pending the outcome of a full disciplinary hearing.

67 Supreme Court of the State of New York, Appellate Division, First Judicial Department, In the Matter of Rudolph W. Giuliani, Admitted as attorney and counselor-at law: Attorney Grievance Committee for the First Judicial Department (Petitioner) and Rudolph W. Giuliani (Respondent) at pp. 6–7.

68 Referring to the New York Appellate Division, First Judicial Department that heard and decided on the petition by the Attorney Grievance Committee to immediately temporarily suspend Rudolph Giuliani's New York law licence.

69 Supreme Court of the State of New York, Appellate Division, First Judicial Department, In the Matter of Rudolph W. Giuliani, Admitted as attorney and counselor-at law: Attorney Grievance Committee for the First Judicial Department (Petitioner) and Rudolph W. Giuliani (Respondent) at p. 2.

70 Supreme Court of the State of New York, Appellate Division, First Judicial Department, In the Matter of Rudolph W. Giuliani, Admitted as attorney and counselor-at law: Attorney Grievance Committee for the First Judicial Department (Petitioner) and Rudolph W. Giuliani (Respondent) at p. 30.

The court referenced the alleged fact that the "broad dissemination of false statements, casting doubt on the legitimacy of thousands of validly cast votes, is corrosive to the public's trust in our most important democratic institutions."[71] It seems to the current author that the court is here referring to an alleged concerted knowing widespread disinformation campaign. In such a circumstance, it is here argued, the First Amendment defence for false and misleading statements, where they occur, whether defamatory or not, does not apply. This since disinformation campaigns are *par excellence* a major threat to the First Amendment free thought and expression rights of the general public and, in some factual scenarios, a potential threat to the vote and other democratic institutions and processes.[72] Disinformation campaigns, especially when (i) widespread with multitudes of unwitting and witting purveyors, and amplified on social media; and (ii) when intended to erode democratic values and institutions arguably also increase the risk for violence and the opportunity for authoritarian forces to fill the vacuum.

## References

### *Literature*

The American Association for the Advancement of Science. The Science of Fake News. *Insights Policy Forum*, Vol. 359, Issue 6380 (March 9, 2018), 1094–1097.

Durkee, A. Sidney Powell's Admission in Dominion Case Could Haunt Her in Michigan as State AG Makes New Move for Sanctions. *Forbes Business* (April 7, 2021) (accessed June 22, 2022).

Molina, M.D., Sundar, S.S. and Le, D. "Fake News" Is Not Simply False Information: A Concept Explication and Taxonomy of Online Content. *American Behavioral Scientist*, Vol. 65, Issue 2 (2021), 180–212.

### *Cases*

Adelson v. Harris, 973 F.Supp.2d 467 (S.D.N.Y. 2013).

Dominion Inc., Dominion Voting Systems Inc., Dominion Voting Systems Corporation v. Rudolph W. Giuliani, United States District Court for the District of Columbia, Civil Action No. 1:21-cv-00213-CJN Defendant's Motion to Dismiss Plaintiffs' Original Complaint (April 7, 2021).

Garrison v Louisiana 379 US, 64 74–75 (1964).

71 "Espousing false factual information to large segments of the public as a means of discrediting the rights of legitimate voters is so immediately harmful to it and warrants interim suspension from the practice of law." Supreme Court of the State of New York, Appellate Division, First Judicial Department, In the Matter of Rudolph W. Giuliani, Admitted as attorney and counselor-at law: Attorney Grievance Committee for the First Judicial Department (Petitioner) and Rudolph W. Giuliani (Respondent) at p. 32.

72 Supreme Court of the State of New York, Appellate Division, First Judicial Department, In the Matter of Rudolph W. Giuliani, Admitted as attorney and counselor-at law: Attorney Grievance Committee for the First Judicial Department (Petitioner) and Rudolph W. Giuliani (Respondent) at p. 32.

Keohane v Stewart 882 P. 2d, 1293. 1299 (Colo. (1994)).
Members of City Council of Los Angeles v Taxpayers for Vincent, 466 US 789, 816 (1984).
Smartmatic U.S.A. Corp, Smartmatic International Holding B.V., and S.G.O. Corporation Limited v. Fox Corporation, Fox News Network LLC, Lou Dobbs, Maria Bartiromo, Jeanine Pirro, Rudolph Giuliani and Sidney Powell. Reply Memorandum of Law in Further Support of Fox Defendants' Motion to Dismiss Pursuant to the First Amendment and CPLR paras 3211(a)(1), (a)(7) and (g) (April 26, 2021) (In the Supreme Court of the State of New York).
Smartmatic U.S.A. Corp, Smartmatic International Holding B.V., and S.G.O. Corporation Limited v. Fox Corporation, Fox News Network LLC, Lou Dobbs, Maria Bartiromo, Jeanine Pirro, Rudolph Giuliani and Sidney Powell Summons (February 4, 2021) (In the Supreme Court of the State of New York).
Supreme Court of the State of New York, Appellate Division, First Judicial Department, in the Matter of Rudolph W. Giuliani, Admitted as Attorney and Counselor-at Law: Attorney Grievance Committee for the First Judicial Department (Petitioner) and Rudolph W. Giuliani (Respondent).
U.S. Dominion Inc., Dominion Voting Systems Inc., and Dominion Voting Systems Corporation v. Fox News Network LLC Complaint, Jury Trial Demanded (March 26, 2021) (In the Superior Court of the State of Delaware).
U.S. Dominion Inc., Dominion Voting Systems Inc., Dominion Voting Systems Corporation v. Rudolph W. Giuliani, Complaint and Demand for a Jury Trial (In the United States District Court for the District of Columbia) (January 25, 2021).
U.S. Dominion Inc., Dominion Voting Systems Inc., Dominion Voting Systems Corporation v. Sidney Powell, Sidney Powell P.C. and Defending the Republic Inc. Defendants' Motion to Dismiss (March 3, 2021) (In the United States District Court for the District of Columbia, Civil Action No. 1.21- cv -00040-CJN).

# 4 The First Amendment Right to Petition the Government for Redress Versus the Intimidation of Elected Officials and Speech Promulgating Disinformation

## United States District Court for the District of Columbia, Representative Eric Swalwell (Plaintiff) v Donald J. Trump (in His Personal Capacity) et al.

Representative Eric Swalwell filed suit against former President Donald J. Trump, Donald Trump Jr., Congressman Mo Brooks and Rudolph Giuliani (former personal lawyer to the former President Trump) for an alleged disinformation campaign that Swalwell alleges led to "the sacking of the United States Capitol on January 6, 2021," and interference in the certification of the results of the U.S. 2020 Presidential election causing a delay in that certification.[1] Swalwell's complaint (civil suit) states in part:

> The Defendants filed frivolous lawsuits, all of which failed. The Defendants tried to intimidate state officials, none of whom caved to the pressure. Out of options and out of time, the Defendants called their supporters to Washington, D.C. on the day Congress met to certify Joe Biden's win, telling them to "Stop the Steal" and "be wild." Thousands came to the District in response. Some planned violence at the Capitol in advance; some were stirred to violence by the Defendants' words on that day. Trump implored the crowd to "fight like hell" and "walk down Pennsylvania Avenue . . . to the Capitol. According to an analysis of cell phone location data, approximately 40% of the rally attendees did just that."[2]
>
> Many members of Congress, including the Plaintiff, were trapped in the House Chamber. . . . Plaintiff and hundreds of others—including police officers, other elected officials, and rank and file workers at the Capitol—were put in mortal danger. . . . The horrific events of January 6 were a direct and

1 United States District Court for the District of Columbia Representative Eric Swalwell (Plaintiff) v Donald J. Trump (in his personal capacity), Donald Trump Jr., representative Mo Brooks (in his personal capacity) and Rudolph Giuliani (Defendants) Complaint, Jury Trial Demanded (March 5, 2021) at p. 1.

2 United States District Court for the District of Columbia Representative Eric Swalwell (Plaintiff) v Donald J. Trump (in his personal capacity), Donald Trump Jr., representative Mo Brooks (in his personal capacity) and Rudolph Giuliani (Defendants) Complaint, Jury Trial Demanded (March 5, 2021) at p. 2.

DOI: 10.4324/9781003153764-4

> foreseeable consequence of the Defendants' unlawful actions. As such, the Defendants are responsible for the injury and destruction that followed.[3]

In his request for relief, Swalwell alleged the following counts regarding the claimed wrongdoing:

(i) *Count 1: Defendants as co-conspirators had violated Swalwell and other particular elected officials' civil rights (as set out in 42 U.S.C. s. 1985).*[4] This by interfering with the official duties of the said elected officials in the certification of the 2020 U.S. Presidential race results which had lawfully rendered Joe Biden U.S. President and Kamala Harris Vice-President. This interference in the certification of the Electoral College results was, Swalwell pleaded, effected by using force, intimidation, or threat;[5]

(ii) *Count 2: Defendants demonstrated neglect to prevent interference with civil rights in violation of 42 U.S.C. s. 1986.* This by failing to prevent the assault on the Capitol that Defendants (according to Swalwell) had conspired no later than January 6, 2021 to incite: "the Defendants commanded the attendance of tens of thousands of individuals at the rally in the District on January 6, 2021 for the purpose of coercing members of Congress to disregard the election results, and further incited thousands to violently storm the Capitol building shortly thereafter. Moreover when it was clear that rioters had stormed the Capitol and Congress was unable to certify the Electoral College vote, the Defendants had the power to stop the rioters but refused, and instead encouraged them."[6]

3 United States District Court for the District of Columbia Representative Eric Swalwell (Plaintiff) v Donald J. Trump (in his personal capacity), Donald Trump Jr., representative Mo Brooks (in his personal capacity) and Rudolph Giuliani (Defendants) Complaint, Jury Trial Demanded (March 5, 2021) at p. 3.

4 42 U.S.C. s. 1985 reads thus as to conspiracy to interfere with civil rights: "(1) Preventing officer from performing duties: If two or more persons in any State or Territory conspire to prevent, by force, intimidation, or threat, any person from accepting or holding any office, trust, or place of confidence under the United States, or from discharging any duties thereof; or to induce by like means any officer of the United States to leave any State, district, or place, where his duties as an officer are required to be performed, or to injure him in his person or property on account of his lawful discharge of the duties of his office, or while engaged in the lawful discharge thereof, or to injure his property so as to molest, interrupt, hinder, or impede him in the discharge of his official duties." 42 U.S. Code s. 1985 (see 42 U.S. Code § 1985 Conspiracy to interfere with civil rights, Legal Information Institute, Cornell Law School).

5 United States District Court for the District of Columbia Representative Eric Swalwell (Plaintiff) v Donald J. Trump (in his personal capacity), Donald Trump Jr., representative Mo Brooks (in his personal capacity) and Rudolph Giuliani (Defendants) Complaint, Jury Trial Demanded (March 5, 2021) at p. 46.

6 United States District Court for the District of Columbia Representative Eric Swalwell (Plaintiff) v Donald J. Trump (in his personal capacity), Donald Trump Jr., representative Mo Brooks (in his personal capacity) and Rudolph Giuliani (Defendants) Complaint, Jury Trial Demanded (March 5, 2021) at p. 51.

(iii) *Count 3: Negligence per se (Violation of D.C. Code sections 22–1322: Incitement to Riot).* Defendants, Swalwell alleged, incited a riot by the false narrative of a stolen 2020 U.S. Presidential election on and weeks before January 6, 2021, violence laced speeches to the mob assembled on January 6, 2021 by the Defendants and their supporters and by the failure for hours to call off the mob from its attack on the Capitol.

(iv) *Count 4: Negligence per se (Violation of D.C. Code sections 22–1321(a)(2): Disorderly Conduct).* Count 4 addressed alleged incitement of violence where such violence is likely to ensue contrary to the interest of public safety. This again was related to the siege of the Capitol on January 6, 2021 and Defendants' alleged role in a) organizing the mob to come to the Capitol and b) inciting the mob violence and the mob's interference with the Electoral College count and certification.

(v) *Count 5: Bias-Related Crimes, Disorderly Conduct and Terrorism D.C. Code sections 22–404,22–1805,22–1321,22–1322(c),22–3152,22–3153,22–3704).* Count 5 refers to a civil cause of action relating to the victimization of the targeted elected officials and others based on a bias that can include "the actual or perceived . . . political affiliation of a victim." Swalwell's complaint also points out that "'Political affiliation' under the statute extends beyond party and includes an individual's stance for or against specific political figures."[7] Swalwell then asserts that "The Defendants and rioters plainly were motivated by the Plaintiff's political affiliation as an opponent of Donald Trump."[8] Swalwell then cites alleged supporting evidence including the following January 6, 2021 statement by Trump: "All of us here today do not want to see our election victory stolen by emboldened radical-left Democrats, which is what they're doing."[9]

Swalwell also alleged violation of various criminal statutes in connection with alleged aiding and abetting of the violence at the Capitol on January 6, 2021.[10] This included also alleged violation of the anti-terrorism statute which "defines an "act of terrorism" as a "specified offense" intended to,

7 D.C. Code § 22–3704(a) Cited in United States District Court for the District of Columbia Representative Eric Swalwell (Plaintiff) v Donald J. Trump (in his personal capacity), Donald Trump Jr., representative Mo Brooks (in his personal capacity) and Rudolph Giuliani (Defendants) Complaint, Jury Trial Demanded (March 5, 2021) at p. 54.

8 United States District Court for the District of Columbia Representative Eric Swalwell (Plaintiff) v Donald J. Trump (in his personal capacity), Donald Trump Jr., representative Mo Brooks (in his personal capacity) and Rudolph Giuliani (Defendants) Complaint, Jury Trial Demanded (March 5, 2021) at p. 54.

9 United States District Court for the District of Columbia Representative Eric Swalwell (Plaintiff) v Donald J. Trump (in his personal capacity), Donald Trump Jr., representative Mo Brooks (in his personal capacity) and Rudolph Giuliani (Defendants) Complaint, Jury Trial Demanded (March 5, 2021) at p. 55.

10 United States District Court for the District of Columbia Representative Eric Swalwell (Plaintiff) v Donald J. Trump (in his personal capacity), Donald Trump Jr., representative Mo Brooks (in his personal capacity) and Rudolph Giuliani (Defendants) Complaint, Jury Trial Demanded (March 5, 2021) at pp. 56–57.

among other things, "influence the policy or conduct of a unit of government by intimidation or coercion"[11] and where the specified offences are particularized under the statute.

(vi) *Count 6 and 7 respectively: Intentional Infliction of Emotional Distress and Negligent Infliction of Emotional Distress.* Swalwell argued, among other things, that "the Defendants . . . are liable to the Plaintiff for aiding and abetting the rioters' acts of intentional infliction of emotional distress."[12]

(vii) *Count 8: Aiding and Abetting Common-Law Assault.* In this count Swalwell in part argued that "The mob terrorized and injured scores of people inside and outside of the Capitol, including the Plaintiff."[13]

(viii) *Count 9: Negligence:* Regarding count nine; Swalwell argued in part that the Defendants owed a duty of care to him and to everyone at the Capitol "to exercise reasonable care in directing the mob's actions." Swalwell argues that instead Defendants breached their duty of care by creating the circumstances that allegedly caused foreseeable violence and danger for Swalwell and other members of Congress and to law enforcement and other security personnel tasked with protecting the Capitol and the congressional members. The Defendants breached their duty of care Swalwell states by "(1) repeating their claims that what was about to occur was a fraud of historical magnitude, (2) blaming the fraud on the Plaintiff and similarly-situated officials, and then, (3) sending the crowd off with exhortations to "fight like hell," to "start taking down names and kicking ass," to have "trial by combat," and to play by "very different rules," all for the literal purpose of "saving the republic."[14]

Swalwell requested from the Court the following forms of relief:

1 Order for actual unspecified money damages to be paid to the Plaintiff (amount to be determined at trial).

11 United States District Court for the District of Columbia Representative Eric Swalwell (Plaintiff) v Donald J. Trump (in his personal capacity), Donald Trump Jr., representative Mo Brooks (in his personal capacity) and Rudolph Giuliani (Defendants) Complaint, Jury Trial Demanded (March 5, 2021) at pp. 56–57.

12 United States District Court for the District of Columbia Representative Eric Swalwell (Plaintiff) v Donald J. Trump (in his personal capacity), Donald Trump Jr., representative Mo Brooks (in his personal capacity) and Rudolph Giuliani (Defendants) Complaint, Jury Trial Demanded (March 5, 2021) at p. 61.

13 United States District Court for the District of Columbia Representative Eric Swalwell (Plaintiff) v Donald J. Trump (in his personal capacity), Donald Trump Jr., representative Mo Brooks (in his personal capacity) and Rudolph Giuliani (Defendants) Complaint, Jury Trial Demanded (March 5, 2021) at p. 61.

14 United States District Court for the District of Columbia Representative Eric Swalwell (Plaintiff) v Donald J. Trump (in his personal capacity), Donald Trump Jr., representative Mo Brooks (in his personal capacity) and Rudolph Giuliani (Defendants) Complaint, Jury Trial Demanded (March 5, 2021) at pp. 62–63.

2 Order for unspecified punitive damages to be paid to the Plaintiff (amount to be determined at trial).
3 Declaration that the Defendants broke the specific laws detailed in the complaint (including certain criminal statutes).
4 Order that the Defendants "provide written notice to the Plaintiff no less than 7 days before any rally or other public event in Washington, D.C., on a day when significant election or election certification activity is taking place, and when the rally is planned to have more than 50 people in attendance, to allow the Plaintiff to determine whether to seek relief from the Court to prevent further violence or disruption to the proper functioning of the federal government."[15]
5 Order that Plaintiff be awarded reasonable attorney fees and costs for the expense in pursuing this investigation and prosecution of the legal action.
6 Grant such further relief as the court deems fit.[16]

Indisputably, the January 6, 2021, mob that descended on the U.S. Capitol was intent on (i) interfering with the certification on that day of the 2020 U.S. Presidential election results and, hence (ii) interfering with the official duties and the "protected political speech" of members of Congress and that of Vice-President Pence regarding certification of the Electoral College vote count. This though 60 courts had in the preceding months *rejected* Trump's attempts to overturn the election results in various key States[17] and his claims of widespread fraud in the 2020 U.S. Presidential election. These courts in so doing arguably thereby indirectly had vetted the legitimacy of the anticipated political speech that was to occur at the Capitol by elected government officials certifying the Electoral College results for the 2020 U.S. Presidential election. This in that these U.S. courts discerned no evidence of widespread fraud or other election irregularities in the 2020 U.S. Presidential election that would have changed the ultimate outcome. This then indirectly rendered the actual Electoral College results, whatever they were to be, legitimate. Furthermore then, on the respectful analysis here, former President's Trump's reply to the

15 United States District Court for the District of Columbia Representative Eric Swalwell (Plaintiff) v Donald J. Trump (in his personal capacity), Donald Trump Jr., representative Mo Brooks (in his personal capacity) and Rudolph Giuliani (Defendants) Complaint, Jury Trial Demanded (March 5, 2021) at p. 64.

16 United States District Court for the District of Columbia Representative Eric Swalwell (Plaintiff) v Donald J. Trump (in his personal capacity), Donald Trump Jr., representative Mo Brooks (in his personal capacity) and Rudolph Giuliani (Defendants) Complaint, Jury Trial Demanded (March 5, 2021), Prayer for Relief, at pp. 63–64.

17 Trump himself confirmed in his reply to the Swalwell complaint that "Mr. Trump and his supporters were engaged in litigation, recounts, and appeals in the weeks and months after the election" (referring to the 2020 U.S. Presidential election). United States District Court for the District of Columbia Representative Eric Swalwell (Plaintiff) v Donald J. Trump (in his personal capacity), Donald Trump Jr., representative Mo Brooks (in his personal capacity) and Rudolph Giuliani (Defendants), Civil Case No. 1:21-cv-00586 APM, Memorandum in Support of Donald J. Trump and Donald Trump Jr.'s Motion to Dismiss (May 24, 2021) at p. 2.

Swalwell complaint that allegedly "Mr. Swalwell comes to this Court directly attacking First Amendment doctrines which lie at the heart of the uniquely American traditions of free speech, free assembly, and freedom to petition the government without fear of reprisal"[18] is misplaced. Rather, considering Trump's failed attempts to overturn several of the State electoral results, it was the mob on January 6, 2021, that attempted to rip away the First Amendment rights of the American public expressed through their votes. The latter by attempting to interfere with the count of the Electoral College vote in the 2020 Presidential election as the first step.

Trump alleges that "In bringing this suit, the Congressman asks this Court to wade into turbulent political waters to decide what controversial speech should be favored. The Court should firmly reject that invitation."[19] The current author, however, argues that the Swalwell suit, as mentioned, concerns the right of the members of the U.S. Congress to engage in the political speech associated with the January 6, 2021 certification of the Electoral College results regarding the U.S. Presidency. It was in fact actually a segment of Trump supporters who, in contravention of the First Amendment, turned violent in their attempt on January 6, 2021, to quash that official political speech based on its content (that political speech by members of Congress and Vice-President Pence connected to the official certification process respecting the 2020 U.S. Presidential Electoral College vote count). There was no First Amendment right, however, that allowed for violence, threats and intimidation directed to ending the certification process nor was there a right to march to and then violently enter the Capitol[20] with the express purpose and result of disrupting the certification process.

President Trump, through counsel, argues in the Swalwell case that "The claims against former President Trump directly contravene the absolute immunity conveyed on the President by the Constitution as a key principle of separation of powers."[21] It is here argued, in contrast, that "absolute immunity" of a President

18 United States District Court for the District of Columbia Representative Eric Swalwell (Plaintiff) v Donald J. Trump (in his personal capacity), Donald Trump Jr., representative Mo Brooks (in his personal capacity) and Rudolph Giuliani (Defendants), Civil Case No. 1:21-cv-00586 APM, Memorandum in Support of Donald J. Trump and Donald Trump Jr.'s Motion to Dismiss (May 24, 2021) at p. 1.

19 United States District Court for the District of Columbia Representative Eric Swalwell (Plaintiff) v Donald J. Trump (in his personal capacity), Donald Trump Jr., representative Mo Brooks (in his personal capacity) and Rudolph Giuliani (Defendants), Civil Case No. 1:21-cv-00586 APM, Memorandum in Support of Donald J. Trump and Donald Trump Jr.'s Motion to Dismiss (May 24, 2021) at p. 1.

20 The January 6, 2021, Trump supporting rally goers were in fact granted a permit for a rally at the ellipse but not for a march to the Capitol.

21 United States District Court for the District of Columbia Representative Eric Swalwell (Plaintiff) v Donald J. Trump (in his personal capacity), Donald Trump Jr., representative Mo Brooks (in his personal capacity) and Rudolph Giuliani (Defendants), Civil Case No. 1:21-cv-00586 APM, Memorandum in Support of Donald J. Trump and Donald Trump Jr.'s Motion to Dismiss (May 24, 2021) at p. 1.

in civil judicial proceedings does *not* apply regarding extra-jurisdictional actions of the President. To have it otherwise would be contrary to fundamental democratic principle, values and democratic rule of law. Absolute immunity applied to non-official actions of a President while in office (even potentially unconstitutional actions) does not reinforce the separation of powers but rather goes far to degrade it. This in that a President with absolute immunity in civil suits also for extra-jurisdictional actions committed while in office would render congressional checks and balances feckless such that there is but one governmental power centre and it lies with the executive. In such a circumstance, Congress would *in effect* be largely but a handmaiden to the executive and the only hope to salvage the democracy would have to be found in an independent judiciary. This is not on the view here what the Framers envisioned in setting out three co-equal branches under the Constitution.

We will not here reach any conclusion on whether President Trump was a co-conspirator with those of his supporters who engaged in the violence at the U.S. Capitol on January 6, 2021. The factual evaluations required in that regard are beyond the scope and intent of this work. Rather, we here focus in this section on some of the main theoretical legal arguments Trump makes in his reply memorandum to the Swalwell complaint. We turn now to selected of those Trump arguments.

> *Trump Contention One—Trump's Speech was Protected by the First Amendment*—Trump was engaged in "protected political speech" and "Well established First Amendment law bars every claim made by Representative Swalwell, showing his real endgame is to use this litigation to score political points."[22]

This Trump argument raises, it is here contended, the question of what exactly constitutes "protected political speech." Trump's reply to the Swalwell civil suit in part states:

> The bulk of Representative Swalwell's allegations against former President Trump and Donald Trump, Jr. center around their promotion of and *speaking at the January 6, 2021 rally at the Ellipse* and *their general political speech* (emphasis added).[23]

22 United States District Court for the District of Columbia Representative Eric Swalwell (Plaintiff) v Donald J. Trump (in his personal capacity), Donald Trump Jr., representative Mo Brooks (in his personal capacity) and Rudolph Giuliani (Defendants), Civil Case No. 1:21-cv-00586 APM, Memorandum in Support of Donald J. Trump and Donald Trump Jr.'s Motion to Dismiss (May 24, 2021) at p. 21.

23 United States District Court for the District of Columbia Representative Eric Swalwell (Plaintiff) v Donald J. Trump (in his personal capacity), Donald Trump Jr., representative Mo Brooks (in his personal capacity) and Rudolph Giuliani (Defendants), Civil Case No. 1:21-cv-00586 APM, Memorandum in Support of Donald J. Trump and Donald Trump Jr.'s Motion to Dismiss (May 24, 2021) at p. 4.

It is well established in American Supreme Court case law that not all political speech is protected speech. It is here contended further that if in fact there is *incitement to violence* as a component of the speech, simply interjecting some placating words amidst that incitement is not a sufficient shield to prevent removal of First Amendment protection for the speech. It is ultimately for the Court to decide if this analysis is applicable to Mr. Trump's January 6, 2021, speech at the ellipse in which he stated, for instance, both of the following lines which appear, on the view here at least, to be contradictory on their face: "[E]veryone here will soon be marching over to the Capitol building to *peacefully and patriotically* make your voices heard (emphasis added)"[24] and "*when you catch someone in a fraud you're allowed to go by very different rules . . . if you don't fight like hell you're not going to have a country anymore* (emphasis added)."[25]

In his reply Trump, referencing U.S. case law, states that the defining feature of First Amendment protection is to "allow for the free trade of ideas."[26] While the foregoing characterization of the core First Amendment meaning is indisputable, it is at the same time the case, it is here contended, that incitement to violence and the imposition by force of a particular narrative (that the 2020 U.S. Presidential election was stolen from Trump through fraud), as alleged by Swalwell, do *not* fall either within the bounds of "the free trade of ideas" or that of protected expressive conduct. Incitement to violence and insurrection, while it most often does reference matters of public concern, is nevertheless *excluded* as "protected political speech" as it undermines rather than promotes self-government in a democratic State. This by sowing chaos, public disorder and destruction and by inherently promoting unfounded bias, authoritarian values and strategies that put the targeted vulnerable at increased risk.

Trump in his reply to Swalwell in fact acknowledges that there are limits to the First Amendment protection for political speech.

> Speech . . . loses its First Amendment protection when there is an incitement to imminent lawless action, rather than mere advocacy. . . . Similarly, speech

24 United States District Court for the District of Columbia Representative Eric Swalwell (Plaintiff) v Donald J. Trump (in his personal capacity), Donald Trump Jr., representative Mo Brooks (in his personal capacity) and Rudolph Giuliani (Defendants), Civil Case No. 1:21-cv-00586 APM, Memorandum in Support of Donald J. Trump and Donald Trump Jr.'s Motion to Dismiss (May 24, 2021) at p. 5.

25 United States District Court for the District of Columbia Representative Eric Swalwell (Plaintiff) v Donald J. Trump (in his personal capacity), Donald Trump Jr., representative Mo Brooks (in his personal capacity) and Rudolph Giuliani (Defendants) Complaint, Jury Trial Demanded (March 5, 2021), at pp. 34–35.

26 United States District Court for the District of Columbia Representative Eric Swalwell (Plaintiff) v Donald J. Trump (in his personal capacity), Donald Trump Jr., representative Mo Brooks (in his personal capacity) and Rudolph Giuliani (Defendants), Civil Case No. 1:21-cv-00586 APM, Memorandum in Support of Donald J. Trump and Donald Trump Jr.'s Motion to Dismiss (May 24, 2021) at p. 21 Citing Virginia v. Black 538 U.S. 343, 358 (2003).

> can be stymied when it announces a "true threat," meaning the speech contains a serious expression of an intent to commit an unlawful act of violence to a particular individual or group of individuals.[27]

Without here reaching any conclusion on the matter of alleged incitement, it is nevertheless noted that the Trump reply does not explain how or why the particular impugned statements made by Trump and his supporters to the "rally" on January 6, 2021, constitute protected political speech and advocacy for a certain position rather than incitement. Instead the reply simply (i) advances the proposition that Trump and his supporters were engaged in protected political speech directed to the rally gathered January 6, 2021, at the ellipse in Washington, D.C. and then (ii) goes on to contend that Swalwell's suit against Trump et al. was an attempt at "Turning district courts into the arbiters of campaign speech."[28] Of course, however, the campaign and the 2020 U.S. Presidential election were in fact over by that date (January 6, 2021), certification by the States of their vote counts had occurred and the Electoral College results were about to be certified by the members of the U.S. Congress in a timely fashion barring any interference. All these facts then will be assessed if the Swalwell case proceeds on the merits question. The Court will determine whether Trump and his supporters engaged in mere protected political speech and advocacy on January 6, 2021, and during the immediate period leading up to the rally and riot or instead were involved in something worrisome that included unprotected speech constituting incitement to violence and insurrection.

Trump in his reply, furthermore, asserted that he and his supporters were engaged in protected speech on January 6, 2021, in that that speech purportedly constituted "petition of the government" regarding a need to remedy a grievance.

> Elections are often hotly contested, and they are certainly a matter of public concern. As Congress is given the duty of deciding whether to certify the votes of electors, Defendants had a right to advocate for their preferred outcome constitutionally-protected.[29]

27 United States District Court for the District of Columbia Representative Eric Swalwell (Plaintiff) v Donald J. Trump (in his personal capacity), Donald Trump Jr., representative Mo Brooks (in his personal capacity) and Rudolph Giuliani (Defendants), Civil Case No. 1:21-cv-00586 APM, Memorandum in Support of Donald J. Trump and Donald Trump Jr.'s Motion to Dismiss (May 24, 2021) at p. 23.

28 United States District Court for the District of Columbia Representative Eric Swalwell (Plaintiff) v Donald J. Trump (in his personal capacity), Donald Trump Jr., representative Mo Brooks (in his personal capacity) and Rudolph Giuliani (Defendants), Civil Case No. 1:21-cv-00586 APM, Memorandum in Support of Donald J. Trump and Donald Trump Jr.'s Motion to Dismiss (May 24, 2021) at p. 24.

29 United States District Court for the District of Columbia Representative Eric Swalwell (Plaintiff) v Donald J. Trump (in his personal capacity), Donald Trump Jr., representative Mo Brooks (in his personal capacity) and Rudolph Giuliani (Defendants), Civil Case No. 1:21-cv-00586 APM, Memorandum in Support of Donald J. Trump and Donald Trump Jr.'s Motion to Dismiss (May 24, 2021) at pp. 26–27.

The difficulty is, however, that the preferred outcome is not, according to U.S. constitutional dictate, to be determined by advocacy once the Electoral College votes are in and waiting to be certified. At that point, the time for advocacy had passed. This especially given that, for instance, Trump and his supporters had lost all legal challenges to the various contested State vote outcomes claiming widespread fraud their having provided no credible evidence to that effect in court.

*Trump Contention Two—Former President Trump enjoys "absolute immunity" from all tort claims:* Trump argued in his reply to Swalwell that as President on January 6, 2021, and the months leading up to that date, he enjoyed absolute immunity from any civil liability regarding the alleged statutory violations that Swalwell outlined in his complaint (violations arising from the January 6, 2021, alleged attempt to overturn the results of the Electoral College vote regarding the 2020 U.S. Presidential election). The U.S. case law, however, makes it clear, by Trump's own admission, that the limitation on Presidential immunity against tort suits is that there is a "requirement that [his] actions fall within the outer perimeter of [his] official duties."[30] Clearly inciting a riot and attempting to interfere and delay the certification of a U.S. Presidential election result (if that is what the court determines occurred in respect of the January 6, 2021, Trump speech and the subsequent mob attack on the Capitol) would *not* fall within even the outer limits of Presidential official duties. There would appear to be then no logical or legal precedent grounded on U.S. case law for the following non-sequitur concerning Trump's alleged absolute immunity in respect of Swalwell's civil suit where Trump states:

> Even when a plaintiff alleges a president's actions exceed his legal authority, the privilege still prohibits litigation. Otherwise, the rule would be swallowed whole by the exception.[31]

The privilege of absolute immunity of the U.S. President from civil liability is to be applied to actions relating to the *official duties foundational to the Office of the Presidency* taken while in office. Hence, *in a sense* the privilege ultimately belongs to the American people to serve their best interest. From the latter perspective

30 United States District Court for the District of Columbia Representative Eric Swalwell (Plaintiff) v Donald J. Trump (in his personal capacity), Donald Trump Jr., representative Mo Brooks (in his personal capacity) and Rudolph Giuliani (Defendants), Civil Case No. 1:21-cv-00586 APM, Memorandum in Support of Donald J. Trump and Donald Trump Jr.'s Motion to Dismiss (May 24, 2021) at p. 8 citing Chastain v. Sundquist, 833 F.2d 311, 315 (D.C. Cir. 1987).

31 United States District Court for the District of Columbia Representative Eric Swalwell (Plaintiff) v Donald J. Trump (in his personal capacity), Donald Trump Jr., representative Mo Brooks (in his personal capacity) and Rudolph Giuliani (Defendants), Civil Case No. 1:21-cv-00586 APM, Memorandum in Support of Donald J. Trump and Donald Trump Jr.'s Motion to Dismiss (May 24, 2021) at p. 8.

then, tort suits in regard to any President's *extra-jurisdictional actions* causing harm while in office to the American people and to their democracy represent litigation in the public interest. Such tort suits are arguably contemplated by the specific articulation of the absolute immunity rule itself—a rule that offers protection against tort suits *only for official acts which are by definition to be constitutionally and statutorily legally sound*. There is thus no "exception" to the aforementioned requirement that the democratic rule of law infuse the application of the absolute immunity privilege. That is there is no allowance for "a president's actions [that] exceed his legal authority" which would "still prohibit litigation."[32]

*Trump Contention Three—The "Political Question Doctrine" Applies*: Trump in his reply to the Swalwell civil suit asserts that the "political question doctrine" applies referencing the doctrine that stipulates that "policy choices" and "values determinations" are not judiciable.[33] Trump argues in his reply that:

> the adjudication of all the allegations against former President Trump would require the Court to make a value determination about what is or is not proper for the President to say at a political speech when advocating for governmental action.[34]

The current author argues, without reaching any conclusion about whether Trump's speech to the rally at the ellipse in Washington, D.C. on January 6, 2021, was incitement to violence, that the court is well within its jurisdiction to decide whether certain speech is incitement to violence and/or insurrection. Incitement to violence and/or insurrection is *not* protected political speech nor shielded speech "on matters of public concern," is antithetical to democratic values and does not reflect speech reflecting a lawful policy choice. Were *all* speech on matters of public concern *ipso facto* "protected speech," there clearly could be no category of "unprotected speech" also then in relation to incitement to violence and/or insurrection. Hence, a more nuanced approach is necessary

32 Contrast with United States District Court for the District of Columbia Representative Eric Swalwell (Plaintiff) v Donald J. Trump (in his personal capacity), Donald Trump Jr., representative Mo Brooks (in his personal capacity) and Rudolph Giuliani (Defendants), Civil Case No. 1:21-cv-00586 APM, Memorandum in Support of Donald J. Trump and Donald Trump Jr.'s Motion to Dismiss (May 24, 2021) at p. 8.

33 United States District Court for the District of Columbia Representative Eric Swalwell (Plaintiff) v Donald J. Trump (in his personal capacity), Donald Trump Jr., representative Mo Brooks (in his personal capacity) and Rudolph Giuliani (Defendants), Civil Case No. 1:21-cv-00586 APM, Memorandum in Support of Donald J. Trump and Donald Trump Jr.'s Motion to Dismiss (May 24, 2021) at p. 11.

34 United States District Court for the District of Columbia Representative Eric Swalwell (Plaintiff) v Donald J. Trump (in his personal capacity), Donald Trump Jr., representative Mo Brooks (in his personal capacity) and Rudolph Giuliani (Defendants), Civil Case No. 1:21-cv-00586 APM, Memorandum in Support of Donald J. Trump and Donald Trump Jr.'s Motion to Dismiss (May 24, 2021) at p. 12.

requiring a detailed case-by-case analysis of all the relevant factual circumstances leading up to and surrounding the impugned speech. The question whether Trump's and his supporters' speech to the rally on January 6, 2021, constituted incitement then, on the view here, is not only justiciable but is a question that, in the current and future American public interest, must be answered.

*Trump Contention Four—The Acquittal on Incitement in an Impeachment Trial Forecloses Re-litigation of the Matter in the Context of a Civil Suit*: In his reply, Trump correctly notes that the U.S. Constitution references those *convicted* in a Senate impeachment trial as yet potentially (depending on the particular case) at risk also of criminal indictment. Trump goes on, however, to argue that since he was acquitted of incitement to insurrection in his second impeachment Senate trial, he is not at risk of having the matter re-litigated either in a civil or criminal proceeding. However, U.S. Const. art. I, para 3, cl. 7 simply sets out that, for those convicted, removal from office (if still in office at the relevant time) and, in some cases, being barred from holding future civil office is the most severe punishment that per the impeachment process can be applied. Thus, any more severe punishment such as imprisonment would have to be imposed only after a criminal judicial process through the courts with the Defendant afforded full constitutional due process protections.

It is here contended that there is nothing in the U.S. Constitution that explicitly states or implies that those acquitted in an impeachment process cannot yet face criminal or civil liability for the same impugned acts. An impeachment process leading to a Senate conviction provides a political and limited practical remedy. This by means of removal from current office (if still in office) and in some instances a bar against the former civil officer holding future civil office. This to protect the public interest. The criminal and civil courts (i) are not mandated to provide political remedies[35] and (ii) operate by different rules of evidence and standards than those applied in an impeachment Senate trial. Hence, on the view here, it would be contrary to the interests of maintaining the democratic rule of law and constitutional values to interpret the U.S. Constitution as foreclosing, *where the relevant evidentiary standard is met*, a criminal or civil case at some point against a current, or more commonly living former President, acquitted or convicted of the same impugned actions in an impeachment trial context. This given the fundamental differences between Senate impeachment trials versus judicial proceedings in a U.S. criminal or civil court context.

For the same reason, it is here contended that *res judicata* and collateral estoppel[36] are also *inapplicable* to the Swalwell suit against former President Trump

35 This in some unusual instances, however, may be one impact where civil liability is established for extra-jurisdictional tortious acts and impeachment processes are thereafter started.

36 "Res judicata precludes further claims by the same parties or their privies after a final judgment on the merits" and "collateral estoppel (issue preclusion) applies when a factual or legal issue is litigated and determined by a valid final judgment." United States District Court for the District of Columbia Representative Eric Swalwell (Plaintiff) v Donald J. Trump (in his

and do not preclude that civil action. On the view here, contrary to former President Trump's argument in his reply to the Swalwell suit, the impeachment acquittal (in regard to whether then U.S. President Trump incited the January 6, 2021, attack on the Capitol in an attempt to halt the certification of the Electoral College results favoring Biden) is *not* the final word on the merits. This as a Senate impeachment proceeding is a qualitatively different category of proceeding than a regular judicial process in that the former involves the legislative branch and the latter, where the courts function constitutionally, act independently from the influence of both the executive and the legislature.

*Trump Contention Five—Swalwell Attempts to Unjustifiably Impose Prior Restraint on Trump's Political Speech:* Trump in his reply argued that (i) Swalwell's request for an order mandating "written notice no less than 7 days before any rally or other public event in Washington, D.C., on a day when significant election or election certification activity is taking place, and when the rally is planned to have more than 50 people in attendance"[37] and (ii) his request for a declaration that the Defendants broke the specific laws detailed in the complaint (including certain criminal statutes) allegedly constitute, according to Trump, a request for unconstitutional court-ordered prior restraint on political speech. Arguably, the aforementioned two requests by Swalwell for relief do *not* constitute prior restraint:[38] (i) The Swalwell request for a court order directing Defendants to provide "written notice no less than 7 days before any rally or other public event in Washington, D.C., *on a day when significant election or election certification activity is taking place*," is intended to ensure the legitimate non-political purpose of no further victimization of police, security and/or members of Congress (as occurred on January 6, 2021) perpetrated by promoters of Trump's unproven 2020 Presidential election fraud claims. This then in consideration of the events of January 6, 2021, at the Capitol and the political speech by Trump and certain of his high-profile supporters that date that preceded the riot and attack on the Capitol.

To argue that a declaration by a court stipulating, for instance, that certain criminal and/or civil statutes were infringed (i.e. statutes as relate to incitement to insurrection, intimidating federal civil officers etc.) is unconstitutional "prior restraint" appears a misplaced argument. This in that such a declaration, should it occur, would be but a legal finding after-the-fact based on the court's assessment of the applicable law and the particular fact pattern involved. Statutes barring

---

personal capacity), Donald Trump Jr., representative Mo Brooks (in his personal capacity) and Rudolph Giuliani (Defendants), Civil Case No. 1:21-cv-00586 APM, Memorandum in Support of Donald J. Trump and Donald Trump Jr.'s Motion to Dismiss (May 24, 2021) at p. 14.

37 See Swalwell Complaint: United States District Court for the District of Columbia Representative Eric Swalwell (Plaintiff) v Donald J. Trump (in his personal capacity), Donald Trump Jr., representative Mo Brooks (in his personal capacity) and Rudolph Giuliani (Defendants) Complaint, Jury Trial Demanded (March 5, 2021) at p. 64.

38 Recall that the U.S. case law provides that there are limited exceptions to the bar on prior restraint imposed, for instance, by the Federal Government.

incitement (i.e. incitement to insurrection) and intimidation of federal civil officers are intended to give advance notice as to what is unlawful behaviour in an effort to prevent such conduct. Hence, a declaration after-the-fact that such a statute was infringed simply declares that the statutory notice was ignored by the Defendant(s) and reaffirms the victims' rights. Such a declaration is *not* prior restraint and is not unconstitutional as it does *not* in any way institute a prior constraint or restriction on *lawful protected* political speech or other lawful political conduct.

### *The Legal Standing Issue in the Tort Suits Brought by Federal Officials Against Trump et al. Relating to the January 6, 2021, Attack on the Capitol*

Swalwell asserts that he can establish legal standing for his suit as a directly injured party in that (i) he suffered emotionally when the rioters entered the Capitol building causing him to fear for his life and to be intimidated by the ongoing mob violence and the specific threats of violence directed also at members of Congress and (ii) he was deprived of his constitutional right in the circumstance to perform his constitutionally mandated official duty as a member of Congress, namely certifying the electoral college 2020 Presidential vote. Swalwell therefore maintains he has articulated a concrete, particularized injury to himself. Whether such an argument is accepted and is sufficient to establish legal standing will be for the court to determine. Constitutional and First Amendment scholars/practitioners who intervened in the case and filed an amicus brief[39] supported the proposition that Swalwell was attempting to carry out his constitutional duty as a federal official in approving the Electoral College vote count when he was prevented from doing so (at least for a time) through threat and intimidation in violation of 42 USC s. 1985(1) (conspiracy to interfere with civil rights).[40] Standing under 42 USC s. 1985(1) actually is grounded in section 3 of the statute:

> The end of Section 1985(3) provides that an individual "injured or deprived" of a legal right as a result of a prohibited conspiracy listed elsewhere in Section 1985 has "an action for the recovery of damages, occasioned by such injury or deprivation, against any one or more of the conspirators" and "individuals have statutory standing if they are "injured or deprived" as a result of the conspiracy to deter someone from acting as a federal officer.[41]

39 Motion for leave to file brief of Amici Curiae Floyd Abrams, Erwin Chemerinsky, Martha Minow and Laurence Tribe in support of plaintiffs, Eric Swalwell, (Plaintiff) v Donald J. Trump et al. (Defendants) United States District Court for the District of Columbia (July 8, 2021).

40 Legal Information Institute, Cornell University 42 USC 1985 (conspiracy to interfere with civil rights).

41 United States District Court for the District of Columbia, Blassingame and Sidney Hemby v. Trump, Brief of Amicus Curiae Campaign Legal Centre Action in Support of the Briefs in Opposition to Defendants motion to Dismiss (July 8, 2021) at p. 5.

The argument underlying all three cases alleging violation of USC 42 1985(1) is that:

> Section 1985(1)'s broad application protects the Federal Officials that the pro-Trump insurrectionists targeted on January 6 because the "text of s. 1985(1) . . . prohibits conspiracies to prevent 'any person' from 'discharging any duties' of an office under the United States." Bray, 506 U.S. at 300; see also Kush, 460 U.S. at 724.[42]
>
> In the wording of Section 1985(1), these are federal officials holding or performing federal duties: Vice President Pence and all members of Congress were tasked to "discharge [their] duties" to manage and ratify the Electoral College votes, and Vice President-elect Harris and President elect Biden were seeking to "accept[ ] or hold[ ]" federal office as a result of that process. 42 U.S.C. s. 1985(1). The Defendants and the insurrectionists conspired together through violence and intimidation to obstruct these federal functions, and successfully delayed them for over five hours.[43]

In *Blassingame* (a suit by Capitol Police Blassingame and Hemby against Trump for their emotional and physical injuries suffered as a consequence of the violent riot at the Capitol on January 6, 2021), an amicus brief in support of the Plaintiffs argues that the meaning of the words "federal civil officer" includes federal Capitol police officers (referring here to the Brief of Amicus Curiae Campaign Legal Centre in support of the Plaintiffs). That amicus brief contends that the term "civil officer" in various parts of the Constitution (i.e. the Ineligibility Clause) *cannot* be interpreted out of the particular context in which it is used (the unique context with its correlated purpose) and be improperly imported to interpret the meaning of those words in the context of, for instance, the 42 USC s. 1985(1) statute.[44] The three tort cases against Trump addressing the riot on January 6, 2021, at the Capitol thus, on the question of legal standing, directly or implicitly advance the argument that

> the Court should reject Defendants' Constitution-as-dictionary arguments, which rely on the faulty premise that a statutory phrase automatically takes on the constitutional definition of the words it uses. Instead, the plaintiffs argue that Congress meant for USC s. 1985(1) to broadly apply to *all* federal

42 United States District Court for the District of Columbia, Blassingame and Sidney Hemby v. Trump, Brief of Amicus Curiae Campaign Legal Centre Action in Support of the Briefs in Opposition to Defendants motion to Dismiss (July 8, 2021) at p. 11.

43 United States District Court for the District of Columbia, Blassingame and Sidney Hemby v. Trump, Brief of Amicus Curiae Campaign Legal Centre Action in Support of the Briefs in Opposition to Defendants motion to Dismiss (July 8, 2021) at p. 12.

44 United States District Court for the District of Columbia, Blassingame and Sidney Hemby v. Trump, Brief of Amicus Curiae Campaign Legal Centre Action in Support of the Briefs in Opposition to Defendants motion to Dismiss (July 8, 2021) at pp. 11–13.

> officials . . . writing in inclusive terms that it protects "any person" holding "any office, trust, or place of confidence under the United States" and/or "any officer of the United States" as they "discharg[e] any duties" of their federal function (emphasis added).[45]

The aforementioned amicus brief summarized the Plaintiffs' position on legal standing in *Blassingame* as follows:

> members of Congress and Vice President Pence are covered under . . . Section 1985(1) because they were "discharge[ing their] duties" as statutory "officers of the United States" to open, count, and ratify the Electoral College votes on January 6. The violent conspiracy to impede the performance of these duties injured Plaintiffs, and they have Section 1985(3) available as a remedy to right those wrongs.[46]

Further, the said amicus brief argued that the Capitol federal police were also fulfilling their *official duties as U.S. federal officers* on January 6, 2021. This in protecting the members of Congress in the latter's discharging of their duty regarding certification of the Electoral College vote result for the 2020 U.S. Presidential election.[47] As such then, the injured Capitol federal police too would be entitled to a remedy under 42 USC s. 1985(3):

> the Plaintiffs in the three related cases—themselves Federal Officials or federal Capitol Police Officers sworn to protect them—were "injured" and "have an action for the recovery of damages against . . . the conspirators. 42 U.S.C. s.1985 (3)[48,49]

### *The First Amendment Issue in the Context of the Blassingame Tort Suit*

*Blassingame* amicus challenged the First Amendment defence advanced by Trump as inapplicable in that:

45 United States District Court for the District of Columbia, Blassingame and Sidney Hemby v. Trump, Brief of Amicus Curiae Campaign Legal Centre Action in Support of the Briefs in Opposition to Defendants motion to Dismiss (July 8, 2021) at pp. 13–14.

46 United States District Court for the District of Columbia, Blassingame and Sidney Hemby v. Trump, Brief of Amicus Curiae Campaign Legal Centre Action in Support of the Briefs in Opposition to Defendants motion to Dismiss (July 8, 2021) at p. 24.

47 United States District Court for the District of Columbia, Blassingame and Sidney Hemby v. Trump, Brief of Amicus Curiae Campaign Legal Centre Action in Support of the Briefs in Opposition to Defendants motion to Dismiss (July 8, 2021) at pp. 5–6.

48 United States District Court for the District of Columbia, Blassingame and Sidney Hemby v. Trump, Brief of Amicus Curiae Campaign Legal Centre Action in Support of the Briefs in Opposition to Defendants motion to Dismiss (July 8, 2021) at p. 6.

49 United States District Court for the District of Columbia, Blassingame and Sidney Hemby v. Trump, Brief of Amicus Curiae Campaign Legal Centre Action in Support of the Briefs in Opposition to Defendants motion to Dismiss (July 8, 2021) at p. 6.

> The First Amendment's protection of free speech does not excuse communications and conduct forming a conspiracy to attack the federal government. That an "agreement . . . to engage in illegal conduct . . . necessarily takes the form of words does not confer upon it, or upon the underlying conduct, the constitutional immunities that the First Amendment extends to speech.[50]

The amicus in *Blassingame* argues that "Defendants' speech is essential evidence of their involvement in the conspiracy and the First Amendment "does not prohibit the evidentiary use of speech to" establish the elements of a Section 1985(1) violation."[51] The amicus went on to clarify that:

> Plaintiffs do not allege that the speech itself is punishable, but identify it as constitutionally unprotected evidence that Defendants engaged in conspiratorial action with the January 6 insurrectionists.[52]

Hence on the view of the Plaintiffs and their amici supporters, this situation triggers *an exception to First Amendment protection of speech* in regard to the inflammatory words spoken to the crowd at the ellipse on January 6, 2021, or any speech connected to pre-planning that took place, if it did, prior to January 6 concerning an attack on the Capitol building. This since that speech allegedly (i) directly or indirectly provoked the unconstitutional attempt to interfere with the ratification of the 2020 Presidential Electoral College vote result through violence pursuant to those words being spoken and (ii) transformed a segment of the crowd into a violent mob either in the moment and/or as according to what was pre-planned if the latter (pre-planning) be the case.

The lawsuit advanced by Congressman Bennie Thompson against Trump et al. in relation to the January 6, 2021 attack on the Capitol[53] also focuses on the alleged civil rights violations implicated and the purported involvement of certain of the Defendants in incitement, and/or other acts such as aiding and abetting and/or participating in the attack. Noteworthy is the fact in that suit that Congressman Thompson names as plaintiffs also a white supremacist group—the Proud Boys. The Thompson complaint is here discussed next.

50 United States District Court for the District of Columbia, Blassingame and Sidney Hemby v. Trump, Brief of Amicus Curiae Campaign Legal Centre Action in Support of the Briefs in Opposition to Defendants motion to Dismiss (July 8, 2021) at p. 24.

51 United States District Court for the District of Columbia, Blassingame and Sidney Hemby v. Trump, Brief of Amicus Curiae Campaign Legal Centre Action in Support of the Briefs in Opposition to Defendants motion to Dismiss (July 8, 2021) at p. 25.

52 United States District Court for the District of Columbia, Blassingame and Sidney Hemby v. Trump, Brief of Amicus Curiae Campaign Legal Centre Action in Support of the Briefs in Opposition to Defendants motion to Dismiss (July 8, 2021) at p. 25.

53 In the United States District Court for the District of Columbia, Hon. Bennie G. Thompson (Plaintiff) v Donald J. Trump (solely in his personal capacity), Rudolph Giuliani, Proud Boys International, LLC, Oath Keepers (Defendants) (February 16, 2021).

## Hon. Bennie G. Thompson (Plaintiff) v Donald J. Trump (in His Personal Capacity), Rudolph W. Giuliani, Proud Boys International LLC and Oath Keepers (Defendants)

In his federal suit, Congressman Thompson alleged violation by the Defendants (Donald J. Trump (in his personal capacity), Rudolph W. Giuliani, Proud Boys International LLC and Oath Keepers) of his right to discharge his official duties as a U.S. congressman to approve the count of the votes of the Electoral College regarding the 2020 U.S. Presidential election.

> Plaintiff, the Honorable Bennie G. Thompson, Member of the United States House of Representatives, brings this action against the Defendants for conspiring to prevent him and other Members of Congress from discharging these official duties, in violation of 42 U.S.C. s. 1985(1). Enacted as the "Ku Klux Klan Act" in 1871, Section 1985(1) was intended to protect against conspiracies, through violence and intimidation that sought to prevent Members of Congress from discharging their official duties. The statute was enacted in response to violence and intimidation in which the Ku Klux Klan and other organizations were engaged during that time period.[54]

This interference with his aforementioned official duties, Thompson alleged, was the intent and effect of what he characterized as the insurrection: "The insurrection at the Capitol . . . a direct, intended, and foreseeable result of the Defendants' unlawful conspiracy."[55] Thompson's suit requests

> compensatory damages to redress the harm to the Plaintiff caused by the Defendants' use of intimidation, harassment and threats of violence to interfere with his discharge of his legally required duty as a Member of Congress and punitive damages to punish the Defendants for the reckless and malicious manner in which they acted and to enjoin and deter a recurrence of this unlawful conduct.[56]

Setting aside who was responsible for the January 6, 2021, violence and intimidation at the U.S. Capitol, such behaviour directed at interfering with federal officials carrying out their official duties is penalized under 42 USC s. 1985(1). Given the Defendants' First Amendment argument in the Swalwell and

54 In the United States District Court for the District of Columbia, Hon. Bennie G. Thompson (Plaintiff) v Donald J. Trump (solely in his personal capacity), Rudolph Giuliani, Proud Boys International, LLC, Oath Keepers (Defendants) (February 16, 2021) at p. 2.

55 In the United States District Court for the District of Columbia, Hon. Bennie G. Thompson (Plaintiff) v Donald J. Trump (solely in his personal capacity), Rudolph Giuliani, Proud Boys International, LLC, Oath Keepers (Defendants) (February 16, 2021) at p. 3.

56 In the United States District Court for the District of Columbia, Hon. Bennie G. Thompson (Plaintiff) v Donald J. Trump (solely in his personal capacity), Rudolph Giuliani, Proud Boys International, LLC, Oath Keepers (Defendants) (February 16, 2021) at p. 4.

Thompson cases, it is not surprising that there has been an ongoing and earnest effort by these Defendants, directly or through their supporters, to rewrite history. This involves falsely framing the events of January 6, 2021, at the U.S. Capitol as largely, if not entirely, a peaceful non-threatening voicing of objection to the certification of the 2020 Presidential Electoral College count and to the recognition of Joseph Biden as the legitimate U.S. President elect. The Defendants (as the amici in support of Swalwell summarize it) contend that "s. 1985(1), at least as applied here, violates their First Amendment right to engage in "political speech."[57]

In Defendants' reply memorandum to the Swalwell suit, they assert that the Swalwell suit in part represents an "attempt at turning important and historic civil rights statutes into political weapons to weaken critical constitutional protections."[58] Yet it is entirely unclear how 42 USC s. 1985(1) could be "turned into a political weapon" since it is triggered only in a context where there is a need *to protect democratic process* through penalizing intimidation directed or threatened against elected officials attempting to carry out their constitutional duties. *In effect, 42 USC 1985(1) protects the political speech of federal elected officials who are entitled to fulfill their constitutional duties unfettered (such as certifying the Electoral College vote on behalf of the people in their electoral district that they represent which process requires certain political speech).* Here then that political speech involved congressional members' approval or disapproval of the Electoral College vote count for the President of the United States relating to the 2020 election. In this case, however, the Capitol mob that entered the building anticipated that the members of Congress would approve the Electoral College vote count if not threatened with and/or subjected to violence to do otherwise. The mob thus sought to interfere with that certification process through violence and intimidation directed to suppressing the political speech of the members of Congress and the Vice-President relating to certification of the 2020 Presidential election result.

The question then becomes whether the Defendant(s) named in the Swalwell and Thompson cases as well as the Blassingame and Hemby case[59] who spoke to the crowd gathered at the ellipse January 6, 2021, but did not march to the Capitol building or enter it that day as part of the riot, were or were not themselves engaged in "protected political speech." The previously mentioned

57 Motion for leave to file brief of Amici Curiae Floyd Abrams, Erwin Chemerinsky, Martha Minow and Laurence Tribe in support of plaintiffs, Eric Swalwell, (Plaintiff) v Donald J. Trump et al. (Defendants) United States District Court for the District of Columbia (July 8, 2021) at p. 2.

58 United States District Court for the District of Columbia Representative Eric Swalwell (Plaintiff) v Donald J. Trump (in his personal capacity), Donald Trump Jr., representative Mo Brooks (in his personal capacity) and Rudolph Giuliani (Defendants), Civil Case No. 1:21-cv-00586 APM, Memorandum in Support of Donald J. Trump and Donald Trump Jr.'s Motion to Dismiss (May 24, 2021) at p. 1.

59 United States District Court for the District of Columbia, Blassingame and Sidney Hemby v. Trump (July 8, 2021).

amici argue that in considering this question, the court ought not restrict itself to focusing only on the two exceptions to First Amendment protection involving (i) speech intended to incite or produce imminent lawlessness or violence and (ii) speech that communicates a serious threat of imminent unlawful violence to a particular person or group of persons, the latter being termed the "true threat" exception.[60] Note that

> Intimidation in the constitutionally proscribable sense of the word is a type of true threat, where a speaker directs a threat to a person or group of persons with the intent of placing the victim in fear of bodily harm or death.[61]

The amici argue that both the foregoing exceptions to First Amendment protection apply to the facts addressed in the three separate January 6 lawsuits brought respectively by (i) Swalwell, (ii) Thompson and (iii) Blassingame et al. However, the amici contend that

> many modern forms of political intimidation do not involve inciting imminent lawless action or threatening to inflict physical violence; and there is uncertainty about the degree of intent that a litigant must prove in order to invoke the true-threat exception.[62]

The more modern forms of subtle intimidation rather include but are not limited to "a wide and ever-expanding range of coercive tactics, including onsite voter harassment and legally baseless offsite threats of legal harm."[63] The amici maintain further that:

> because the political-intimidation statutes share common terms that implicate speech—"conspire," "intimidate," "threat"—they are collectively vulnerable to erosion by inapt interpretations and applications of the First Amendment. Here, for example, the defendants assert that the plaintiffs' s. 1985(1) claims

60 Motion for leave to file brief of Amici Curiae Floyd Abrams, Erwin Chemerinsky, Martha Minow and Laurence Tribe in support of plaintiffs, Eric Swalwell, (Plaintiff) v Donald J. Trump et al. (Defendants) United States District Court for the District of Columbia (July 8, 2021) at p. 3.

61 Motion for leave to file brief of Amici Curiae Floyd Abrams, Erwin Chemerinsky, Martha Minow and Laurence Tribe in support of plaintiffs, Eric Swalwell, (Plaintiff) v Donald J. Trump et al. (Defendants) United States District Court for the District of Columbia (July 8, 2021) at p. 10.

62 Motion for leave to file brief of Amici Curiae Floyd Abrams, Erwin Chemerinsky, Martha Minow and Laurence Tribe in support of plaintiffs, Eric Swalwell, (Plaintiff) v Donald J. Trump et al. (Defendants) United States District Court for the District of Columbia (July 8, 2021) at p. 4.

63 Motion for leave to file brief of Amici Curiae Floyd Abrams, Erwin Chemerinsky, Martha Minow and Laurence Tribe in support of plaintiffs, Eric Swalwell, (Plaintiff) v Donald J. Trump et al. (Defendants) United States District Court for the District of Columbia (July 8, 2021) at p. 11.

> cannot survive First Amendment scrutiny unless they fall within one of two carefully circumscribed exceptions to First Amendment coverage, the "incitement" exception . . . and the "true threat" exception.[64]

Said amici counter-argue, however, that the court should also consider, in addition to the "incitement" and "true threat" exceptions to First Amendment protections,

> the long-recognized, categorical exception to First Amendment coverage for speech that is integral to the commission of a crime or tort—speech, in other words, that is the very vehicle by which a crime or tort is committed. That exception is peculiarly appropriate here, where the speech in question is integral to antidemocratic conduct that federal law has proscribed for 150 years (emphasis added).[65]

It seems to the current author that the suite of three First Amendment cases relating to the events of January 6, 2021, and challenging the constitutionality of the speech by Trump et al. (the named Defendants in these cases)[66] are of profound significance beyond the recovery of damages for the plaintiffs and a ruling on whether the statute 42 USC s. 1985(1) was violated. These cases, the current author maintains, raise the issue of the distinction between (1) protected political speech *versus* (2) inflammatory and intimidating speech that is allegedly a vital propaganda component of a disinformation campaign and may be integral to certain crimes. The latter speech is directed to incitement and subverting the constitutional functioning of targeted democratic institutions and to thwart the execution of specific democratic processes. That speech furthermore potentially but not necessarily may lead to violence. In contrast, protected political speech may attack political perspectives, practices and policies but involves no intimidation or actual threats of imminent violence and is unrelated to the potential for criminal conduct. Protected speech may be directed to altering policies and decisions where such a shift is expected to occur consistent with democratic norms and jurisdictional authorities. In the case of January 6, 2021, however, the Electoral College votes had already been certified by electoral State officials (many of them Republican) and there was no constitutional process for the Vice-President

64 Motion for leave to file brief of Amici Curiae Floyd Abrams, Erwin Chemerinsky, Martha Minow and Laurence Tribe in support of plaintiffs, Eric Swalwell, (Plaintiff) v Donald J. Trump et al. (Defendants) United States District Court for the District of Columbia (July 8, 2021) at p. 4.

65 Motion for leave to file brief of Amici Curiae Floyd Abrams, Erwin Chemerinsky, Martha Minow and Laurence Tribe in support of plaintiffs, Eric Swalwell, (Plaintiff) v Donald J. Trump et al. (Defendants) United States District Court for the District of Columbia (July 8, 2021) at p. 4.

66 Referring here to the following federal cases: (i) Eric Swalwell (Plaintiff) v Donald J. Trump et al., (ii) Blassingame and Sidney Hemby v. Trump and (iii) Hon. Bennie G. Thompson v Donald J. Trump et al.

to decertify these State vote counts and return them to the respective States for reconsideration.

The impugned speech by the named high-profile Defendants[67] addressing the crowd at the ellipse on January 6, 2021, was *not* speech that addressed a feasible legitimate shift in tact by members of Congress in the process of vetting the Electoral College vote. There was then no lawful shift in process that could conceivably have effected a change in outcome of the 2020 Presidential Electoral certification process as contemplated by the U.S. constitutionally set out election system. This was the case in part as there was no evidence of widespread fraud or voting irregularities established by Trump and his allies through the courts in the approximately 60 failed lawsuits they had filed trying to overturn the 2020 U.S. Presidential election results.[68] There was a demonstrated lack of objective basis thus to challenge the State certifications of the vote in the respective States. Indeed, a federal court in Colorado has gone so far as to impose sanctions on counsel who, without proper investigation of witnesses and so-called reasonable inquiry into all the alleged evidence of widespread fraud, advanced a lawsuit in relation to the 2020 U.S. Presidential election mostly citing *failed* other such lawsuits. That Colorado suit

> purported to be a class action lawsuit on behalf of all American registered voters, alleging a vast conspiracy between four governors, secretaries of state, and various election officials of Michigan, Wisconsin, Pennsylvania and Georgia; along with Dominion, a private supplier of election and voting technology; the social media company Facebook; CTCL, a non-profit organization dedicated to making elections more secure and inclusive; as well as Facebook founder Mark Zuckerberg and his wife Priscilla Chan.[69]

The complaint was that (i) the Defendants purportedly had infringed the constitutional right of 160 million registered American voters to vote for Donald J. Trump in the 2020 Presidential election[70] and that (ii) alleged varied mechanisms

67 Trump et al. as set out in the three cases here mentioned Eric Swalwell (Plaintiff) v Donald J. Trump et al.; Blassingame and Sidney Hemby v. Trump and Hon. Bennie G. Thompson v Donald J. Trump et al.

68 See United States District Court for the District of Colorado, Kevin O'Rourke et al. v. Dominion Voting Systems et al., Order Granting Defendants' Motion for Sanctions, August 3, 2021 at pp. 32–36 (under title "Numerous lawsuits making similar allegations had failed—meaning that more investigation was required" starting at p. 32) and pp. 37–44 (under title "Both Independent and Republican Sources had Publicly Refuted Claims that the Election had been "Rigged" or that Dominion Machines had "Flipped" Votes" starting at p. 37).

69 United States District Court for the District of Colorado, Kevin O'Rourke et al. v Dominion Voting Systems et al., Order Granting Defendants' Motion for Sanctions (August 3, 2021) at pp. 4–5.

70 United States District Court for the District of Colorado, Kevin O'Rourke et al. v Dominion Voting Systems et al., Order Granting Defendants' Motion for Sanctions (August 3, 2021) at p. 2.

had been employed for accomplishing that objective purportedly including, but not necessarily limited to, the "coordinated effort" to

> change voting laws without legislative approval, use unreliable voting machines, alter votes through an illegitimate adjudication process, provide illegal methods of voting, count illegal votes, suppress the speech of opposing voices, disproportionally and privately fund only certain municipalities and counties, and other methods, all prohibited by the Constitution.[71]

Based on that claim, the plaintiffs sought a "determination from a federal court in Colorado that the actions of multiple state legislatures, municipalities, and state courts in the conduct of the 2020 election should be declared legal nullities."[72] Crucially, the Colorado federal court in this case noted that:

> While Plaintiffs' counsel insist that the lawsuit was not intended to challenge the election or reverse the results, the effect of the allegations and relief sought would be to sow doubt over the legitimacy of the Biden presidency and the mechanisms of American democracy (the actual systems of voting) in numerous states.[73]

Aside from the lack of evidence of widespread election fraud and other election irregularities to assert the claim, the court also held the plaintiffs lacked standing as they had not articulated particularized injury in regards to each of the alleged victims.[74] Rather, the injury was "generalized, affecting everyone in the same way."[75] The plaintiffs were thus held *not* to have standing to bring this "generalized grievance" claim. Further, the Colorado Court in this case held it had no jurisdiction: "[T]here was no legal or factual basis to assert personal jurisdiction in Colorado for actions taken by sister states' governors, secretaries of state, or other election officials, in those officials' home states."[76]

71 United States District Court for the District of Colorado, Kevin O'Rourke et al. v Dominion Voting Systems et al., Order Granting Defendants' Motion for Sanctions (August 3, 2021) at p. 5.
72 United States District Court for the District of Colorado, Kevin O'Rourke et al. v Dominion Voting Systems et al., Order Granting Defendants' Motion for Sanctions (August 3, 2021) at p. 5.
73 United States District Court for the District of Colorado, Kevin O'Rourke et al. v Dominion Voting Systems et al., Order Granting Defendants' Motion for Sanctions (August 3, 2021) at p. 6.
74 United States District Court for the District of Colorado, Kevin O'Rourke et al. v Dominion Voting Systems et al., Order Granting Defendants' Motion for Sanctions (August 3, 2021) at pp. 13–14.
75 United States District Court for the District of Colorado, Kevin O'Rourke et al. v Dominion Voting Systems et al., Order Granting Defendants' Motion for Sanctions (August 3, 2021) at pp. 14–15.
76 United States District Court for the District of Colorado, Kevin O'Rourke et al. v Dominion Voting Systems et al., Order Granting Defendants' Motion for Sanctions (August 3, 2021) at p. 19.

The judge in the Colorado case furthermore found the affidavits submitted by plaintiffs to be replete with conclusory statements based on suspicion, belief and rumour as well as "unverified and questionable media reports" rather than on any first-hand knowledge of voter fraud or other irregularities in the 2020 U.S. Presidential election.[77] The Colorado court thus imposed sanctions on the attorneys in the case on the basis that "a reasonable attorney admitted to practice before the district court" would not have filed such a complaint with the court (even setting aside the standing and jurisdictional barriers to the suit) given (i) the aforementioned issues with the legal and factual basis for the plaintiffs' claims and (ii) the failure of the attorneys to first conduct a "reasonable and competent inquiry" into the claims and the purported evidence allegedly supporting them.[78]

> Lawyers who conceive of a lawsuit seeking $160 billion dollars, making allegations questioning the validity of a Presidential election, and the fairness of the basic mechanisms of American democracy, must conduct extensive independent research and investigation into the validity of the claims before filing suit.[79]

The court in the Colorado case found that such a thorough independent investigation of the claims of widespread irregularities in the 2020 U.S. Presidential election had not taken place before the case was filed and hence in part for that reason sanctions were imposed on the plaintiffs' attorneys.

It is striking that the Colorado case plaintiffs' claim of widespread irregularities in the U.S. 2020 Presidential election has been found to be inadequately investigated.[80] That claim filed by Trump's attorneys also in other States amounts to an allegation of mass violation of the civil rights[81] of American registered voters. Yet attorneys for Trump and certain of his most high-profile supporters deny the reality of the grievous violation of the civil rights (arising from the January 6, 2021, attack on the U.S. Capitol Building) of the elected members of Congress

77 United States District Court for the District of Colorado, Kevin O'Rourke et al. v Dominion Voting Systems et al., Order Granting Defendants' Motion for Sanctions (August 3, 2021) at pp. 7–8.

78 United States District Court for the District of Colorado, Kevin O'Rourke et al. v Dominion Voting Systems et al., Order Granting Defendants' Motion for Sanctions (August 3, 2021) at pp. 23–26.

79 United States District Court for the District of Colorado, Kevin O'Rourke et al. v Dominion Voting Systems et al., Order Granting Defendants' Motion for Sanctions (August 3, 2021) at p. 32.

80 The Colorado court held that "The Court need not draw conclusions about the truth of the factual allegations in the Complaint and Amended Complaint to impose sanctions based on inadequate inquiry." United States District Court for the District of Colorado, Kevin O'Rourke et al. v Dominion Voting Systems et al., Order Granting Defendants' Motion for Sanctions (August 3, 2021) at p. 52.

81 United States District Court for the District of Colorado, Kevin O'Rourke et al. v Dominion Voting Systems et al., Order Granting Defendants' Motion for Sanctions (August 3, 2021) at p. 20.

charged with carrying out their official duties in final vetting of the Electoral College vote and of their staff as well as of the police and other security charged with defending the Capitol who were brutally attacked on that day (with tragically some deaths ensuing) and that of the American registered voters who cast their vote for President and Vice-President in the free and fair U.S. Presidential election of November 2020.

Since there was no evidence of widespread voter fraud or other irregularities in the 2020 Presidential election (as assessed by multiple federal courts), the certification of the Electoral College vote by the members of Congress and the Vice-President for that election was essentially a *pro forma* constitutionally mandated exercise. The alleged attempt to disrupt that constitutional process by professing in the political speeches addressing the crowd at the ellipse near the Capitol complex that there was both (i) a legitimate basis linked to widespread voter fraud for doing so and (ii) a window of opportunity afforded by the Constitution still existing to stop the ratification of the Electoral College vote count for U.S. President was arguably nothing more than political disinformation involving ***unprotected*** political speech. That inflammatory political speech, at a minimum, allegedly risked imminent violence given the date, the locale and the imminent vetting process of the Electoral College votes that was to take place January 6, 2021. The risk of violence was arguably apparent to reasonable persons in that the mob that descended on the Capitol Building could not in any scenario have accomplished its goals through peaceful speech as the goals were beyond what was constitutionally permissible (to stop the certification of a free and fair U.S. Presidential election that produced a clear winner). Whether the Defendants' speech directed to the crowd at the ellipse was in fact integral to either or both the commission of a crime(s) or of violation of civil statute (i.e. USC 42 1985(1)) is something the court will hopefully definitively determine. (Note that the exception to First Amendment protection regarding speech integral to statutory violations includes both criminal and civil violations: "The exception applies not only to speech integral to proscribed criminal conduct but also to speech integral to civilly actionable conduct").[82]

Arguably the January 6, 2021, Defendants' speech at the ellipse in Washington, D.C. referenced in said lawsuits cannot thus be categorized as protected political speech in that:

1 The speech was, on the view here, intimidating and threatening in its literal and implied content.
2 The speech was arguably directed at stopping the certification of the Electoral College vote count when there was no constitutional mechanism or reason for doing so in the circumstance.

82 Motion for leave to file brief of Amici Curiae Floyd Abrams, Erwin Chemerinsky, Martha Minow and Laurence Tribe in support of plaintiffs, Eric Swalwell, (Plaintiff) v Donald J. Trump et al. (Defendants) United States District Court for the District of Columbia (July 8, 2021) at p. 13.

Defendant Trump and his supporters have since January 6, 2021, sought to put in place laws at the State level that would allow for replacement of members of the State Electoral College where the outcome of an election was challenged by the Republican legislature in that State (potentially with no objective legitimate criteria set out for proving the constitutionally grounded basis for the same). This political strategy lays bare that the absence of the latter possibility in relation to the 2020 U.S. Presidential election was a key missing piece for guaranteeing the ultimate alleged objective of the Defendant-defined Republican-favored electoral outcome (i.e. decertification of the Electoral vote count pursuant to a fair and free election where the clear winner is not the one endorsed by the Republican legislature, as a foregone conclusion, to be the winner, namely the Republican nominee). Indeed, one could argue that laws at the State level that (i) would allow for replacement of members of the State Electoral College and/or (ii) revocation of the Secretary of State's certification of the State Presidential election results[83] and (iii) even where the outcome of an election is challenged by the in-power Party legislature despite no evidence of widespread significant voting or other irregularities are themselves potential violations of 42 USC s. 1985(1). This in that such laws allow for possible interference with the ability of State members of the Electoral College to faithfully and dutifully carry out their official constitutional duties as federal officers regarding the U.S. Presidential election vote count.[84] Such laws thus can serve to erode the democratic rule of law and equal participation in the vote.

It is important to consider also that "Post-election, the former President and his supporters' claims of the vote being 'stolen' or 'rigged' resulted in, among other things, serious threats to the safety of both public election officials and private employees of Dominion."[85] The democratic process held insofar as the fact that (i) the counting of the Electoral College votes proceeded in a manner consistent with constitutional requirements and (ii) the 2020 Presidential election results of a free and fair election were not overturned. Nevertheless, the threats of and/or actual violence against those in various capacities protecting the democracy is a stark indicator that the democratic rule of law itself is under attack in the U.S. Put differently, the purported disinformation campaign regarding a *falsely alleged* rigged 2020 U.S. Presidential election arguably contributed to the January 6, 2021, attack on the Capitol and jeopardized the peaceful transfer of Presidential power: "The peaceful transition of Presidential power has been described as "the

83 NBC News online Dartunorro Clark "Arizona GOP lawmaker introduces bill to give Legislature power to toss out election results" (January 28, 2021).

84 Forbes online. Trump Allies Suggest Electoral College Could Overturn a Biden Win. Here's Why That (Probably) Wouldn't Work. (November 5, 2020): "Federal law instructs states to set their policies for choosing electors before Election Day, and although states are not outright required to follow this guideline, Congress could decline to accept any electors chosen by states who violate the rule when it certifies the results."

85 United States District Court for the District of Colorado, Kevin O'Rourke et al. v Dominion Voting Systems et al., Order Granting Defendants' Motion for Sanctions (August 3, 2021) at p. 45.

ultimate expression of the rule of law and of a society governed by the law, not by individual rulers."[86] The First Amendment does *not* transform political rhetoric that is part and parcel of a disinformation campaign that includes intimidation and concrete threats targeting the democratic rule of law into protected political speech. Rather, the relevant case law clearly sets such speech outside the boundaries of First Amendment protection.[87] Were it otherwise (as allegedly former President Trump and his allies arguably would have it), the First Amendment itself would serve to eviscerate the democratic legal and other foundational human rights values underpinning the U.S. Constitution.

## References

### *Materials*

Forbes Online. Trump Allies Suggest Electoral College Could Overturn a Biden Win. Here's Why That (Probably) Wouldn't Work. (November 5, 2020) (accessed August 8, 2021).

Legal Information Institute, Cornell Law School, 42 U.S. Code § 1985.Conspiracy to Interfere with Civil Rights www.law.cornell.edu/uscode/text/42/1985 (accessed July 11, 2021).

Motion for Leave to File Brief of Amici Curiae Floyd Abrams, Erwin Chemerinsky, Martha Minow and Laurence Tribe in Support of Plaintiffs, Eric Swalwell, (Plaintiff) v Donald J. Trump et al. (Defendants) United States District Court for the District of Columbia (July 8, 2021).

NBC News online Dartunorro Clark. Arizona GOP Lawmaker Introduces Bill to Give Legislature Power to Toss Out Election Results. (January 28, 2021) www.nbcnews.com/politics/politics-news/arizona-gop-lawmaker-introduces-bill-give-legislature-power-toss-out-n1256097 (accessed August 6, 2021).

Q&A between Daniel I. Weiner and Tim Lau, Why the Presidential Transition Process Matters, Brennan Center for Justice (November 13, 2020) www.brennancenter.org/our-work/research-reports/why-presidential-transition-process-matters (accessed August 9, 2021).

### *Cases*

Chastain v. Sundquist, 833 F.2d 311, 315 (D.C. Cir. 1987).

In the United States District Court for the District of Columbia, Hon. Bennie G. Thompson (Plaintiff) v Donald J. Trump (Solely in His Personal Capacity),

86 United States District Court for the District of Colorado, Kevin O'Rourke et al. v Dominion Voting Systems et al., Order Granting Defendants' Motion for Sanctions (August 3, 2021) at pp. 46–47. See Q&A between Daniel I. Weiner and Tim Lau, Why the Presidential Transition Process Matters, Brennan Center for Justice (November 13, 2020).

87 For a discussion on exceptions to First Amendment protections, see Motion for leave to file brief of Amici Curiae Floyd Abrams, Erwin Chemerinsky, Martha Minow and Laurence Tribe in support of plaintiffs, Eric Swalwell, (Plaintiff) v Donald J. Trump et al. (Defendants) United States District Court for the District of Columbia (July 8, 2021).

Rudolph Giuliani, Proud Boys International, LLC, Oath Keepers (Defendants) (February 16, 2021).
United States District Court for the District of Colorado, Kevin O'Rourke et al. v Dominion Voting Systems et al. Order Granting Defendants' Motion for Sanctions (August 3, 2021) https://law.justia.com/cases/federal/district-courts/colorado/codce/1:2020cv03747/203235/136/ (accessed August 9, 2021).
United States District Court for the District of Columbia, Blassingame and Sidney Hemby v. Trump (July 8, 2021) https://campaignlegal.org/sites/default/files/2021-07/CLC%20Action%20Amicus%20Brief%202021.07.08%20FILE%20STAMPED%20%28Thompson%29.pdf (accessed August 9, 2021).
United States District Court for the District of Columbia, Blassingame and Sidney Hemby v. Trump, Brief of Amicus Curiae Campaign Legal Centre Action in Support of the Briefs in Opposition to Defendants motion to Dismiss (July 8, 2021).
United States District Court for the District of Columbia Representative Eric Swalwell (Plaintiff) v Donald J. Trump (In His Personal Capacity), Donald Trump Jr., Representative Mo Brooks (In His Personal Capacity) and Rudolph Giuliani (Defendants), Civil Case No. 1:21-cv-00586 APM, Memorandum in Support of Donald J. Trump and Donald Trump Jr.'s Motion to Dismiss (March 24, 2021).
United States District Court for the District of Columbia Representative Eric Swalwell (Plaintiff) v Donald J. Trump (In His Personal Capacity), Donald Trump Jr., Representative Mo Brooks (In His Personal Capacity) and Rudolph Giuliani (Defendants) Complaint, Jury Trial Demanded (March 5, 2021).
Virginia v Black 538 U.S. 343, 358 (2003).

# 5 The First Amendment Rights of Public School Students

The Snapchat Case

## The Snapchat Case: Mahanoy Area School District v B.L. (Decision of the Supreme Court of the United States, Issued June 23, 2021)

The robustness of the democratic rule of law is indicated in part by the strength of freedom of expression rights in the society. Further, the extent to which protected speech exists for the most vulnerable amongst us is a good indicator as to whether that constitutional right of freedom of expression is in jeopardy. Hence, this chapter examines first a case involving the First Amendment rights of schoolchildren who, being denied the vote on account of age ineligibility, have only their voice to rely on in protesting the particular acts of government to which they object.

## Background to the Case

B.L. was at the relevant time a 14-year-old junior at Mahanoy Area High School which is part of the Mahanoy Area School District. She joined the junior varsity cheerleading squad at the school. In May of her freshman year, B.L. tried out for the next year's squad. A condition was placed on all those trying out that they agree to abide by the following cheer rules if chosen:

> These rules—the "Cheerleading Rules" or "Rules"—state: "Please have respect for your school, coaches, teachers, other cheerleaders and teams. Remember you are representing your school when at games, fundraisers, and other events. Good sportsmanship will be enforced, this includes foul language and inappropriate gestures." . . . (the "Respect Provision"). The Rules also warn: "There will be no toleration of any negative information regarding cheerleading, cheerleaders, or coaches placed on the internet." . . . (the "Negative Information Rule").[1]

The evidence revealed that the cheerleading coaches involved in the B.L. case were not required to obtain the School District's approval to adopt or enforce

1 Cheerleading Rules for Mahanoy Area High School Cited in B.L. v. Mahanoy Area Sch. District 376 F. Supp. 3d 429 (M.D. Pa. 2019) Decided (March 21, 2019) (United States District Court for the Middle District of Pennsylvania) at p. 2.

DOI: 10.4324/9781003153764-5

these cheerleading rules and that the rules had in fact been previously adopted without any apparent School District objection.[2] B.L. and her mother reviewed the rules and then both signed a document indicating B.L. would abide by the aforementioned cheerleading rules if chosen for a Mahanoy School cheer squad. B.L. was unsuccessful in her cheerleading tryouts for the senior varsity cheer squad and was once again placed on the junior varsity squad though she was in her sophomore year at school. In comparison, a certain incoming freshman at B.L.'s high school was selected for the varsity cheerleading squad which B.L found quite distressing and unfair. This was reflected in her *first* contentious snapchat referenced in the following excerpt from the District Court judgement in the case:

> B.L., a student at Mahanoy Area High School, was dismissed from the cheerleading squad for uttering "fuck school, fuck softball, fuck cheer, fuck everything" off school grounds on a Saturday through a snapchat message.[3]

It is important to note that given the nature of snapchat (snapchat messages are only available for a limited time, cannot be accessed from the web and can be viewed only temporarily),[4] B.L. likely considered her snapchat rant to be a private communication between her and her 250 Snapchat "followers"; some of whom were fellow students at her high school, including some who were cheerleaders. She posted the message with a selfie in the company of a friend with both having their middle fingers raised, dressed in street clothes and sent the snapchat with picture from a local *off-campus* store. That snapchat was followed up soon after with another:

> She posted a follow-up snapchat message right after the profanity-laced chat that read "Love how me and [my friend] get told we need a year of jv before we make varsity but that [] doesn't matter to anyone else?"[5]

The latter snapchat appears to indicate that B.L. and her friend felt (correctly or incorrectly) that the selection process for the (senior) varsity cheerleading squad at their school had been inequitable with differing requirements for certain individuals allegedly being applied. The first snapchat, through a circuitous route, came to the attention of B.L.'s cheer coaches in the form of a screenshot shown them (which B.L. had not intended). There seems to be a lack of consistency

2 B.L. v. Mahanoy Area Sch. District, 376 F. Supp. 3d 429 (M.D. Pa. 2019) Decided (March 21, 2019) (United States District Court for the Middle District of Pennsylvania) at p. 2.
3 B.L. v. Mahanoy Area Sch. District, 376 F. Supp. 3d 429 (M.D. Pa. 2019) Decided (March 21, 2019) (United States District Court for the Middle District of Pennsylvania) at p. 1.
4 B.L. by Levy v. Mahanoy Area Sch. District, 289 F.Supp.3d 607, 610 n. 1 (M.D. Pa. 2017).
5 B.L. v. Mahanoy Area Sch. District, 376 F. Supp. 3d 429 (M.D. Pa. 2019) Decided (March 21, 2019) (United States District Court for the Middle District of Pennsylvania) at p. 2. Note jv here refers to the junior varsity cheerleading squad.

in the District Court versus Appeals Court judgement references to the facts of the case insofar as to whether a screenshot of the second B.L. snapchat was also shown to the cheer coaches. The District Court appeared to find that screenshots of *both* contentious B.L. snapchats were shown to the cheer coaches at B.L.'s school by one or more other cheerleaders:

> One of those cheerleaders, Coach Gnall's daughter, came across the *Snaps*, took screen shots of *them* (as they were not publicly viewable), and brought them to the coaches' attention. . . . Meanwhile, with the weekend now over, word of B.L.'s *Snaps* spread through the school. . . . Several students, "both cheerleaders and non-cheerleaders . . . approached Coach Luchetta-Rump to express their concerns that the *Snaps* were inappropriate (emphasis added).[6]

The Appeals Court, however, in its delineation of the facts appears to report on only a screenshot of the *first snapchat* shown to the cheer coaches:

> One of B.L.'s teammates took a screenshot of her *first snap* and sent it to one of MAHS's two cheerleading coaches. That coach brought the screenshot to the attention of her co-coach, who, it turned out, was already in the know: "Several students, both cheerleaders and non-cheerleaders," had approached her, "visibly upset," to "express their concerns that [B.L.'s] [s]naps were inappropriate."[7]

Despite the apparent inconsistency between the District Court's and the Appeals Court's recitation of the facts as to whether the cheer coaches also saw a *screenshot* of the *second* B.L. snapchat (as evidenced in the excerpts shown earlier illustrating the disparity), both lower courts appeared to have considered that the coaches disciplined B.L. based only on her *first snapchat* (a profanity-laced rant about, amongst other things, school and cheer). Be that as it may, it appears more likely than not that the *content* of the first and second B.L. snapchats came to be known to both of the cheer coaches since both snapchats were being discussed by students at the school ("word of B.L.'s snaps [plural] spread through the school").[8] This is unsurprising in that many if not all of the selected students (some of whom were cheerleaders as well) who followed B.L.'s snapchats likely saw both contentious snapchats. These students then were reported to have communicated their distress about these snapchats to the cheer coaches and sometime later, B.L. was disciplined in regard to her snapchat off-campus speech. It is to be noted, however, that neither of B.L.'s snapchats at the centre

6 B.L. v. Mahanoy Area Sch. District 376 F. Supp. 3d 429 (M.D. Pa. 2019) Decided (March 21, 2019) (United States District Court for the Middle District of Pennsylvania) at p. 2.

7 B.L. v. Mahanoy Area Sch. District, 964 F.3d 170 (3d Cir. 2020) (United States Court of Appeals for the Third Circuit) at p. 2.

8 B.L. v. Mahanoy Area Sch. District, 376 F. Supp. 3d 429 (M.D. Pa. 2019) at p. 2.

of this case identified the high school or school district involved or named the cheer coaches, members of the cheer teams or other students.

It is important to recall that B.L., prior to the snapchat incident, had inquired of the coaches whether a year of junior varsity cheer was a prerequisite for moving forward to join the senior varsity cheer squad and was informed that it was. This was a fact B.L. referenced in her second contentious snapchat as here previously mentioned. Thus, the cheer coaches were already aware of the likely source of B.L.'s anger and frustration and what had exacerbated it (i.e. not making the senior varsity cheer squad despite her experience on the junior squad while an incoming freshman at her school in fact did make the senior varsity cheer team).[9] This given the conversation they had had with B.L. and her mother regarding the established selection criteria for making the senior varsity cheer squad which conversation well preceded the impugned snapchat communication(s). Given the aforementioned, let us reconsider then the contention of the Appeals Court in the case that "although B.L.'s second snap *contains information* about the varsity team's acceptance of an incoming freshman, nothing in the record suggests B.L.'s punishment was based on that snap or *the information it revealed* (emphasis added)."[10] However it appears, as previously here discussed, that the coaches had or in all probability had knowledge of at least the content of both contentious off-campus B.L. snapchat communications. If the latter is the case, it is difficult to comprehend how or why the second snapchat therefore, in practice, would not have influenced the disciplinary decision-making in B.L.'s case. On the view here then, it more probably was the entire context which led the cheer coach or coaches to fear that "chaos" would ensue if they did not stiffly discipline B.L. If that was the case, then the coaches' fear of "chaos" would likely have been based on a concern that some others on the cheer team may have come to endorse B.L.'s view that the selection process was unfair regarding the senior varsity cheer squad (as implied in B.L.'s second snapchat). If this analysis is correct, the cheer coaches likely further feared that B.L.'s two snapchats, especially the more specific second one charging an inequitable selection process for senior varsity cheer, would facilitate a lack of faith in the cheer coaches and an undermining of cheer team cohesion and morale. On the respectful view here, had the issue been just the first snapchat and its profanity, (i) the discipline likely would not have been so severe. This is evidenced by the fact that others on the team (*the evidentiary record revealed*) had received a much less severe punishment for disrespectful behaviour (including profanity) relating to speech about cheerleading and (ii) the "negative information rule" ("There will be no toleration of any negative information regarding cheerleading, cheerleaders, or coaches placed

9 There is no mention in the court judgements in *Mahanoy* to anything in the evidentiary record that reveals why the incoming freshman at B.L.'s high school (referenced in B.L.'s second snapchat) was able to join the senior varsity cheer squad without having experience on the junior varsity cheer squad.

10 B.L. v. Mahanoy Area Sch. District, 964 F.3d 170 (3d Cir. 2020) (United States Court of Appeals for the Third Circuit) at p. 18.

on the internet")[11] would not have been invoked since the first B.L. snapchat conveyed no particular or substantive information but rather expressed a rather global emotion of frustration.

### *The Parties' Arguments on the Constitutional First Amendment Challenge Brought by B.L.*

Let us turn now then to the First Amendment issue core to the case and the application of the constitutional law to the facts of the case. If B.L.'s constitutional First Amendment rights were *not* waived by her signing the cheer rules, this raises the question whether (i) the school bar against her expressing a good faith opinion while *off-campus* that conveyed, according to the school, both disrespect and some negative information about the cheer programme (without mentioning any school-identifying information) was overbroad and whether (ii) the discipline applied pursuant to her expressing that opinion was a violation of her First Amendment right regardless of whether her impugned off-campus communication did or had the possibility of causing significant disruption to the cheer programme and/or school functioning more generally (the off-campus B.L. snapchat communications did ultimately reach the larger school community beyond those she had intended to be the audience. The intended audience were her limited followers on Snapchat including some classmates and selected cheer team members, but the snapchats factually did not actually cause significant disruption at school). B.L. was suspended from the cheerleading programme for a year[12] as discipline ostensibly for the first snapchat alone and

> During . . . attempts to return to the cheerleading squad, Plaintiff was told that the school had the right to discipline her for "disrespecting the school," and that the coaches believed that her Snap was "demeaning to [the coach], the school, and the rest of the cheerleaders."[13]

Both B.L. snapchats at issue originated off-campus but came to be discussed by others in the cheerleading programme while they were on campus, and hence, this caused some relatively minor disruption in terms of class time devoted to that discussion. However, according to the School District itself in its court submissions, no actual significant or severe disruption occurred as a result of B.L.'s snapchat (or snapchats). Nor did the School District claim that the snapchat it designated at issue (the first profanity-laced snapchat) would foreseeably in the

11 Cheerleading Rules for Mahanoy Area High School. Cited in B.L. v. Mahanoy Area Sch. District 376 F. Supp. 3d 429 (M.D. Pa. 2019) Decided March 21, 2019 (United States District Court for the Middle District of Pennsylvania) at p. 2.

12 B.L. was *not* as part of the discipline barred, however, from trying out for the senior varsity cheer squad the following year.

13 B.L. by Levy v. Mahanoy Area Sch. District, 289 F.Supp.3d 607, 613 (M.D. Pa. 2017) at p. 2.

future cause significant disruption to the extra-curricular cheer programme or to school programming more widely. Yet the cheer coach who disciplined B.L. (with the concurrence of the other coach) justified the discipline to B.L. and her family based on an expressed fear that B.L.'s snapchat undermined the coaching programme and would cause significant disruption ("chaos") essentially by lowering respect for the coaches and the programme:

> "B.L. was disciplined for violating the Respect Provision and the Negative Information Rule of the Cheerleading Rules. . . ." Even though electronic squabbling amongst cheerleaders at the High School "is a fairly typical occurrence," the coaches felt the need to enforce the Rules against B.L. "to 'avoid chaos' and maintain a 'team-like environment. . . ." The cheerleading coaches would not have suspended B.L. from the team if her Snaps had not referenced cheerleading, "though" (emphasis added).[14]

At the same time, the cheer coaches did *not* testify at any evidentiary hearing as to, in their opinion, any alleged actual or contemplated foreseeable *severe disruption* to the cheer team or cheer programming or to school programming as a result of B.L.'s snapchat(s). One cheer coach testified at an evidentiary hearing that she disciplined B.L. due to B.L.'s use of profanity in referencing cheerleading in the first snapchat *not* due to "any possibility of disruption."[15] There seems to be some inconsistency then in the record between documentary evidence on what B.L. and her parents were told or at least understood as to why B.L. was receiving a year suspension from the cheer squad and the testimony of the coach that there was no concern that B.L.'s snapchat had or foreseeably would cause significant disruption to school functioning and/or to the cheer programme.

It is noteworthy that B.L. was disciplined, according to her high school cheer coaches, for allegedly violating *both* the "Respect" Provision and the "Negative Information Rule," though the *first* disparaging snapchat actually contains no specific information nor articulated complaint (i.e. no reference to varsity cheer squad selection criteria) that might be expected to trigger the negative information rule. There would seem then to be no meeting of the *Tinker* disruption standard on the facts of this case nor a basis for application of discipline being based, in part, on the negative information cheer rule.

The question put to the Supreme Court of the United States in this case as framed by the Mahanoy Area School District (the Petitioner) is as follows:

> Whether Tinker v. Des Moines Independent Community School District, 393 U.S. 503 (1969), which holds that public school officials may regulate

14 B.L. v. Mahanoy Area Sch. District, 376 F. Supp. 3d 429 (M.D. Pa. 2019) at pp. 2–3. Note there is a reference here to "snaps" (snapchats) plural citing the submission by the School District.

15 See In the Supreme Court of the United States, Mahanoy Area School District (Petitioner) v. B.L. et al. (Respondents), Brief in Opposition (Respondents' Brief) at p. 16.

> speech that would materially and substantially disrupt the work and discipline of the school, applies to student speech that occurs off-campus.[16]

In contrast, the question put to the Supreme Court of the United States as articulated by the Respondent (B.L. et al.) in opposition is as follows:

> Whether the court of appeals correctly held that a public high school violated the First Amendment when it punished a student for her colorful expression of frustration, made in an ephemeral Snapchat on her personal social media, on a weekend, off-campus, containing no threat or harassment or mention of her school, and that did not cause or threaten any disruption of her school.[17]

The Respondents (B.L. et al.) took the position at the United States Supreme Court that *Tinker* sets out an additional limited *exception* to the First Amendment bar against message-based (content-based) suppression of speech (in addition to the exceptions allowing school regulation of threatening, harassing, bullying speech, or speech connected to cheating which both parties agreed could be suppressed by the school even if originating off-campus). That ***additional exception***, according to the Respondents, allows school officials to regulate offensive speech that is likely to cause disruption due to the strongly held opposing views of other students but that exception, the Respondents argued, would only apply in a school supervised or school sanctioned contexts.[18] Thus, the aforementioned category of ***disruptive speech***, according to the Respondents, ***can be barred off-campus but only in a context that is school supervised or has the imprimatur of the school in some fashion***. The Respondents argued that expanding *Tinker* beyond the aforementioned restricted exceptions would be excessively onerous. This in that students would constantly have to monitor their own off-campus speech lest it not be protected by the First Amendment even though it did not fall into any of the First Amendment exceptions to protection already here discussed and did not occur in a school supervised or sanctioned context.[19]

Respondents (B.L. et al.) also argued that such pervasive school regulation of student speech off-campus (as suggested by the Mahanoy Area School District would be acceptable if the speech caused or foreseeably could cause substantive

16 In the Supreme Court of the United States, Mahanoy Area School District (Petitioner) v. B.L. (Respondent), On writ for Certiorari to the United States Court of Appeals for the Third Circuit, Brief for the Petitioner at p. I.

17 In the Supreme Court of the United States, Mahanoy Area School District (Petitioner) v. B.L. et al. (Respondents), Brief in Opposition (Respondents' Brief) at p. i.

18 In the Supreme Court of the United States, Mahanoy Area School District v. B.L., A Minor, By and Through her Father, Lawrence Levy and her Mother, Betty Lou Levy, Transcript of Oral Argument Before the Supreme Court of the United States (April 28, 2021) at pp. 61–62.

19 In the Supreme Court of the United States, Mahanoy Area School District v. B.L., A Minor, By and Through her Father, Lawrence Levy and her Mother, Betty Lou Levy, Transcript of Oral Argument Before the Supreme Court of the United States (April 28, 2021) at p. 62.

school disruption) would interfere with parental responsibilities. Counsel for the Respondents gave the hypothetical example of a father not feeling he is, in a practical sense, at liberty to bring his daughter to a Black Lives Matter protest about mistreatment of a black student at his daughter's school. This since the father would likely be worried that his daughter might post a photo on social media of the Black Lives Matter protest and, consequently, be suspended from school for allegedly causing school disruption connected to the likely strong conflicting positions of other students at that same school and their reaction to the post.[20]

Respondents further argued that if the school could discipline for speech posted on the Internet by one of its students that might cause disruption at the school in some respect *even though* (i) the communication originated *off-campus*, (ii) did *not* involve threats, harassment, bullying or cheating and (iii) was *not* uttered in a school supervised or sanctioned context, this would contradict *Tinker*.[21] The rule to be deciphered from *Tinker* then, as put forth by the Respondents (B.L. et al.), was articulated as (i) the school having broad authority to regulate student speech when the student is on-campus or under school supervision and the student speech at issue is likely to cause substantial disruption to school functioning or interfere significantly with the rights of other students and (ii) the school having the *same* (not more) authority as other entities such as the city when it comes to regulating off-campus student speech that is in a non-school supervised or sanctioned context where that speech is protected by the First Amendment with any exceptions to that protection which might apply.[22]

Thus, the Respondents held that *off-campus speech* (i) that is *not* one of the exceptions (bullying, harassing or threatening speech or speech connected to facilitating cheating, all of which are inherently disruptive to normal school functioning) and/or (ii) *off-campus speech* that is likely to cause a disruptive response at school *simply due to the highly charged opposing views of others* and where that speech was uttered in a context where the school has no supervisory role in regard to the speaker is "protected speech."[23] That is, such off-campus student speech meeting one or more of the aforementioned criteria does *not* fall into any First Amendment exception category and hence is *not* subject to regulation

20 In the Supreme Court of the United States, Mahanoy Area School District v. B.L., A Minor, By and Through her Father, Lawrence Levy and her Mother, Betty Lou Levy, Transcript of Oral Argument Before the Supreme Court of the United States (April 28, 2021) at p. 62.

21 In the Supreme Court of the United States, Mahanoy Area School District v. B.L., A Minor, By and Through her Father, Lawrence Levy and her Mother, Betty Lou Levy, Transcript of Oral Argument Before the Supreme Court of the United States (April 28, 2021) at p. 64.

22 In the Supreme Court of the United States, Mahanoy Area School District v. B.L., A Minor, By and Through her Father, Lawrence Levy and her Mother, Betty Lou Levy, Transcript of Oral Argument Before the Supreme Court of the United States (April 28, 2021) at pp. 66–67.

23 For example speech posted on the Internet by the student at home over the weekend in a forum that is not school sanctioned or supervised (i.e. posted on the student's personal Snapchat or Facebook account).

by the school authorities and is instead "protected speech." The Respondents maintained then that students enjoy robust free speech protections for their off-campus speech that occurs in a non-school supervised or school sanctioned context even if that speech is disruptive through causing offence as long as that speech does not meet the criteria for a First Amendment exception to protection or otherwise interfere with others' rights.[24]

According to the Respondents then, *Tinker* allows content-based suppression also of off-campus speech but only *in a school-supervised or school-sanctioned context* or a circumstance bearing the school's imprimatur *and where that speech does or likely will cause significant disruption to the school's mission to educate and even if the speech suppressed is religious or political.*[25] The Respondents also emphasized that while the school can also regulate off-campus student threats, bullying and/or harassment targeting the school in some way and also school cheating, the school cannot regulate all off-campus student speech based simply on its offensive content which might be disruptive in causing offence.[26]

The Petitioners (the School District), in contrast, argued at the United States Supreme Court that (i) *Tinker* does *not* apply to controversial political, religious or other speech *off-campus as long as the speech did not "target" or reference the school in some way* and (ii) that this is the rule *Tinker* allegedly sets out even if such off-campus student speech does cause disruption to the educational agenda on the school campus. The school cannot, in the view of the Petitioners, constitutionally regulate such off-campus student speech falling into the aforementioned category.[27] The complexity of this position involves in part, however, how to handle cases where the off-campus student speech is political or religious for the main, for instance, but also references the school, or a teacher and/or a student. If the school response turns out to be inconsistent across such various cases, then this would reflect the vagueness in the application of the School District's proposed rule regarding when the school can constitutionally regulate *off-campus* student speech.[28] Judge Alito made specific reference to this concern as to how

24 In the Supreme Court of the United States, Mahanoy Area School District v. B.L., A Minor, By and Through her Father, Lawrence Levy and her Mother, Betty Lou Levy, Transcript of Oral Argument Before the Supreme Court of the United States (April 28, 2021) at pp. 74–75.

25 In the Supreme Court of the United States, Mahanoy Area School District v. B.L., A Minor, By and Through her Father, Lawrence Levy and her Mother, Betty Lou Levy, Transcript of Oral Argument Before the Supreme Court of the United States (April 28, 2021) at pp. 74–75.

26 In the Supreme Court of the United States, Mahanoy Area School District v. B.L., A Minor, By and Through her Father, Lawrence Levy and her Mother, Betty Lou Levy, Transcript of Oral Argument Before the Supreme Court of the United States (April 28, 2021) at p. 75.

27 In the Supreme Court of the United States, Mahanoy Area School District v. B.L., A Minor, By and Through her Father, Lawrence Levy and her Mother, Betty Lou Levy, Transcript of Oral Argument Before the Supreme Court of the United States (April 28, 2021) at pp. 15, 45–46.

28 In the Supreme Court of the United States, Mahanoy Area School District v. B.L., A Minor, By and Through her Father, Lawrence Levy and her Mother, Betty Lou Levy, Transcript

the school is to apply a rule in regulating off-campus school speech when the rule depends so much on the specific case facts and context.[29]

Further, the Petitioners acknowledged that issues arise in determining whether the education rights of other students have in fact been significantly infringed and/or the educational agenda on campus has been severely compromised by the disruption caused by certain off-campus student speech that references the school in some way. Such is the requirement to meet the "substantial disruption" standard under *Tinker* which standard is not met merely by evidence that some listeners took offence at the particular student's off-campus speech.[30] The question also arises in this case as to whether the school has additional or more expansive regulatory power in regard to speech (i) uttered off-campus and (ii) in a context that is *not* school sanctioned or supervised and does not have the school's imprimatur *if the student is a member of an extracurricular programme* such as cheer. That question was *not* answered by the courts below that found, in the first instance, that B.L. in fact did *not* violate the cheer rules by posting her vague off-campus snapchats that did not name the school, the coaches or members of the cheer squad.[31] Thus, these courts held that there was no need in order to decide the case to get to the question whether the school has more expansive regulatory power over students' off-campus speech if the students involved are members of extracurricular programmes such as cheer.

## *Selected Highlights of the District Court Ruling*

The District Court held that B.L.'s off-campus obscenity-laced snapchat rant (the first snapchat) was constitutionally protected speech under the First Amendment and that she had *not* waived her constitutionally based free expression rights by signing the cheer rules. A. Richard Caputo, United States District Judge, had previously granted B.L.'s motion for a preliminary injunction on the imposition of the discipline (removal from the cheer programme for one year). Judge Caputo found that holding otherwise would "allow school children to serve as Thought Police—reporting every profanity uttered—for the District."[32]

---

of Oral Argument Before the Supreme Court of the United States (April 28, 2021) at pp. 16–17.

29 In the Supreme Court of the United States, Mahanoy Area School District v. B.L., A Minor, By and Through her Father, Lawrence Levy and her Mother, Betty Lou Levy, Transcript of Oral Argument Before the Supreme Court of the United States (April 28, 2021) at p. 17.

30 In the Supreme Court of the United States, Mahanoy Area School District v. B.L., A Minor, By and Through her Father, Lawrence Levy and her Mother, Betty Lou Levy, Transcript of Oral Argument Before the Supreme Court of the United States at p. 7.

31 See In the Supreme Court of the United States, Mahanoy Area School District v. B.L., A Minor, By and Through her Father, Lawrence Levy and her Mother, Betty Lou Levy, Transcript of Oral Argument Before the Supreme Court of the United States (April 28, 2021) at p. 71.

32 B.L. by Levy v. Mahanoy Area Sch. District, 289 F.Supp.3d 607, 613 (M.D. Pa. 2017).

The District Court Judge denied the School District's motion for summary dismissal of the case holding that the evidence reveals that B.L.'s constitutional rights were violated by the School District in imposing discipline for her snapchat which did *not* specifically reference the school or name any cheer coaches.

The District Judge found that in the B.L. snapchat case, the *Tinker standard* of the impugned speech causing actual or likely foreseeable substantial school disruption had *not* been met. This was evidenced by the record since "at the only evidentiary hearing in the case, the School District did not even argue that the speech caused disruption,"[33] and the coaches testified that they did not expect the snapchat (the first one) to cause significant disruption in future. The court found also that B.L.'s obscenity-laced first snapchat did *not* bear the imprimatur of the school or the school's cheer squad or reference either so could not be held to have undermined either. Further then B.L.'s snapchats could *not* be said to have been disruptive to school functioning or the cheer programme to a level required under the *Tinker* standard or to have met the precedential case law standard for discipline related to the use of obscenity. Hence, the District Court found it *unnecessary* to consider whether *Tinker* applied to off-campus speech in cases where that speech did or could cause severe disruption to school functioning in some respect (i.e. regarding regular school programming and/or extracurricular school programming).[34] The District Court also held that the School District was vicariously liable for the coaches' violation of B.L. First Amendment rights as the "District admits it 'approved or ratified' the Cheerleading Rules pursuant to which B.L. was punished."[35]

### *Selected Highlights of the Appeals Court Ruling*

The Appeals Court held that *Tinker* does *not* apply to off-campus speech such as B.L.'s snapchats at issue. This in the first instance in that the snapchats were *not connected to the school* through a school-supervised activity or occurring in a context that carries the school's imprimatur. Recall also that (i) B.L. did not name the school, the School District, the coaches, teachers nor any cheer team members or other classmates in her snapchats and that (ii) the impugned communication(s) were not made using school property such as school computers or using communication vehicles identified with the school such as a school newspaper and

33 B.L. by Levy v. Mahanoy Area Sch. District, 289 F.Supp.3d 607, 613 (M.D. Pa. 2017) Mem. 5 n.7, Oct. 5, 2017, ECF No. 12, No. 3:17-cv-1734 (M.D. Pa.) Cited in In the Supreme Court of the United States, Mahanoy Area School District (Petitioner) v. B.L. et al. (Respondents), Brief in Opposition (Respondents' Brief) at p. 15.

34 "The court [referencing the District Court] reasoned that it did not need to determine whether Tinker applied to B.L.'s speech because, even assuming it did, the undisputed evidence showed that the Tinker standard was not met." B.L. v. Mahanoy Area Sch. District 376 F. Supp. 3d 429 (M.D. Pa. 2019) at p. 16.

35 B.L. v. Mahanoy Area Sch. District, 376 F. Supp. 3d 429 (M.D. Pa. 2019) Decided (March 21, 2019) (United States District Court for the Middle District of Pennsylvania) at p. 7.

did not occur in a school-sponsored online forum.[36] Hence, the Appeals Court for the Third Circuit in this case held it did *not* need to decide the disruption question. The Court of Appeals, however, suggested that off-campus student speech that is threatening or harassing may be an exception that is unprotected by the First Amendment though the court declined to address that question since B.L.'s contentious impugned communication(s) by snapchat at the heart of this case were *not* contended by any party to have been threatening, harassing or bullying.[37]

Interestingly, the Mahanoy Area School District argued that (i) B.L.'s snapchat (the first obscenity-laced snapchat) was "vulgar," "low-value" speech and so was allegedly subject to more extensive regulation by the school than would be the case for more civil, content-based speech[38] and that (ii) the first snapchat expressed *no opinion and hence was unprotected by the First Amendment.*[39] The School District's legal strategy/arguments hence focused on the *first* B.L snapchat (the profanity-laced snapchat). The Appeals Court rejected both these arguments. The Appeals Court stated that "There is no doubt B.L.'s snap [referring to the first snapchat] was "imbued with elements of communication and . . . thus deserving of First Amendment protection."[40] It is noteworthy also in this regard that B.L. was informed by the school that she was disciplined for violating both the "respect" and the "negative information" cheer rules. Contending that B.L. had violated the "negative information rule" seems inconsistent, however, with the school's contention that B.L. was disciplined for the *first* snapchat; one that expressed, *in the school's view*, little if any actual informational content and no opinion. In contrast, the second B.L. snapchat undisputedly referenced an alleged unfair selection process for the senior varsity cheer team (without identifying the school or the name of the cheer squad involved). It seems at least plausible thus that the second snapchat triggered the heightened level of discipline in B.L.'s case and the school's reliance in part in that disciplining on the negative information rule. While the lower courts did *not* make such a finding, on the respectful view here, the evidentiary record contains inconsistencies that raise a question about what role, if any, the second B.L. snapchat may have played in the discipline imposed on B.L. for her impugned off-campus speech.

The Appeals Court furthermore (i) concurred with the District Court that B.L. had *not* waived her First Amendment rights by agreeing to the cheer rules and

36 B.L. v. Mahanoy Area Sch. District, 964 F.3d 170 (3d Cir. 2020) (United States Court of Appeals for the Third Circuit) (Decided June 30, 2020) at p. 11.
37 B.L. v. Mahanoy Area Sch. District, 964 F.3d 170 (3d Cir. 2020) (United States Court of Appeals for the Third Circuit) (Decided June 30, 2020) at p. 11.
38 B.L. v. Mahanoy Area Sch. District, 964 F.3d 170 (3d Cir. 2020) (United States Court of Appeals for the Third Circuit) (Decided June 30, 2020) at p. 17.
39 B.L. v. Mahanoy Area Sch. District, 964 F.3d 170 (3d Cir. 2020) (United States Court of Appeals for the Third Circuit) (Decided June 30, 2020) at p. 17.
40 B.L. v. Mahanoy Area Sch. District, 964 F.3d 170 (3d Cir. 2020) (United States Court of Appeals for the Third Circuit) (Decided June 30, 2020) at p. 17.

signing the relevant school document outlining those rules and that (ii) to condition participation in the cheer programme on a waiver of free expression rights would in any case be to violate the "unconstitutional conditions doctrine."[41] The Appeals Court also held that the school could not, using the rationale of teaching students civility, extend its regulatory power over students to their off-campus speech occurring in a context unconnected to any off-campus school-sponsored event or activity and lacking the school's imprimatur: "Otherwise, we give school administrators the power to quash student expression deemed crude or offensive—which far too easily metastasizes into the power to censor valuable speech and legitimate criticism."[42]

### *Dissenting Off-Campus Student Speech: Controversies Over When Protection Under the First Amendment Applies*

The Mahanoy Area School District argued that the landmark *Tinker* case rule should be extended to off-campus student speech in the alleged proper instance (i) even if the speech is non-threatening, non-bullying and non-harassing and (ii) even if the off-campus student speech did not occur in a school supervised or sanctioned context or in some respect under the school imprimatur. This on the rationale that off-campus speech can, in certain cases when the school is targeted in such speech, cause "substantial disruption" on campus that goes beyond listeners just taking offence. If the latter be the case, the Mahanoy School District argued, the off-campus school speech would *not* be protected speech.

The *Tinker* case is a 1960s case concerning high school students who, *on the school campus*, peacefully expressed dissent. Their dissent had to do with their objecting to the Vietnam War and advocating for a Christmas truce. The form of expression they chose was the wearing of a black armband.

> The school officials banned and sought to punish petitioners for a silent, passive expression of opinion, *unaccompanied* by any disorder or disturbance on the part of petitioners. There is here no evidence whatever of petitioners' interference, actual or nascent, with the schools' work or of collision with the rights of other students to be secure and to be let alone. Accordingly, this

41 B.L. v. Mahanoy Area Sch. District, 964 F.3d 170 (3d Cir. 2020) (United States Court of Appeals for the Third Circuit) (Decided June 30, 2020) at p. 17. See Fuhr, E.J. The Doctrine of Unconstitutional Conditions and the First Amendment. *Case Western Reserve Law Review*, Vol. 39, Issue1 (1989), 97 (Abstract): "The doctrine of unconstitutional conditions posits that if the government is prohibited from directly limiting the exercise of constitutional rights in a given situation, the government may not achieve the same result indirectly by offering benefits subject to the condition that the recipients waive their constitutional rights."

42 B.L. v. Mahanoy Area Sch. District, 964 F.3d 170 (3d Cir. 2020) (United States Court of Appeals for the Third Circuit) (Decided June 30, 2020) at p. 19.

case does not concern speech or action that intrudes upon the work of the schools or the rights of other students (emphasis added).[43]

Importantly, on the view here, the Supreme Court of the United States (USSC) acknowledged that the student conscientious objectors to the Vietnam War here (the student petitioners in the *Tinker* case) were trying to sway other students and school personnel to their view opposing the continuation of the war:

> the record does not demonstrate any facts which might reasonably have led school authorities to forecast substantial disruption of or material interference with school activities, and no disturbances or disorders on the school premises in fact occurred. . . . Their deviation consisted only in wearing on their sleeve a band of black cloth, not more than two inches wide. *They wore it to exhibit their disapproval of the Vietnam hostilities and their advocacy of a truce, to make their views known, and, by their example, to influence others to adopt them.* They neither interrupted school activities nor sought to intrude in the school affairs or the lives of others. *They caused discussion outside of the classrooms*, but no interference with work and no disorder (emphasis added).[44]

It is a key point, the current author maintains, that the Supreme Court of the United States in *Tinker* did *not* consider as inherently disruptive the *peaceful advocacy of one's dissenting views* in an effort to sway others' opinion on the matter at hand to one's own. In the snapchat case, B.L. arguably was conveying to certain selected others on the cheer squad who were her friends, and to certain other classmates, her view that the cheer selection process for the senior varsity cheer team at their school was unfair. She may have wished to commiserate with some of these students who may have agreed with her and with her Snapchat followers who might be, she likely hoped, at least persuaded to perceive the same alleged aforementioned injustice she did.

The potential for a coalition of student dissenters being formed due to B.L.'s snapchats (students who dissented (correctly or incorrectly)) from the expected and accepted school wisdom that selection of the senior varsity cheer squad at the school was fair likely raised serious concerns for the Mahanoy Area School District cheer coaches. The latter possibility, as here discussed, then may have been the actual basis for the School District imposing significant discipline and justifying this in terms of B.L.'s alleged significant violation of both the "respect" and "negative information" cheer rules purportedly potentially causing the cheer programme to

43 John F. Tinker and Mary Beth Tinker, Minors, etc., et al., Petitioners, v. Des Moines Independent Community School District et al. 393 U.S. 503, 89 S. Ct. 733 Decided (February 24, 1969) para 13.

44 In the Supreme Court of the United States John F. Tinker and Mary Beth Tinker, Minors, etc., et al., Petitioners, v. Des Moines Independent Community School District et al. 393 U.S. 503, 89 S. Ct. 733 at para 28.

come into disrepute and interfering with team cohesion. The lower courts in the case however, it will be recalled, found that the record did not reveal actual or foreseeable substantial on-campus disruption relating to B.L.'s snapchats.[45] The Mahanoy Area School District personnel did *not*, as mentioned, testify at the evidentiary hearing that in fact substantial disruption had or foreseeably would occur due to B.L.'s impugned snapchat(s). In any case, on the *Tinker* standard, it is here argued, express or tacit concerns that a student's *peaceful expression of opinion-based*[46] *dissent*[47] may attract further student adherents at his or her school to that view is *not* the proper basis for the proposition that certain off-campus student speech is unprotected by the First Amendment and meets the *Tinker* disruption standard. *Tinker* instructs that even with regard to on-campus speech:

> the prohibition of expression of one particular opinion, at least without evidence that it is necessary to avoid material and substantial interference with schoolwork or discipline, is not constitutionally permissible.[48]

The *Tinker* majority also cited with approval the following which goes to the issue of student peaceful dissent and advocacy being "protected speech"—what Tinker refers to as "pure speech" (that is expression that is *not* inherently by its content objectively likely to be causative of substantial disruption to school process or to interfere in the rights of other students though perhaps being speech offensive and upsetting others and rather just expresses an opinion):[49]

> In our system, state-operated schools may not be enclaves of totalitarianism. School officials do not possess absolute authority over their students. *Students in school as well as out of school are "persons" under our Constitution. They are possessed of fundamental rights which the State must respect*, just as they themselves must respect their obligations to the State. *In our system, students may not be regarded as closed-circuit recipients of only that which the State chooses to communicate. They may not be confined to the expression of those*

45 B.L. v. Mahanoy Area Sch. District, 964 F.3d 170 (3d Cir. 2020) (United States Court of Appeals for the Third Circuit) at pp. 20–21.
46 Referring here to speech which is not an incitement to violence, nor bullying, threatening. harassing nor hate speech.
47 Referring here to dissenting speech where the content of the speech is non-harassing, not threatening nor bullying in any way.
48 In the Supreme Court of the United States John F. Tinker and Mary Beth Tinker, Minors, etc., et al., Petitioners, v. Des Moines Independent Community School District et al. 393 U.S. 503, 89 S. Ct. 733 Decided (February 24, 1969) at para 19.
49 In the Supreme Court of the United States John F. Tinker and Mary Beth Tinker, Minors, etc., et al., Petitioners, v. Des Moines Independent Community School District et al. 393 U.S. 503, 89 S. Ct. 733 Decided (February 24, 1969) at para 7: "As we shall discuss, the wearing of armbands in the circumstances of this case was entirely divorced from actually or potentially disruptive conduct by those participating in it. It was closely akin to 'pure speech' which, we have repeatedly held, is entitled to comprehensive protection under the First Amendment."

> *sentiments that are officially approved.* In the absence of a specific showing of constitutionally valid reasons to regulate their speech, students are entitled to freedom of expression of their views. As Judge Gewin, speaking for the Fifth Circuit, said, *school officials cannot suppress "expressions of feelings with which they do not wish to contend."*[50]

The Mahanoy Area School District argued that the requirements set out in *Tinker* that (i) the speech must target the school in some way and (ii) must be or foreseeably would be substantially disruptive to the school would prevent any overreach in the school authorities punishing on or off-campus student speech. Extending *Tinker* to off-campus speech with the aforementioned provisos, in the view of the Mahanoy Area School District, thus is constitutionally sound. On the analysis here, however, such an extension would capture improperly also that student content-based peaceful dissenting speech falling into the category of "protected speech" as opposed to one of the speech categories relating to a court-determined limited exception to the First Amendment. Let us consider then the issue of the scope of so-called disruptive off-campus student speech which encompasses also (i) speech that is disruptive because it represents and advocates for a certain peaceful dissent while *not* causing or likely to cause substantial disruption to school process or to interfere with the rights of other students and (ii) where the speech occurred out of a school context entirely (it was speech that did *not* take place in a school supervised or school sanctioned context and did *not* have the school imprimatur in any way) and whether such speech is protected under the First Amendment.

## The Core Issue: Democracy, "Good Trouble" and Peaceful Dissenting Speech

The *Mahanoy Area School District v B.L.* snapchat case[51] raises a number of legal sub-issues, but we should not lose sight of what is, on the view here, a core issue embedded in the case. That core issue is whether public school students are constitutionally permitted to peacefully, non-violently raise their voices on or off-campus (in a non-school context) in protest to what they perceive, correctly or incorrectly, as a social wrong or injustice. When children are suppressed in speaking their minds on campus or off-campus (the latter in a non-school context) in a peaceful manner—including on what, at times, to adults may seem as comparatively trivial matters—the question arises as to whether they are also learning to

50 In the Supreme Court of the United States John F. Tinker and Mary Beth Tinker, Minors, etc., et al., Petitioners, v. Des Moines Independent Community School District et al. 393 U.S. 503, 89 S. Ct. 733 Decided (February 24, 1969) at para 20 (citing Burnside v. Byars, 363 F.2d 744, 749 (1966)).

51 In the Supreme Court of the United States, Mahanoy Area School District v. B.L., A Minor, By and Through her Father, Lawrence Levy and her Mother, Betty Lou Levy, Transcript of Oral Argument Before the Supreme Court of the United States (April 28, 2021).

later suppress their voices on significant societal issues. The amicus brief by the College Athlete Advocates contends that this issue is embedded in the *Mahanoy Area School District v B.L.* case:

> This case implicates the ability of students playing competitive sports, at all educational levels, to express themselves about the social and political issues they care about—and to engage in safety motivated whistleblowing about conditions within their own athletic programs—without fear of retaliation.[52]

The College Athlete Advocates Amici in the case argued that the position of the Mahanoy Area School District and its supporters, if accepted by the court, would also cause unconstitutional suppression of whistleblower speech at the high school and college levels. This since, on this amici view, "the District and its supporting amici would have the Court define complaining about the athletic program as a punishable act of 'disruption' unprotected by the First Amendment."[53] The College Athlete Advocates amici highlighted cases in their brief in which the Supreme Court of the United States has applied a certain speech standard in a First Amendment school case involving a K–12 school, and the lower courts have generalized that holding to college-age adult students as well.[54] The College Athlete Advocates amici rejected the notion that because the cheerleading programme was a discretionary government benefit which B.L. *chose* to engage with, her constitutional First Amendment rights could therefore somehow be properly *less protected* when she spoke out in a non-school context off-campus and critiqued the cheerleading programme and the coaches without providing identifying information.[55] The College Athlete Advocates amici also expressed concern that social media posts may be misinterpreted by school administrators who may not share the ethnic and cultural experiences of the poster and that the unreviewable power of the school to punish such off-campus speech will likely thus have a disproportionately adverse effect on so-called racialized minorities.[56]

52 Mahanoy Area School District v. B.L., A Minor, By and Through her Father, Lawrence Levy and her Mother, Betty Lou Levy, Brief Amicus Curiae, College Athlete Advocates in support of the respondents, Supreme Court of the United States No. 20–255 (March 31, 2021) at pp. 2–3.

53 Mahanoy Area School District v. B.L., A Minor, By and Through her Father, Lawrence Levy and her Mother, Betty Lou Levy, Brief Amicus Curiae, College Athlete Advocates in support of the respondents, Supreme Court of the United States No. 20–255 (March 31, 2021) at p. 3.

54 Mahanoy Area School District v. B.L., A Minor, By and Through her Father, Lawrence Levy and her Mother, Betty Lou Levy Brief Amicus Curiae, College Athlete Advocates in support of the respondents, Supreme Court of the United States No. 20–255 (March 31, 2021) at p. 3.

55 Mahanoy Area School District v. B.L., A Minor, By and Through her Father, Lawrence Levy and her Mother, Betty Lou Levy Brief Amicus Curiae, College Athlete Advocates in support of the respondents, Supreme Court of the United States No. 20–255 (March 31, 2021) at p. 3.

56 Mahanoy Area School District v. B.L., A Minor, By and Through her Father, Lawrence Levy and her Mother, Betty Lou Levy Brief Amicus Curiae, College Athlete Advocates in support

These College Athlete Advocates amici contend further that the issue of the profanity used in the impugned first snapchat in this case (i) clouds the central First Amendment rights issue and (ii) puts at risk the exercise of freedom of expression by athletes on matters of critical concern whether that be in relation to, for instance, abuse in the athletic programme or a social injustice in the wider community:

> No one has a legally enforceable duty to complain politely about the government. To enforce a "mandatory politeness rule," under threat of punishment, will guarantee that abuse festers undetected.[57]
>
> Now, imagine that colleges are equipped with the ***judicially sanctioned authority to retaliate against anyone who speaks in the context of sports in a "disruptive" way***. This is a recipe for making the already-abusive conditions for athletes exponentially worse, cutting off the only viable source of rescue. . . . The Court should not lose sight of the fact that it is dealing with young and vulnerable speakers in a position of extreme power differential (emphasis added).[58]

It is a relevant fact to consider in evaluating the merits of the arguments advanced by the Mahanoy Area School District and by the student B.L. in this case that American children ("children" being defined for our purposes here as persons under 18 years of age) are barred from the vote.[59] The latter is a most precious and consequential form of free expression denied them notwithstanding their First Amendment constitutional right. Children in the United States, even of age 16 to under 18, have no say in the election or appointment of public officials including school authorities or regarding the policies that regulate the children's lives in important ways including at school. Hence, the suppression of children's voices in peaceful dissent or whistleblowing or self-advocacy raised through social media off-campus in a *non-school* supervised or school sanctioned context is especially impactful given children's socio-political vulnerability. It is particularly striking then, on the current author view, that the Mahanoy Area School District would argue, as it did, that the student B.L. waived her First Amendment right

---

of the respondents, Supreme Court of the United States No. 20–255 (March 31, 2021) at p. 12.

57 Mahanoy Area School District v. B.L., A Minor, By and Through her Father, Lawrence Levy and her Mother, Betty Lou Levy Brief Amicus Curiae, College Athlete Advocates in support of the respondents, Supreme Court of the United States No. 20–255 (March 31, 2021) at p. 13.

58 Mahanoy Area School District v. B.L., A Minor, By and Through her Father, Lawrence Levy and her Mother, Betty Lou Levy Brief Amicus Curiae, College Athlete Advocates in support of the respondents, Supreme Court of the United States No. 20–255 (March 31, 2021) at pp. 14–15.

59 Grover, S.C. *Young People's Human Rights and the Politics of Voting Age* (New York: Springer, 2011).

by signing the school rules for cheer.[60] The latter seems a gross overestimation of the School District's authority in potentially infringing on the constitutional rights of a vulnerable party. In fact, the District Court judge in this case held that B.L. and her mother had *not* waived B.L.'s First Amendment rights[61] given the power differential between the school authorities (including the cheer coaches) and the other parties (B.L. and her mother):

> neither B.L. nor her mother had bargaining equality with the coaches or the school. Cheerleading Rules were not subject to negotiation; and B.L. and her mother were not represented by counsel when they agreed B.L. would abide by the Rules. Additionally, conditioning extracurricular participation on a waiver of a constitutional right is coercive.[62]

Thus, the District Judge in the case found there had been no "voluntary, knowing, and intelligent waiver of [B.L.'s] . . . First Amendment rights."[63]

At the same time, off-campus student speech that (i) references the school in some way and (ii) occurs in a school supervised or school sanctioned context or under the school's imprimatur and *substantially disrupts* or foreseeably will disrupt the on-campus school functioning (i.e. so as to infringe other students' right to access their education in a peaceful and productive, supportive learning environment) is not acceptable nor protected. Hence, the issue in *Mahanoy* becomes whether there is *any* legitimate private space (virtual or otherwise) for students to get into "good trouble" off-campus through speech ("good trouble" in the sense of peacefully demanding reflection on whether the *status quo* in some respect at school or in the wider context is equitable). Put somewhat differently: Can students ever voice disruptive non-violent dissent off-campus that is beyond the reach of school regulation? If such *peaceful but provocative* truly off-campus speech[64] referencing a school in some way is suppressed in every instance where it causes or foreseeably could cause *disruption in the sense of upset or offence* to at least some school officials and some students on campus, the further issue arises as to whether that is counterproductive to educating for democracy. This in

60 "The District maintains that both B.L. and her mother voluntarily waived B.L.'s First Amendment rights by signing the 'Application for Cheerleading Tryouts' (which conditioned participation on abiding by the Cheerleading Rules)." See B.L. v. Mahanoy Area Sch. District, 376 F. Supp. 3d 429 (M.D. Pa. 2019) Decided (March 21, 2019) (United States District Court for the Middle District of Pennsylvania) at p. 6.

61 Referring here to an alleged waiver of the student's First Amendment rights based on signing the school document setting out the rules for participating in the cheerleading programme.

62 B.L. v. Mahanoy Area Sch. District, 376 F. Supp. 3d 429 (M.D. Pa. 2019) Decided (March 21, 2019) (United States District Court for the Middle District of Pennsylvania) at p. 6.

63 B.L. v. Mahanoy Area Sch. District, 376 F. Supp. 3d 429 (M.D. Pa. 2019) Decided (March 21, 2019) (United States District Court for the Middle District of Pennsylvania) at p. 6.

64 Referencing here off-campus student speech that is *not* occurring in a school supervised or sanctioned context or in any way under the school's imprimatur. The same question might be raised legitimately about such provocative speech if on-campus.

that the message conveyed—intentionally or not—by such ***blanket suppression*** of off-campus provocative speech would be that students are not to think critically about the socio-cultural immediate context in which they are located or about the more global situation which also directly or indirectly intrudes upon and affects or will significantly affect their lives.[65] If the latter be the case, it is the converse of the message conveyed by Congressman John Lewis who communicated the following to the younger generation:

> You are never too young or too old to lead. To get into trouble—good trouble, necessary trouble. . . . When you see something that is not right, not fair; not just; stand up, say something; speak up and speak out.[66]

To further inform our thinking about off-campus student speech and when it is in fact-based on fundamental human rights and democratic constitutional values—"protected speech," let us consider what constitutes "the right to education" under international human rights law. While the United States is only a signatory to the *Convention on the Rights of the Child* and has not ratified this international treaty and so is not bound by it (unlike all other members of the United Nations General Assembly), considering the articulation of the right to education in that legal instrument is yet instructive. This as it reflects a global consensus amongst nations on children's human rights despite the 196 States Parties to the Convention having vastly different cultures and social norms and understandings of childhood.

Articles 28 and 29 of the Convention on the Rights of the Child (the CRC) state in part:

> **CRC Article 28**
>
> States Parties recognize the right of the child to education, and . . . . they shall, in particular . . . take all appropriate measures to ensure that school discipline is administered in a manner consistent with the child's human dignity and in conformity with the present Convention.[67]
>
> **CRC Article 29**
>
> 1. States Parties agree that the education of the child shall be directed to: (a) The development of the child's personality, talents and mental and physical abilities to their fullest potential; (b) *The development of respect for human rights and fundamental freedoms, and for the principles enshrined in the Charter of the United Nations*. . . . (d) *The preparation of the child for responsible life in a free*

65 Climate change and the COVID-19 pandemic has surely illustrated the interconnectedness of the global community and its challenges.

66 Congressman John Lewis Address, Harvard Commencement 2018.

67 Convention on the Rights of the Child, entry into force (September 2, 1990), Article 28.

> *society*, in the spirit of understanding, peace, tolerance, equality of sexes, and friendship among all peoples, ethnic, national and religious groups and persons of indigenous origin (emphasis added).[68]

Clearly, the global consensus is that the right to education entails learning, in part through schooling, to respect fundamental human rights and freedoms, and to have high regard for the human dignity of all persons. In particular also, the right to education includes "The preparation of the child for responsible life in a free society" (CRC Article 29). Also note that discipline is to be administered "in manner consistent with the child's human dignity and in conformity with the present Convention" (CRC Article 28). One would not expect based on the CRC articulation of the right to education then that the peaceful expression by a student off-school campus of dissent (dissent that is not threatening, bullying or harassing) should be disciplined by school authorities. Other articles (Articles 12 and 13) of the *Convention on the Rights of the Child* in fact guarantee children's participation and freedom of expression rights particularly in regard to decisions that affect them personally in a significant manner:

> **Article 12**
>
> 1.States Parties shall assure to the child who is capable of forming his or her own views the right to *express those views freely in all matters affecting the child*, the views of the child being given due weight in accordance with the age and maturity of the child (emphasis added).[69]
>
> **Article 13**
>
> 1. *The child shall have the right to freedom of expression; this right shall include freedom to seek, receive and impart information and ideas of all kinds*, regardless of frontiers, either orally, in writing or in print, in the form of art, or *through any other media of the child's choice.*
>
> 2. *The exercise of this right may be subject to certain restrictions, but these shall only be such as are provided by law and are necessary:*
>
> (a) For respect of the rights or reputations of others; or
> (b) For the protection of national security or of public order . . . or of public health or morals (emphasis added).[70]

Hence, Articles 12 and 13 of the "Convention on the Rights of the Child" "read together set out the child's freedom of expression rights as central to the child's

68 Convention on the Rights of the Child, entry into force (September 2, 1990), Article 29.
69 Convention on the Rights of the Child, entry into force (September 2, 1990), Article 12.
70 Convention on the Rights of the Child, entry into force (September 2, 1990), Article 13.

democratic participation rights and permit only those restrictions on that freedom of expression such as are genuinely necessary and consistent with democratic values.

Now to return to the facts of the snapchat case at hand and recap this author's interpretation of the circumstantial evidence in the larger case context. On the view here, arguably, it would appear that it likely was *not* B.L.'s first obscenity-laced snapchat that singularly led to her being significantly disciplined by the cheer coach. Recall that B.L.'s first snapchat in the view of the School District relayed no identifying or substantive information or opinion. It is difficult thus to endorse the view that obscenities themselves referring in part to cheer (as in the first snapchat) without any context to make sense of what precipitated the tirade and without identifying information (as in the case of B.L.'s snapchats) would be sufficient to lower respect in the school community for the cheer coaches or damage the good reputation of the cheer programme or the school as appears to be directly or indirectly alleged by the coaches (and School District). Had the issue of the use of obscenity been the only one, it seems likely the discipline imposed on B.L. would not have been so severe as the one-year suspension from the cheerleading programme which she received. Indeed in this regard, it is noteworthy that one of the coaches involved in the case (the record reveals) had previously administered a lesser discipline to a different student for profanely referring to another cheerleading team (that discipline being imposed based on the obscenity and not any fear of disruption of the Mahanoy high school cheer programme).[71] The District Court Judge determined that "B.L.'s mere off-campus profanity is what upset Coach Luchetta-Rump, not the potential for chaos about which the District's evidence, at best, raises 'metaphysical doubt.'"[72] On the analysis here, however, it may have been the follow-up snapchat (which B.L. sent almost immediately after the first snapchat) and which contained the specific implied claim of inequity in the selection process for the senior varsity cheerleading squad at her (unnamed) high school that was the prime issue that resulted in the significant discipline (the one-year suspension by the cheer coaches of B.L. from the cheerleading programme).

The courts did not address whether B.L. was correct in her claim of inequity in the selection process for the senior varsity cheerleading squad and no presumption is made here on that question. In fact, whether or not B.L. was correct in her claim of inequity in the selection process for the senior varsity cheer squad at her school is irrelevant to the First Amendment question at the heart of this case—namely her constitutional right to express this view off-campus in her private virtual space. At the same time, whistleblowing as "protected speech" is key to those in power meeting their duty of trust to the public and to vulnerable persons in particular.

71 B.L. by Levy v. Mahanoy Area Sch. District, 289 F.Supp.3d 607, 613 (M.D. Pa. 2017) United States District Court, M.D. Pennsylvania, Decided (October 5, 2017) at p. 12.

72 B.L. by Levy v. Mahanoy Area Sch. District, 289 F.Supp.3d 607, 613 (M.D. Pa. 2017) United States District Court, M.D. Pennsylvania, Decided (October 5, 2017) at p. 12.

B.L. was, on the view here, entitled to have her opinion on the cheerleading senior varsity selection process equity issue and to express it off-campus in a private virtual space as she did (and likely also on-campus). To argue otherwise is, it is here contended, to suggest that students' First Amendment rights are less than those of other citizens: "[T]he First Amendment protects students engaging in off-campus speech to the same extent it protects speech by citizens in the community at large."[73] The cheerleading coaches were free and presumably in a position to rebut B.L.'s claim of inequity in the senior varsity cheer selection process at her high school. That they, on the view here, took a different route—imposing the significant discipline of suspending B.L. from the cheer programme for one year based on (if this analysis is correct) both snapchats—is a testament on the respectful view here to the lack of toleration of dissent. This even where that dissent was peacefully though arguably offensively expressed (if one considers both of B.L.'s impugned snapchats together). That dissent then related (on the view here) to a key issue, namely equity in the cheer programme with regard to the selection criteria and process for the senior varsity cheer squad. The latter issue apparently needed resolution which would require, unsurprisingly, free and open discussion and clarification. The approach taken by the high school cheer coaches in this case would arguably do little if anything to resolve any doubts about equity that others besides B.L. may have had about fairness in the selection process for choosing members of the senior cheer varsity squad. It seems plausible in fact that the coaches may have been concerned that others on both the junior and senior varsity cheerleading squads would begin to raise questions (justified or not) about equity in the cheerleading senior varsity selection process. This should the cheer coaches support B.L.'s right to raise such issues and trigger an open discussion amongst all those in the cheer programme (junior and senior varsity level) and their coaches. Hence, B.L.'s raising of this controversial issue and her dissenting view that the cheer selection criteria and process for the senior varsity cheer team was not fair was, it would seem, judged by the coaches to be dissent "beyond the pale"—that is, as speech unduly disruptive to the cheer programme, team cohesion and morale. On the latter standard, it is difficult to discern what meaningful controversial dissenting speech (but speech that is, at the same time, *not* threatening, harassing or bullying in nature) would be tolerated under the cheer rules of the Mahanoy Area School District and by the cheer coaches at B.L.'s high school.

On the analysis here, B.L.'s speech in her first and second snapchats expressing negative emotions about cheer and raising a question about the equity in the cheer selection process for the senior varsity cheer squad would be protected speech under the First Amendment. This since (i) she was off-campus in a non-school supervised, non-school sanctioned private virtual space and not in any way speaking under the school imprimatur when she uttered that speech and (ii) the

73 B.L. by Levy v. Mahanoy Area Sch. District, 289 F.Supp.3d 607, 613 (M.D. Pa. 2017) at p. 13 Citing J.S. ex rel. Snyder v. Blue Mountain Sch. District, 650 F.3d 915, 926 (3d Cir. 2011) (*en banc*).

speech did *not* fall under one of the limited exceptions to First Amendment protections but rather was arguably "pure speech" just expressing an opinion without giving identifying information about the school or any individual connected to the issue (i.e. no name of a cheer coach or student was provided in either of B.L.'s contested snapchats) .

Whether B.L.'s first snapchat with its profanity would allow the school to constitutionally impose some reasonable punishment based on the profanity *per se* and not the opinion expressed (disdain for cheerleading, school etc.) had she delivered it *on campus* through her snapchat is an open question. The obscenity B.L. used, while common especially amongst many high schoolers, no doubt represents a breach of decorum and is not particularly conducive to cordial respectful interaction between those in the school when discussing controversial opposing viewpoints. However, B.L. was not using the vulgarity in an open classroom forum. Whether B.L.'s first snapchat meets the standard set in United States Supreme Court (USSC) case precedent for profane speech (speech that incorporates obscenity or blasphemous language) that can be regulated by schools when it occurs on campus or in a school-regulated context is thus contentious.[74] The USSC in *Mahanoy* importantly found that "*the vulgarity in B. L.'s posts encompassed a message*, an expression of B. L.'s irritation with, and criticism of, the school and cheerleading communities (emphasis added)."[75] This complicates the matter in that this vulgar first B.L. snapchat confounds *opinion* with vulgar and obscene language. Hence, if suppressed through school discipline had the first snapchat been sent while on campus, that could have conveyed to the students the message that the *criticism* of the cheer programme communicated by B.L. was impermissible. This might auger for First Amendment protection especially since the USSC in *Mahanoy* found that "the school . . . presented no evidence of any general effort to prevent students from using vulgarity outside the classroom."[76] Furthermore, notwithstanding the "respect" cheer rule, it is *not* the case that being a member of an extra-curricular programme such as cheer affords the student any less First Amendment protection.

That B.L.'s contested speech originated off-campus in a non-school context was communication posted on snapchat that provides only a temporary posting (is self-deleting) and was *not* intended to be seen by the coaches or others outside of those who followed B.L. on her snapchat social media are highly relevant facts

74 See Bethel School District No. 403 v. Fraser (1986). This author is in accord with the dissent in the Bethel case. Stevens in his dissent in that case quoted from *Gone With the Wind* the line, "Frankly, my dear, I don't give a damn." Stevens argued that "if a student is to be punished for using offensive speech, he is entitled to fair notice of the scope of the prohibition and the consequences of its violation. The interest in free speech protected by the First Amendment and . . . the Due Process Clause . . . combine to require this conclusion."

75 In the Supreme Court of the United States, Mahanoy Area School District (Petitioner) v. B.L. et al. (Respondents), No. 20–255, Opinion (June 23, 2021) at p. 10.

76 In the Supreme Court of the United States, Mahanoy Area School District (Petitioner) v. B.L. et al. (Respondents), No. 20–255, Opinion (June 23, 2021) at p. 10.

in considering the anti-vulgarity interest of the school. The snapchats at issue would not have been communicated to the coaches and others outside B.L.'s circle of followers on her snapchat account but for the classmate "informer." That B.L. chose snapchat—a medium in which the communications self-delete after a short time—to vent her frustration and did not identify the school or cheer coaches suggests that her snapchats were *not* intended to disrupt the cheer programme or team cohesion (i.e. they were not akin to a petition circulated to find students who would endorse a view that the senior varsity cheer programme was allegedly unfair in terms of selection and that the selection criteria for the senior varsity squad must be changed for instance). Rather, the two snapchats taken together were B.L.'s attempt to vent and communicate "her truth" about the *perceived* unfairness she saw in the selection for the senior varsity cheer squad at her high school. "B.L. testified that she used Snapchat for spontaneous communication with her friends, in the same way she would talk to them if they were together in person outside of school."[77]

It would seem to be the case that B.L. regarded her not being selected to be on the senior varsity cheer team as a "fait accompli"—something she knew she could not change through negative snapchats. Hence, her first snapchat was but an obscenity-laced emotional rant expressing anger and frustration. The second snapchat provided an alleged explanation (from her perspective) as to the reason for her rant. This view is bolstered by the fact that B.L. and her mother had asked the coaches whether students on the senior varsity cheer team had to spend a year in junior varsity first and were told that this was the case even though, to their later knowledge, a certain incoming freshman had made the senior varsity cheer squad. B.L.'s second snapchat made reference to this latter alleged fact without naming the incoming freshman involved or commenting on her or his cheer skills or the strength of the senior varsity cheer squad. Hence, on the view here, the contention that B.L. intended to or did weaken the cohesion of the cheer squad is but speculation, though apparently there was some evidence that some members of the cheer programme were somewhat disgruntled by the B.L. off-campus snapchats at issue in this case. The cheer squad, however, would not in fact have been, prior to B.L.'s snapchats, and as the record revealed, a group of adolescents working in perfect harmony without some internal disputes and upset feelings often playing out in their Internet communications. On the uncontested evidence available on the issue of disruption introduced in the case, B.L.'s snapchats did *not* appear to have caused a substantive disruption in the cheer programme or in the level of performance proficiency or cohesion of the cheer squads involved.

The question can justifiably be raised as to whether *off-campus* student speech that (i) raises a legitimate issue regarding equity and social justice and/or (ii) expresses a view (political, religious etc.) about some controversial matter is protected under the First Amendment *even if it causes substantial disruption* and

77 In the Supreme Court of the United States, Mahanoy Area School District (Petitioner) v. B.L. et al. (Respondents), Brief in Opposition (Respondents' Brief) at p. 3.

some lack of cohesion in a school as long as it does not fall into one of the First Amendment exception categories. One could argue that that would depend, in large part, on what "disruption" precisely means in practice in that instance. If it means simply facilitating peaceful, critical, *informed* reflection and debate on such an issue in the proper place and time at school, on the view here, that would be off-school campus "protected student speech." Thus, in contrast, disruptive controversial student speech off-campus, even in a non-school context, that *referred somehow to the school* and which was based in *disinformation grounded on hate*, would *not* meet the latter qualifying test for "student protected speech."[78] Being inundated by the latter speech would be an interference with the education rights of other students. This since all students are entitled to access the truth in terms of the most scientifically and historically accurate information available on any topic being addressed and to understand dissenting views and whether these are grounded in any valid supporting demonstrable evidence or are based mostly or entirely on disinformation and propaganda. When it comes to issues such as equity and sensitive issues relating to a school such as abuse of athletes, all students are entitled to the truth.

*It is thus important to acknowledge that not all dissenting student speech is inherently substantially disruptive in a manner that is adverse to the educational agenda/objective and programme* (i.e. the agenda of developing critical thinkers, and informed independently minded individuals competent to participate in a democratic society). Dissenting student *off-campus* peaceful speech, it is here contended, is more likely to cause *untoward* substantive disruption to the school programmes proper or to extra-curricular school programmes when (i) no dedicated scheduled actual and/or virtual space is provided generally for respectful, peaceful on-campus discussion of dissenting student views and (ii) the effort by teachers and administrators is to suppress the expression of any significant student dissent and criticism of the school even in regards to off-campus student speech that does *not* meet the test for a First Amendment exception to protection. Suppression by schools of such peaceful student dissenting speech that occurred off-campus, on the analysis here, is a violation of the First Amendment. On the analysis here then, any substantial school disruption in response to peaceful off-campus student dissenting speech is in practice most often correlated with the inadequate particular school's response to student dissent generally rather than with the content of that student dissent *per se*. Recall in the latter regard

78 Ironically, across America there is a debate amongst mostly parents and politicians regarding teaching about U.S. racist colonialist history and its vestiges. At the same time, most teachers are dedicated to teaching history with fidelity and in full context and hence lament the attempts to suppress the aforementioned sensitive information in school curriculum and discussion. They fear the potential consequences for democracy of such information suppression, namely the proliferation of false and/or misleading historical narratives perpetuated on social media and in the larger society left uncontested in the schools, thus undermining concerns about and possible remedies directed to eliminating or reducing *current* intergenerational inequities. See Ray, R. and Alexander Gibbons. Why Are States Banning Critical Race Theory? (Brookings) (2021).

that importantly *Tinker* requires that it is ***the contested speech in itself*** that is the proximate cause of the substantial school disruption (by interfering with school functions or with the rights of other students) to negate the First Amendment protection for student speech and not the "heckler's veto."[79]

On the view here, it would appear that in *Mahanoy Area School District v B.L.*, the aforementioned *Tinker* disruption standard for regulation of student speech was in practice diluted by the school.[80] The cheer coaches were, on the analysis here, led to significantly discipline B.L. for off-campus speech uttered in a private virtual forum (her personal Snapchat account), in part at least, as (i) they were arguably led by their own "***heckler's veto***" and, to some degree, also (i) by the mild grumbling of some cheerleaders who had seen or learned of B.L.'s snapchats and were upset by them. There was no evidence that B.L's off-campus snapchats as described were ***inherently*** such speech content as to lead to objectively interfering with the rights of others or compromising school functioning in any substantive way. For instance, B.L.'s snapchats did ***not*** reference the school involved nor the specific cheer squad and did ***not*** advocate that anyone drop out of the junior or senior cheer varsity squad at any school. Further, with regard to the first snapchat, the United States Supreme Court in *Mahanoy* found that since B.L.'s contested vulgar speech was off-campus and not in a forum where the school was in ***loco parentis***, the school's interest in promoting civil student speech in this instance was weakened.[81]

Arguably, the end result of ***overreach*** by school authorities in suppressing ***all*** opinion-based off-campus disruptive student speech that (i) references the school in some way and (ii) where that dissenting speech has content to which the school objects is that students may ***not*** come to "honor and cherish a First Amendment that their lived experience teaches them to be a valueless abstraction."[82] Central questions in this case, it is here contended, include (i) whether the specific facts of this snapchat case reveal overreach or not in the school authorities' punishment of ***this*** particular student's off-campus speech and (ii) what, if any, would be the broader implications for student First Amendment rights off-campus if the Supreme Court of the United States were to have upheld the School District's position. Such a ruling would have, on the view here, established that the ***blanket test of "actual or school perceived foreseeable substantive school disruption"*** would be sufficient to rationalize discipline for ***any*** student off-campus speech which references the school in some

79 In the Supreme Court of the United States, Mahanoy Area School District v. B.L., A Minor, By and Through her Father, Lawrence Levy and her Mother, Betty Lou Levy, Transcript of Oral Argument Before the Supreme Court of the United States (April 28, 2021) (Petitioner Argument) at p. 5.

80 That *Tinker* standard referred to on-campus speech, and hence one would expect it should also apply to off-campus student speech of the same quality.

81 In the Supreme Court of the United States, Mahanoy Area School District (Petitioner) v. B.L. et al. (Respondents), No. 20–255, Opinion (June 23, 2021) at pp. 9–10.

82 Mahanoy Area School District v. B.L., A Minor, By and Through her Father, Lawrence Levy and her Mother, Betty Lou Levy, Brief Amicus Curiae, College Athlete Advocates in support of the respondents, Supreme Court of the United States No. 20–255 (March 31, 2021) at p. 8.

way and meets that test, that is in the Mahanoy School District case "the disciplinarian perceives [the] student speech as contrary to "maintaining team cohesion and respect for the coach's authority."[83] This regardless of the particulars which stimulated the disruptive student speech and whether that speech was a legitimate, informed commentary on an issue of student concern and was, for example peaceful critique and advocacy (i.e. regarding such school-relevant matters as athlete safety, fairness and the like). In this regard, consider that the basic argument and proposition of the College Athlete Advocate amicus brief in this case is that:

> Schools are asking the Court for authority to police off-campus speech because they do not like students second-guessing their decisions, and if given the authority they seek, they will use it to silence dissent. This is not speculation.[84]

The College Athlete Advocates Amici maintain that:

> Of all of the off-campus behaviors that might spill over and provoke discord in the locker room, schools are interested in regulating only one: Criticism of government employees. And that is the one that the Constitution most fiercely protects.[85]

Indeed, one could argue that the *potential* for so-called disruption associated with good faith peaceful student criticism of school (government) employees and how they regulate on a particular matter is a necessary and essential part of the democratic process and hence does not weaken the First Amendment protection of student speech.[86]

### *The United States Supreme Court Justices Seeking to Formulate a Narrow Opinion*

It is here suggested that at least some of the justices on the Supreme Court of the United States (USSC) in *Mahanoy Area School District v B.L.* unnecessarily sought

83 Mahanoy Area School District v. B.L., A Minor, By and Through her Father, Lawrence Levy and her Mother, Betty Lou Levy Brief Amicus Curiae, College Athlete Advocates in support of the respondents, Supreme Court of the United States No. 20–255 (March 31, 2021) at p. 16.

84 Mahanoy Area School District v. B.L., A Minor, By and Through her Father, Lawrence Levy and her Mother, Betty Lou Levy Brief Amicus Curiae, College Athlete Advocates in support of the respondents, Supreme Court of the United States No. 20–255 (March 31, 2021) at p. 18.

85 Mahanoy Area School District v. B.L., A Minor, By and Through her Father, Lawrence Levy and her Mother, Betty Lou Levy Brief Amicus Curiae, College Athlete Advocates in support of the respondents, Supreme Court of the United States No. 20–255 (March 31, 2021) at p. 19.

86 This principle arguably applying to both on-campus and off-campus student speech.

to narrow their decision on the critical issue of the freedom of expression rights of students under the age of majority when ostensibly in their own private sphere off-campus (i.e. communication posted on personal social media accounts). A prime complicating factor is whether the particular contested student "off-campus" speech (in the sense of being speech uttered outside the brick and mortar school and the school grounds) was yet uttered in the school context and how the latter is to be defined (i.e. speech uttered that targets the school audience and concerns a school topic and/or speech uttered in a school supervised or sanctioned context or forum or under the school imprimatur in some way).

Justice Kavanaugh expressed the view that there is an alleged need to resist writing a treatise on the First Amendment in *Mahanoy Area School District v B.L.* and agreed with Justice Breyer that part of the reason for this is that the range of pertinent hypotheticals that might arise cannot be forecasted.[87] Malcolm Stewart, Deputy Solicitor General, Department of Justice, Washington, D.C., for the United States, as amicus curiae, supporting the Petitioner concurred on this point during oral argument before the USSC.[88]

In the United States Supreme Court (USSC) opinion in *Mahanoy*, Justice Breyer, writing for the majority, states:

> we do *not* now set forth a broad, highly general First Amendment rule stating just what counts as "off campus" speech and whether or how ordinary First Amendment standards must give way off campus to a school's special need to prevent, e.g. substantial disruption of learning-related activities or the protection of those who make up a school community.[89]

Thus, the USSC did *not* endorse the Mahanoy Appeals Court definition of off-campus speech as generally applicable which definition was as follows:

> We hold today that *Tinker* does not apply to off campus speech—that is, speech that is outside school-owned, -operated, or -supervised channels and that is not reasonably interpreted as bearing the school's imprimatur.[90]

It is here argued that since (i) the United States Supreme Court (USSC) in *Mahanoy* did *not* adopt the definition of "off-campus" student speech offered

87 In the Supreme Court of the United States, Mahanoy Area School District v. B.L., A Minor, By and Through her Father, Lawrence Levy and her Mother, Betty Lou Levy, Transcript of Oral Argument Before the Supreme Court of the United States (April 28, 2021) at p. 56.

88 In the Supreme Court of the United States, Mahanoy Area School District v. B.L., A Minor, By and Through her Father, Lawrence Levy and her Mother, Betty Lou Levy, Transcript of Oral Argument Before the Supreme Court of the United States (April 28, 2021) at pp. 56–57.

89 In the Supreme Court of the United States, Mahanoy Area School District (Petitioner) v. B.L. et al. (Respondents), No. 20–255, Opinion (June 23, 2021) at pp. 6–7.

90 B.L. v. Mahanoy Area Sch. District. 964 F.3d 170 (3d Cir. 2020) (United States Court of Appeals for the Third Circuit) (Decided June 30, 2020) at p. 14.

by the Appeals Court in this case and (ii) did so *without* substituting an alternate definition it found more suitable, the *non-applicability* as a general rule (save for some specified limited First Amendment exceptions) to off-campus student speech of the *Tinker* substantive disruption high standard for the triggering of school's regulatory power over student speech is seriously undermined if not negated. *Off-campus student speech, for purposes of this discussion, is defined by the current author as student speech occurring in a context that is not in any way under the school's imprimatur or auspices and in a context not normally perceived by the vast majority of the general public as a school-related or other context*[91] *in which the school would be expected to have and to exercise its constitutional legitimate regulatory power over certain student speech.* Keeping that definition in mind, it is here argued that the aforementioned narrow judicial approach by the USSC in *Mahanoy* results, by default, in an unconstitutional extension of the school's regulatory power over "off-campus" student speech where (i) that speech somehow refers to the school and is (ii) deemed by the school to pose a risk for or to have caused substantial disruption in the school even when the speech itself was not objectively inherently disruptive (i.e. the disruption was due to others' reactions to or anticipated response to the contentious off-campus student speech). This then, it is here argued, significantly increases the risk for overreach by the school in exercising regulatory power over, in particular, off-campus student speech in violation of the students' First Amendment free speech rights,

This author concurs with the USSC in *Mahanoy* that the contemporary school environment leads to some considerable complexity in distinguishing between truly "off-campus" versus "on-campus" student speech.[92] However, the current author argues, with respect, that this is no legally supportable rationale for the Court to shirk from the opportunity to provide a workable definition of off-campus student speech and a general rule as to when the school's power to regulate student speech off-campus is constitutional and when such regulation of student off-campus speech violates the First Amendment. Of course, no general such definition and rule will be a perfect fit in every fact scenario and there may be complexities in future difficult cases that require exceptions or refinements to the general rule. Despite such aforementioned complications, on the view of the current author, with respect, the USSC nevertheless inappropriately in *Mahanoy* largely, if not entirely, *shifted the responsibility in practice to the schools themselves without the Court's guidance (through its judgement in Mahanoy) to determine*

91 Referring to the limited exceptions, First Amendment situations of bullying, harassing or threatening student speech or speech that undermines the integrity of the school functioning, that is speech involved in promoting or actualizing cheating on exams etc.

92 A virtual space allows for *distance education* but this is still *on-campus* activity where it is a school-supervised or a school-provided modality of learning. In this regard, see the USSC statement on its hesitancy to agree with the Appeals Court in *Mahanoy* that *Tinker* is *ipso facto* inapplicable to all so-called off-campus student speech; that hesitancy being related "particularly [to] the advent of computer-based learning." (In the Supreme Court of the United States, Mahanoy Area School District (Petitioner) v. B.L. et al. (Respondents), No. 20–255, Opinion (June 23, 2021) at p. 6).

*what constitutes "off-campus" student speech and what types of off-campus speech that are school-related in some way may yet be vulnerable to school regulation as "unprotected speech."* In so doing, the Court consequently left it to the schools to determine the scope of the school's alleged constitutional regulatory power over certain off-campus school-related student speech perhaps even where the speech does *not* fall into the traditional First Amendment exceptions (bullying, harassing or threatening speech or speech that directly compromises the integrity of the school, that is relates to cheating or interferes with the rights of others at school) but is rather "pure speech" simply peaceably expressing a highly contentious viewpoint.

It is here respectfully argued then that the resistance from the outset of several USSC justices in *Mahanoy Area School District v B.L.* to writing an opinion that would set out a general rule on First Amendment protection of off-campus student speech rather than one narrowly tailored only to the very specific facts of the case before them was misguided. Such an approach sidesteps the children's right to have their First Amendment rights vis-a-vis the school clarified as to peaceful, non-harassing, non-threatening political or religious or other controversial or critical speech that (i) somehow implicates the school but was uttered off-campus in every meaningful sense and (ii) did or foreseeably likely would cause some substantive school disruption *due to others' potential reaction to it* but concerned topics necessary to bring to light such as maltreatment of disabled students at the school or some other such serious matter of social injustice and human rights violations or expressed an opinion on any issue as "pure speech" that was not inherently disruptive.

Writing a very narrow USSC opinion in *Mahanoy Area School District v B.L.* as to whether *Tinker* applies *in this particular case on these specific facts* does little to address the aforementioned fundamental questions which relate to the proper scope of the child's First Amendment speech rights in or out of the school context (the "out-of-school context" not being always directly correlated simply with whether the speech originated off the physical school campus). This is especially damaging for children in that their free expression rights are already highly regulated at school (on campus) and given that they do not have the vote to express a protest. A narrow opinion on the First Amendment issues in *Mahanoy Area School District v B.L.*, it is here respectfully contended, thus inadequately serves the public interest in proper clarification of the scope of the constitutional protection of the free expression rights of children notwithstanding school regulatory powers. Such an approach, it is here argued, is ultimately likely be ineffective in deterring the unconstitutional punishment/suppression by school authorities of critical off-campus student speech, that is of speech disciplined due to the school's objecting to the *lawful* opinion-based content of the speech that occurred in a non-school supervised/non-school sanctioned context and also that was speech not otherwise under a school imprimatur.

Furthermore, the legal uncertainty that results from a narrow opinion by the USSC in *Mahanoy*, on the view here, likely will have a detrimental overall effect in inadvertently reinforcing a "chilling" of off-campus student speech. In the latter regard, recall the words of the Court of Appeals in the *Mahanoy v B.L.* case: "[L]egal uncertainty of any kind is undesirable, uncertainty in this context creates unique problems. Obscure lines between permissible and impermissible speech have an independent chilling effect on speech."[93] The USSC (i) *avoiding* formulating a *rigorous* standard and test in *Mahanoy* (for relaxing First Amendment protection regarding school regulation of off-campus student speech) and (ii) being reticent to tackle some of the more complex contemporary First Amendment questions generated by off-campus student speech posted on social media in particular,[94] it is here contended, inadvertently undermines the democratic rule of law. This in that, in practice, it is likely to perpetuate schools overreach and impunity in often regulating off-campus student speech in circumstances that are unconstitutional. It is here respectfully suggested then that it is overdue time to reconsider the purported wisdom of the notion that where the courts are presented with compelling fundamental constitutional issues (i) they should, if they can, offer a narrow opinion relating only to the particular facts of a specific case such that the opinion will likely not be relevant in any substantive way to other difficult cases involving similar issues or (ii) avoid the constitutional question altogether if the case can be decided on another basis. This is especially an inapt strategy, it is here argued, when the protection of the constitutional rights of a vulnerable group such as students under the age of majority is in continued jeopardy as a result.[95] With these points in mind, let us consider then the judgement that was ultimately rendered by the United States Supreme Court in *Mahanoy Area School District v B.L.* and whether it can be fairly critiqued as too narrow.

## The United States Supreme Court Opinion in *Mahanoy Area School District v B.L.*

In *Mahanoy Area School District v B.L.*,[96] the United States Supreme Court held that *on the specific facts of the case*, B.L.'s free expression interest overrode any special interests the school may have had in penalizing B.L.'s speech in an effort to curtail such off-campus school speech. The Court agreed with the lower courts that B.L.'s speech did *not* fall into one of the special categories that would trigger the school's regulatory interests (for example B.L.'s speech was deemed *not* to

93 B.L. v. Mahanoy Area Sch. District, 376 F. Supp. 3d 429 (M.D. Pa. 2019) at p. 11.

94 Questions such as "Does the school have constitutional authority to discipline for some or all off-campus opinion-based student speech posted on personal social media if that speech causes significant disruption to the school where that speech is not bullying threatening or harassing?"

95 Note that Justice Ambro concurred with the majority opinion of the Appeals Court in the B.L. snapchat case. However, Judge Ambro dissented based on an endorsement of judicial restraint suggesting it would have been wise not to "formulate a rule of constitutional law broader than . . . required by the precise facts" of the B.L. case (see B.L. v. Mahanoy Area Sch. District. 964 F.3d 170 (3d Cir. 2020) at p. 19.

96 In the Supreme Court of the United States, Mahanoy Area School District (Petitioner) v B.L. et al. (Respondents), No. 20–255, Opinion (June 23, 2021).

constitute bullying or threats nor targeting of a person or persons) and did not cause any substantive disruption at school. The USSC appears to have construed the facts to be that the cheer coaches had seen *both* of B.L.'s contested snapchats. This raises the possibility that B.L. was punished in consideration of both of her impugned snapchats (the Appeals Court held that only the first snapchat figured into the school's discipline of B.L.).[97]

The Court further noted certain points that it considered key in the case: (i) The school is not in *loco parentis* in regard to overseeing student off-campus speech that occurs in a non-school context; (ii) the school's regulation of off-campus as well as on-campus speech would be quite onerous for students since it would mean 24-hour regulation of their speech by the school. Hence, the Court concluded: "That means courts must be more skeptical of a school's efforts to regulate off-campus speech, for doing so may mean the student cannot engage in that kind of speech at all."[98] and (iii) "the school itself has an interest in protecting a student's unpopular expression, especially when the expression takes place off campus, because America's public schools are the nurseries of democracy."[99] The Court maintained that in view of the aforementioned three factors, the school was constrained in the degree to which it could *constitutionally* regulate off-campus student speech. Given the aforementioned broader legal perspective and the specific facts of the case, the United States Supreme Court ruled in this particular matter that (i) B.L.'s off-campus snapchat posts were protected by the First Amendment. She was properly exercising her free speech rights in expressing criticism of the cheerleading programme as the specific content of her posts *did not trigger any of the First Amendment exceptions* that would have placed her posts outside of the First Amendment protection (Interestingly, the USSC held—contrary to the suggestion by the School District—that B.L.'s first snapchat also conveyed an opinion and constituted protected speech and was not just vulgar speech subject to greater school regulation even if off-campus speech: "And the vulgarity in B. L.'s posts encompassed a message of criticism."[100]); (ii)

> B. L.'s posts appeared outside of school hours from a location outside the school. *She did not identify the school in her posts or target any member of the school community with vulgar or abusive language.* B. L. also transmitted her speech through a personal cellphone, to an audience consisting of her private circle of Snapchat friends.[101]

97 In the Supreme Court of the United States, Mahanoy Area School District (Petitioner) v B.L. et al. (Respondents), No. 20–255, Opinion (June 23, 2021) at p. 2.
98 In the Supreme Court of the United States, Mahanoy Area School District (Petitioner) v B.L. et al. (Respondents), No. 20–255, Opinion, Syllabus (June 23, 2021).
99 In the Supreme Court of the United States, Mahanoy Area School District (Petitioner) v B.L. et al. (Respondents), No. 20–255, Opinion, Syllabus (June 23, 2021).
100 In the Supreme Court of the United States, Mahanoy Area School District (Petitioner) v B.L. et al. (Respondents), No. 20–255, Opinion (June 23, 2021) Syllabus.
101 In the Supreme Court of the United States, Mahanoy Area School District (Petitioner) v B.L. et al. (Respondents), No. 20–255, Opinion, Syllabus (June 23, 2021).

These latter factors undercut the school's interest in restraining and penalizing B.L.'s off-campus speech that was at issue; (iii) the fact that the *school was not in loco parentis* and that B.L.'s speech at issue was on her off-school hours and off-campus also undercut the school's interest in curbing her vulgar language; (iv) "The school's interest in preventing disruption is not supported by the record, which shows that discussion of the matter took, at most, 5 to 10 minutes of an Algebra class";[102] and (v) "Likewise, there is little to suggest a substantial interference in, or disruption of, the school's efforts to maintain cohesion on the school cheerleading squad."[103]

The current author wishes to focus on the Supreme Court's pronouncement in its *Mahanoy Area School District v B.L.* ruling that "the school itself has an interest in protecting a student's unpopular expression, especially when the expression takes place off campus, because America's public schools are the nurseries of democracy."[104] That important perspective seems belied in the ruling by the Court's emphasis on the fact that B.L.'s contested off-campus speech at issue (as per the record) did *not* cause substantial disruption either at school in classes or to the cohesion of the cheerleading squad and would not foreseeably do so. On the view here, the Court in this case thus missed the opportunity to address whether the school could have constitutionally interfered with B.L.'s contested off-campus speech *if it had disrupted* class and/or the cohesion of the cheerleading squad. This even though the speech was not bullying, threatening, targeting and did not fit into any other of the clear exceptions that would have put it outside of First Amendment protection (i.e. advocating or inciting violence) and moreover was off-campus dissenting critical speech in a completely non-school private context. The Court also could have more substantively, on the respectful view here, have revisited *Tinker* to consider whether there are instances when disruptive unpopular or critical student speech even on-campus might yet be protected by the First Amendment, for example where speech discloses some important truths that are in the public interest to know and urgent for the school community to know.

## References

### *Literature*

Grover, S.C. *Young People's Human Rights and the Politics of Voting Age* (New York: Springer, 2011).

102 In the Supreme Court of the United States, Mahanoy Area School District (Petitioner) v B.L. et al. (Respondents), No. 20–255, Opinion, Syllabus (June 23, 2021).

103 In the Supreme Court of the United States, Mahanoy Area School District (Petitioner) v B.L. et al. (Respondents), No. 20–255, Opinion, Syllabus (June 23, 2021).

104 the Supreme Court of the United States, Mahanoy Area School District (Petitioner) v B.L. et al. (Respondents), No. 20–255, Opinion, Syllabus (June 23, 2021).

### *Materials*

Congressman John Lewis Address, Harvard Commencement (May 24, 2018) www.youtube.com/watch?v=XRjAzepG-bA (accessed May 8, 2021).
Fuhr, E.J. The Doctrine of Unconstitutional Conditions and the First Amendment. *Case Western Reserve Law Review*, Vol. 39, Issue 1 (1989), 97 (Abstract).
Ray, R. and Gibbons. Why Are States Banning Critical Race Theory? (Brookings) (2021) www.brookings.edu/blog/fixgov/2021/07/02/why-are-states-banning-critical-race-theory/ (accessed October 26, 2021).
United Nations, Office of the High Commissioner for Human Rights, Convention on the Rights of the Child Entry into Force (September 2, 1990) www.ohchr.org/en/professionalinterest/pages/crc.aspx (accessed May 10, 2021).

### *Cases*

B.L. by Levy v. Mahanoy Area Sch. District, 289 F.Supp.3d 607, 613 (M.D. Pa. 2017) United States District Court, M.D. Pennsylvania (Decided October 5, 2017).
B.L. v. Mahanoy Area Sch. District, 376 F. Supp. 3d 429 (M.D. Pa. 2019) (Decided March 21, 2019) (United States District Court for the Middle District of Pennsylvania).
B.L. v. Mahanoy Area Sch. District, 964 F.3d 170 (3d Cir. 2020) (United States Court of Appeals for the Third Circuit) (Decided June 30, 2020).
Burnside v. Byars, 363 F.2d 744, 749 (1966).
In the Supreme Court of the United States, Bethel School District No. 403 v. Fraser (1986).
In the Supreme Court of the United States, John F. Tinker and Mary Beth Tinker, Minors, etc., et al., Petitioners, v. Des Moines Independent Community School District et al. 393 U.S. 503, 89 S. Ct. 733 (Decided February 24, 1969) www.law.cornell.edu/supremecourt/text/393/503 (accessed May 13, 2021).
In the Supreme Court of the United States, Mahanoy Area School District (Petitioner) v B.L. et al. (Respondents), Brief in Opposition (Respondents' Brief) www.scotusblog.com/case-files/cases/mahanoy-area-school-District-v-b-l/ (accessed May 8, 2021).
In the Supreme Court of the United States, Mahanoy Area School District (Petitioner) v B.L. et al. (Respondents), No. 20–255, Opinion (June 23, 2021).
In the Supreme Court of the United States, Mahanoy Area School District v B.L., A Minor, By and Through her Father, Lawrence Levy and Her Mother, Betty Lou Levy, Brief Amicus Curiae, College Athlete Advocates in Support of the Respondents, Supreme Court of the United States No. 20–255 (March 31, 2021) www.scotusblog.com/case-files/cases/mahanoy-area-school-District-v-b-l/ (accessed May 8, 2021). In the Supreme Court of the United States, Mahanoy Area School District v B.L., A Minor, by and Through her Father, Lawrence Levy and Her Mother, Betty Lou Levy, Transcript of Oral Argument before the Supreme Court of the United States (April 28, 2021) www.supremecourt.gov/oral_arguments/argument_transcripts/2020/20-255_1p24.pdf (accessed May 17, 2021).

# 6 The Democratic Rule of Law, Religious Freedom and the Public Interest

## Different Cases, Different Equities to Consider

### Ryan Klaassen et al. v the Trustees of Indiana University

#### *Background*

Eight university students filed a complaint in the United States District Court for the Northern District of Indiana against the Trustees of the Indiana University regarding the university's imposition on students (staff and faculty) of mandatory COVID mitigation measures, including proof of COVID vaccination if these students were to be on campus in person in fall 2021. The suit is a civil one and seeks declaratory and injunctive relief in respect of the university's mandatory COVID vaccination requirement. The student complainants allege (i) violation of their Fourteenth Amendment constitutional rights: "IU's Mandate violates the liberty protected by the Fourteenth Amendment to the U.S. Constitution, which includes rights of personal autonomy and bodily integrity, and the right to reject medical treatment"[1] and (ii) infringement of the State's vaccine passport law that "prohibits state and local units (including Indiana University ('IU')) from requiring or issuing vaccine 'passports' that indicate an individual's COVID immunization status."[2] Certain exemptions are available to the Indiana University students (faculty and staff) on what the complainants consider to be an "extremely limited and narrow set of criteria."[3] Those exemptions are set out by the university in the following terms:

- Religious exemptions per Indiana state law.
- Ethical objection.
- Medical exemptions with documentation from your provider of an allergy to the COVID-19 vaccines or their components.

1 United States District Court for the Northern District of Indiana, Ryan Klaassen et al. v The Trustees of Indiana University, Complaint for Declaratory and Injunctive Relief (June 21, 2021) at p. 1.

2 United States District Court for the Northern District of Indiana, Ryan Klaassen et al. v The Trustees of Indiana University, Complaint for Declaratory and Injunctive Relief (June 21, 2021) at pp. 1–2.

3 United States District Court for the Northern District of Indiana, Ryan Klaassen, et al. v The Trustees of Indiana University, Complaint for Declaratory and Injunctive Relief (June 21, 2021) at p. 4.

DOI: 10.4324/9781003153764-6

- Medical deferrals for the following circumstances with a note from your provider:
  - (i) Active pregnancy or active breastfeeding only if the provider is requesting an exemption. The exemption lasts only until you're no longer actively pregnant or actively breastfeeding. Pregnancy and breastfeeding are not contraindications for vaccination.
  - (ii) Immunocompromised individuals only with provider request for an exemption and only for those who have recent (within the past 3–6 months) hematopoietic or solid organ transplant, or on active treatment with Rituximab within the past 3–6 months.
  - (iii) Have received COVID-specific monoclonal antibodies in the past 90 days.
- An online program exemption for students who are in a 100% online program with no on-campus component. This must be an online program; not simply taking all online classes.[4]

The complainants' petition to the Court states that

> IU's [Indiana University's] mandate does not include an exemption for those with natural immunity to COVID, including those who have previously been infected and fully recovered, or those students [sic] with a medical condition where the COVID vaccination is contra-indicated, even under their attending physician's advice.[5]

Since the complainants' petition was filed, medical evidence has emerged showing clearly—if this was not so apparent earlier—that those who have been exposed to COVID and recovered may still become re-infected. Further, the CDC has recently reported a study that indicates that those who have been fully vaccinated and had no previous documented COVID-19 infection are much better protected from hospitalization due to COVID than those who were previously infected but unvaccinated.[6]

The Indiana University mandatory vaccination policy further stipulates that persons who receive an exemption from Indiana University for mandatory vaccination and plan to attend on-campus are required to

> participate [in] mitigation testing twice a week, a mandatory quarantine if exposed to someone who tests positive for COVID, mandatory face masks

4 Indiana University, COVID-19 Frequently Asked Questions.

5 United States District Court for the Northern District of Indiana, Ryan Klaassen, et al. v The Trustees of Indiana University, Complaint for Declaratory and Injunctive Relief (June 21, 2021) at p. 5.

6 Centers for Disease Control and Prevention (CDC) *Early Release*, October 29, 2021, 70 Laboratory-Confirmed COVID-19 Among Adults Hospitalized with COVID-19-Like Illness with Infection-Induced or mRNA Vaccine-Induced SARS-CoV-2 Immunity—Nine States (January–September 2021).

> in public spaces, and a mandatory return to their home address if the campus has a serious outbreak of the virus[7]

and "These Extra Requirements apply to all types of exemptions, regardless of which exemption an individual qualifies."[8] Failure to comply with the extra requirements as an exempted student will, according to the policy of the university, result in discipline by the university that might include termination of student status.[9]

The District Court for the Northern District of Indiana that heard the case on the preliminary injunction matter noted that "Twice the United States Supreme Court has upheld state authority to compel reasonable vaccinations."[10] The court acknowledged the students' constitutionally protected liberty interest under the Fourteenth Amendment that includes refused forced medical treatment that is unwanted. However, the court articulated that constitutional right to bodily autonomy as follows:

> Given this due process protection of liberty, longstanding constitutional law prevents a public university—an arm of the State—from mandating a vaccine for its students *unless it has rationally pursued a legitimate interest in public health for its campus community* (emphasis added).[11]

The court set out that a preliminary injunction would issue only if the students presented "a *strong* showing that they will likely succeed on the merits of their claims, that they will sustain irreparable harm, and that the balance of harms and the public interest favor such a remedy (emphasis added)."[12]

The eight student complainants included seven students who, it appears from the text of the District Court ruling, had obtained religious exemptions from Indiana University and one student without an exemption who believes she would

7 United States District Court for the Northern District of Indiana, Ryan Klaassen, et al. v The Trustees of Indiana University, Complaint for Declaratory and Injunctive Relief (June 21, 2021) at pp. 5–6.

8 United States District Court for the Northern District of Indiana, Ryan Klaassen, et al. v The Trustees of Indiana University, Complaint for Declaratory and Injunctive Relief (June 21, 2021) at p. 6.

9 United States District Court for the Northern District of Indiana, Ryan Klaassen, et al. v The Trustees of Indiana University, Complaint for Declaratory and Injunctive Relief (June 21, 2021) at p. 6.

10 United States District Court for the Northern District of Indiana, Ryan Klaassen, et al. v The Trustees of Indiana University, South Bend Division, Opinion and Order, Cause No. 1:21-CV-238 DRL (July 18, 2021) at p. 1.

11 United States District Court for the Northern District of Indiana, Ryan Klaassen, et al. v The Trustees of Indiana University, South Bend Division, Opinion and Order, Cause No. 1:21-CV-238 DRL (July 18, 2021) at p. 1.

12 United States District Court for the Northern District of Indiana, Ryan Klaassen, et al. v The Trustees of Indiana University, South Bend Division, Opinion and Order, Cause No. 1:21-CV-238 DRL (July 18, 2021) at p. 2.

not qualify for an exemption under Indiana University rules. All the students objected to the imposition by Indiana University of COVID mitigation measures as a condition of on-campus attendance at the university regardless of the fact that specified accommodations were built into the plan for those who obtained exemptions from the university for having to show proof of vaccination. The District Court in brief held that "These students aren't likely to succeed on the merits."[13] The court accepted that the case was a constitutional challenge alleging that the State—through Indiana University, an arm of the State—had purportedly encroached on the liberty rights of the complainants in violation of the Fourteenth Amendment by imposing COVID mitigation measures as a condition of on-campus attendance at the university. The court held that the liberty interest at issue in the case was *not* reflective of a fundamental right and hence the standard was that of rational review: The infringement would be upheld if the restriction imposed on the complainant students was "rationally related to a legitimate state interest."[14] Although in the United States "No case to date has decided the constitutionality of whether a public university, such as Indiana University, may mandate that its students receive a COVID-19 vaccine,"[15] there is U.S. Supreme Court case law on States having "the power, within constitutional limits, to pass laws that 'provide for the public health, safety, and morals.'"[16] In *Jacobson*,[17] the leading case, the United States Supreme Court affirmed that States had broad authority to enforce vaccination mandates amongst other health measures to protect the general public health stating that:

> The Constitution gave Massachusetts broad deference: a court should only intervene "if a statute purporting to have been enacted to protect the public health, the public morals, or the public safety, has no real or substantial relation to those objects, or is beyond all question, a plain, palpable invasion of rights secured by the fundamental law . . ."[18] ". . . only 'regulations so

13 United States District Court for the Northern District of Indiana, Ryan Klaassen, et al. v The Trustees of Indiana University, South Bend Division, Opinion and Order, Cause No. 1:21-CV-238 DRL (July 18, 2021) at p. 31.

14 United States District Court for the Northern District of Indiana, Ryan Klaassen, et al. v The Trustees of Indiana University, South Bend Division, Opinion and Order, Cause No. 1:21-CV-238 DRL (July 18, 2021) at p. 35.

15 United States District Court for the Northern District of Indiana, Ryan Klaassen, et al. v The Trustees of Indiana University, South Bend Division, Opinion and Order, Cause No. 1:21-CV-238 DRL (July 18, 2021) at p. 31.

16 United States District Court for the Northern District of Indiana, Ryan Klaassen, et al. v The Trustees of Indiana University, South Bend Division, Opinion and Order, Cause No. 1:21-CV-238 DRL (July 18, 2021) at p. 36.

17 Jacobson v. Massachusetts, 197 U.S. 11 (1905) addressed Cambridge Massachusetts mandatory vaccination for smallpox programme that offered no exemptions for religious objectors.

18 United States District Court for the Northern District of Indiana, Ryan Klaassen, et al. v The Trustees of Indiana University, South Bend Division, Opinion and Order, Cause No. 1:21-CV-238 DRL (July 18, 2021) at p. 38.

arbitrary and oppressive in particular cases [would] justify the interference of the courts to prevent wrong and oppression.'"[19]

It is noteworthy also in considering the Indiana University Klaassen et al. case that "the State of Indiana requires all public university students to receive vaccinations for diphtheria, tetanus, measles, mumps, rubella, and meningococcal disease, save for religious and medical exemptions."[20] Note also that selected of the case law relied upon by the District Court in the Indiana University case (the mandated COVID mitigation measures case) referenced mandated measures imposed upon university students to fulfil an obligation to a compelling public interest. In such cases, the court involved had ruled that these mandated measures imposed for the sake of a pressing general public interest (where the restriction of the right has a substantive relation to achieving the public interest objective) were *not* inconsistent with protection of the liberty interest afforded by the Fourteenth Amendment. For example in *Hamilton v. Regents of the University of California*, 293 U.S. 245, 264 (1934), the United States Supreme Court ruled that compelled military service of the students as a condition of their attendance at the University of California was constitutional. This is not to imply that the government is owed complete deference where there is a compelling public interest to be served. In the case at hand, Indiana University recognized this by offering students certain categories of exemptions from a vaccination mandate (e.g. a religious exemption) that involve accommodations entailing *alternative* COVID mitigation measures (e.g. testing twice a week and certain other mandatory measures as applied).

### *The Fourteenth Amendment and the Indiana University Vaccine Mandate*

The students in the Indiana University case argue that they are being denied a benefit from the government—the right to attend the university of their choice on campus which they would be able to attend/continue to attend for face-to-face classes but for the mandatory COVID mitigation measures imposed by the university. Those measures, according to the student complainants, infringe their constitutionally protected liberty interest (more specifically their right to bodily autonomy and to medical privacy).[21] The District Court in the Indiana University case distinguished court precedents where an individual's refusal of medical

19 United States District Court for the Northern District of Indiana, Ryan Klaassen, et al. v The Trustees of Indiana University, South Bend Division, Opinion and Order, Cause No. 1:21-CV-238 DRL (July 18, 2021) at pp. 38–39.

20 United States District Court for the Northern District of Indiana, Ryan Klaassen, et al. v The Trustees of Indiana University, South Bend Division, Opinion and Order, Cause No. 1:21-CV-238 DRL (July 18, 2021) at p. 40.

21 United States District Court for the Northern District of Indiana, Ryan Klaassen, et al. v The Trustees of Indiana University, South Bend Division, Opinion and Order, Cause No. 1:21-CV-238 DRL (July 18, 2021) at pp. 48–49.

treatment affected only him or her from those cases in which the medical treatment addressed "a collective enemy."[22] The latter applies to the instant case in that the "collective enemy" is COVID (a highly infectious virus spread in large part through the air) where the individual who refuses the vaccine may potentially severely adversely affect the health of others in the community by spreading the infection. This is particularly the situation post the arrival of the much more infectious and virulent Delta variant. Indeed, even some fully vaccinated persons have become infected (though at a significantly lower rate than vaccinated persons) and potentially then might unintentionally spread the infection to others especially if that infected person is symptomatic, but there is also a risk even if that person is non-symptomatic.

The District Court ruling in the instant Indiana University mandatory COVID mitigation measures case then balances the compelling public interest and Fourteenth Amendment objectives assessing whether (i) the restrictive measures taken by the university are legitimately connected to the public health interest objective (preventing to the degree possible the spread of COVID among the Indiana University community and from that community beyond) and whether (ii) the university adopted the least restrictive measures possible under the circumstances. Here one indicia of respect for the Constitution and implementing the least restrictive measures available was to offer certain exemptions and alternate COVID mitigation measures for students who objected to the mandatory vaccination against COVID as a condition of on-campus attendance at Indiana University. All but two of the students applied for and were granted a religious exemption—only one student did not apply for any exemption, as mentioned, due to a self-perception of being unable to meet the qualifying criteria and the other student would qualify for a religious exemption if and when that student should apply for that category of exemption (as apparently occurred).

This Indiana University case is an instance where a religious exemption as applied by an arm of government (here Indiana University) arguably did *not* undermine the public interest (in this instance a public health interest). This given the implementation of mandatory alternate COVID mitigation measures imposed on those faculty, students and staff of the university who qualified for a religious (or medical) exemption. Thus, since reasonable accommodations were provided to the student complainants who qualified for an exemption (such that they could opt out of the mandatory vaccination requirement and adopt as an alternative the other COVID mitigation measures specified by the university), the "unconstitutional conditions doctrine" did not apply. That is the students were *not* deprived of a benefit—that benefit being attending Indiana University on campus—through the indirect means of imposition of an unconstitutional condition for that on-campus attendance.

22 United States District Court for the Northern District of Indiana, Ryan Klaassen, et al. v The Trustees of Indiana University, South Bend Division, Opinion and Order, Cause No. 1:21-CV-238 DRL (July 18, 2021) at p. 50.

### *The First Amendment Rights and the Indiana University Vaccine Mandate*

The student complainants in the Indiana University case further maintained that the university was violating their constitutional fundamental right to freedom of religion. The District Court, however, rejected this argument based on case precedent. The court held that neutral, generally applicable law *rationally connected to a compelling public interest* is constitutional even if it blocks access to a government benefit where (i) the individual, on religious or other grounds, refuses not only to comply with a mandatory requirement but *also* (ii) *refuses all reasonable accommodations.* In describing the situation in the Indiana University instant case, the court put the situation thus:

> The vaccine mandate is a neutral rule of general applicability. It applies to all students, whether religious or not. It doesn't discriminate among religions. Indeed, the university has chosen to enable the practice of religion by providing a religious exemption to this vaccination requirement—one that the university, on this record, has freely granted to students if they request it, no questions asked. This is consistent with the Constitution.[23]

The Court of Appeals in the Indiana University case affirmed the District Court decision based in part on case precedent that a State may mandate vaccination against a highly infectious disease doing so in the public interest (citing *Jacobson v Massachusetts*, 197 US 11 (1905) where a State's mandated smallpox vaccination programme for all members of the public during a smallpox epidemic was deemed constitutional even without exemptions being offered to any category of adults). The Appeals Court highlighted the fact that Indiana University in offering accommodations avoided potential constitutional challenge based on any absence of exemptions for qualified students (staff and faculty). Indeed, the Appeals Court held that there was only a justiciable controversy at all in that one of the complainant students did not qualify for an exemption based on the criteria the university had set out for religious or medical exemptions.[24]

Interestingly, the Appeals Court in *Ryan Klaassen et al. v The Trustees of Indiana University* noted that there may be, in the proper circumstances, permissible constitutional restrictions in a university context to even fundamental rights such as the First Amendment right to freedom of religion:

> Other conditions of enrollment are normal and proper. The First Amendment means that a state cannot tell anyone what to read or write, but a state

23 United States District Court for the Northern District of Indiana, Ryan Klaassen, et al. v The Trustees of Indiana University, South Bend Division, Opinion and Order, Cause No. 1:21-CV-238 DRL (July 18, 2021) at p. 54.

24 United States Court of Appeals for the Seventh Circuit, No. 21–2326 Ryan Klaassen et al. v The Trustees of Indiana University Decided (August 2, 2021) at p. 3.

> university may demand that students read things they prefer not to read and write things they prefer not to write. A student must read what a professor assigns, even if the student deems the books heretical, and must write exams or essays as required. . . . If conditions of higher education[25] may include . . . following instructions about what to read or write, it is hard to see a greater problem with medical conditions[26] that help all students remain safe when learning.[27]

Note that the United States Supreme Court *denied review* of the Indiana University mandatory COVID-19 vaccination requirements for on-campus attendance. Hence, these university requirements (which allowed for certain exemptions with mandatory alternate mitigation measures) were left standing as constitutional (the lower court decision was not reversed).[28]

In the next case to be examined, on the analysis here, the situation is quite contrary to that in the Indiana University COVID mitigation measure case involving religious and specified medical exemptions. In *Fulton et al. v City of Philadelphia et al.*,[29] it is here argued, the United States Supreme Court (USSC) elevated the religious freedom of a private agency *in its performance of a public function* on behalf of government (as an agent of government) above a complex of compelling public interests. This by means of affirming a religious exemption that, in the particular circumstance, did not, on the respectful view here, meet constitutional muster. Indeed, it will here be argued that in certain ways, the USSC ruling in *Fulton* importantly erodes the public interest in the fundamental right to equality under the law.

## Fulton et al. v City of Philadelphia et al. No. 19–123. Decided June 17, 2021 (United States Supreme Court)

The Fulton case, discussed next, concerns the role of private foster agencies contracted by the city of Philadelphia *to perform a public function*, namely to do home studies on prospective foster families and *certify those families that qualify to foster under State statutory criteria.* The case more specifically concerns Catholic Social Services (CSS) as petitioner in this case:

25 Referring to conditions the university sets for attendance at the university generally and, in some cases, as in the instant Indiana University case, medical requirements for attendance on campus.

26 Referring here to the Indiana University vaccination mandate or failing that an accommodation if one qualifies that allows for alternate COVID mitigation measures as a substitute for the vaccination.

27 United States Court of Appeals for the Seventh Circuit, No. 21–2326 Ryan Klaassen et al. v The Trustees of Indiana University Decided (August 2, 2021) at pp. 3–4.

28 SCOTUSblog Klaassen v. Trustees of Indiana University: Application for injunctive relief denied by Justice Barrett (August 12, 2021).

29 Fulton et al. v City of Philadelphia et al No. 19–123. Decided (June 17, 2021) (United States Supreme Court).

> CSS holds the religious belief that marriage is a sacred bond between a man and a woman. *Because CSS believes that certification of prospective foster families is an endorsement of their relationships*, it will not certify unmarried couples—regardless of their sexual orientation—or same-sex married couples. But other private foster agencies in Philadelphia will certify same-sex couples, and no same-sex couple has sought certification from CSS (emphasis added).[30]

After a newspaper article documented the aforementioned position of CSS in providing certification for prospective foster families, the city of Philadelphia "informed CSS that unless it agreed to certify same-sex couples the City would no longer refer children to the agency or enter a full foster care contract with it in the future.":[31]

> The City explained that the refusal of CSS to certify same-sex married couples violated both a non-discrimination provision in the agency's contract with the City as well as the non-discrimination requirements of the citywide Fair Practices Ordinance.[32]

Catholic Social Services and three affiliated foster parents filed suit seeking to block the City's referral freeze in respect of contracting CSS foster care services arguing that the freeze violated the Free Exercise and Free Speech Clauses of the First Amendment. The Complainants lost at both the District and Appeal levels with those courts holding that the City's non-discrimination requirement was neutral and generally applicable (did not favor one religion over another) and hence constitutional. The United States Supreme Court (USSC), however, *reversed* the lower court ruling, holding instead that "The refusal of Philadelphia to contract with CSS for the provision of foster care services unless CSS agrees to certify same-sex couples as foster parents violates the Free Exercise Clause of the First Amendment."[33]

On the respectful view here, the USSC did *not*, though necessary, put at the core of its analysis the fact that CSS was performing a public function. The latter as a contracted *agent of the State* certifying prospective foster families under State statute requirements and, as such, CSS was required to act in the public interest. This then allowed the Court, on the respectful view here, to disregard compelling public interest claims that augured *against* granting CSS a religious exemption.

30 Fulton et al. v City of Philadelphia et al. No. 19–123. Decided (June 17, 2021) (United States Supreme Court) Syllabus at p. 1.
31 Fulton et al. v City of Philadelphia et al. No. 19–123. Decided (June 17, 2021) (United States Supreme Court) Syllabus at p. 1.
32 Fulton et al. v City of Philadelphia et al. No. 19–123. Decided (June 17, 2021) (United States Supreme Court) Syllabus at p. 1.
33 Fulton et al. v City of Philadelphia et al. No. 19–123. Decided (June 17, 2021) (United States Supreme Court) Syllabus at p. 2.

That exemption entailed CSS being *excluded* from the prohibition against applying discriminatory practices in its rendering of said certification services on behalf of the government. Let us examine then the presumptions that underpin the Supreme Court's central ruling that the religious freedom and free speech rights of Catholic Social Services guaranteed under the First Amendment were violated by the City of Philadelphia (in that the City required CSS to comply with its non-discriminatory policies):

### *USSC Contention One*

> The City's actions burdened CSS's religious exercise by forcing it either to curtail its mission or to certify same-sex couples as foster parents in violation of its religious beliefs . . . the City has burdened CSS's religious exercise through policies that do not satisfy the threshold requirement of being neutral and generally applicable.[34]

*Counter-argument*: The burden placed on CSS's religious exercise was both constitutional and not undue. In acting as an agent of government in providing foster care services for the City of Philadelphia, the CSS should have well understood the requirement of non-discrimination in the provision of such services including with respect to unmarried couples and same-sex couples whether married or not. Indeed, it was arguably instead CSS that placed an undue burden on the First Amendment rights of potential prospective foster parent applicants to CSS who would be hoping to be certified by CSS as acceptable foster families under State statute. Such couples would have only a few options—curtail their free speech rights and unlawfully not disclose to CSS their status as unmarried and/or a same-sex couple or seek services at another agency providing certification of foster families. There is no constitutional reason, it is here argued, why prospective foster couples should have a reduced chance of certification *in a timely fashion* due to their marital status or sexual orientation their having been filtered out of consideration by an additional agency (CSS).

### *USSC Contention Two*

The USSC further held that "the contract as a whole contains no generally applicable non-discrimination requirement"[35] and therefore CSS had a valid claim regarding purported violation of its First Amendment rights. The Court referred in this regard to section 3.21 of the City's contract with private foster agencies

34 Fulton et al. v City of Philadelphia et al. No. 19–123. Decided (June 17, 2021) (United States Supreme Court) Syllabus at p. 2.
35 Fulton et al. v City of Philadelphia et al. No. 19–123. Decided (June 17, 2021) (United States Supreme Court) Syllabus at p. 3.

to provide a public function, namely certification services. That section of the contract states:

> Rejection of Referral. Provider shall not reject a child or family including, but not limited to, . . . prospective foster or adoptive parents, for Services based upon . . . their . . . sexual orientation . . . unless an exception is granted by the Commissioner or the Commissioner's designee, in his/her sole discretion. Supp. App. to Brief for City Respondents 16–17 (emphasis added).[36]

*Counter-argument*: Any discretionary exemption the City may have offered to the non-discrimination requirement relating to sexual orientation and/or marital status of the prospective foster (or adoptive couple) would, on the analysis here, in the normal course have been unconstitutional. The latter by blocking, without a compelling public interest justification, such couples from equal treatment under the State statute governing the certification process and qualifying criteria. *It is also of import that the City made it clear to the Court that neither the Commissioner nor the Commissioner's designee had had any intention of offering CSS an exemption allowing that agency to discriminate on religious grounds against unmarried and/or same-sex couples in its provision of certification as an agent of government.*[37] Further, as one amicus in the case put it in regard to non-discrimination, it is to be noted that:

> These [non-discrimination] policies are not some incidental feature of the foster system. They are central to its purpose. By maximizing the number of available families and preventing harmful prejudice, non-discrimination rules serve the best interests of children.[38]

Indeed, the current author would argue further that abandonment of the City's non-discrimination requirement in the certification of foster families by CSS violates the child's constitutional right to security of the person. This by potentially depriving that child of the enhanced chance he or she would otherwise have for a timely foster placement were CSS to apply the non-discrimination requirement and thus also certify suitable same-sex married or unmarried couples and heterosexual unmarried couples. This is especially the case given the "acute shortage of foster parents" in the United States.[39]

36 Fulton et al. v City of Philadelphia et al. No. 19–123. Decided (June 17, 2021) (United States Supreme Court), Opinion, Cited at p. 7.

37 It is not mentioned in the judgement what circumstances would allow for such an exemption by the City, but presumably such would be the very exceptional case and would consider the best interest of the particular child as the first priority in this foster care context.

38 Fulton et al. v City of Philadelphia et al. No. 19–123. Decided (June 17, 2021) (United States Supreme Court), Brief for Lutheran Child and Family Services of Illinois in Support of Respondents (City of Philadelphia et al.) (August 20, 2020) at p. 2.

39 Washington Post Editorial Board, "The crisis in foster care," Wash. Post (January 11, 2020). Cited in Fulton et al. v City of Philadelphia et al. No. 19–123. Decided (June 17, 2021)

Further, the child's constitutional First Amendment religious freedom right[40] is impinged by the screening out by CSS of same-sex and unmarried couples as prospective foster or adoptive families. It may be the case that the child's religious views do or may ultimately align with those of the rejected prospective foster parents who were automatically precluded from certification on discriminatory grounds relating to sexual orientation and/or marital status. In any case, the child is faced with a roadblock (at least for a time) created by CSS in regard to the child's opportunity to be placed in a foster family with non-discriminatory attitudes/perspectives about sexual orientation and/or marital status and the value and sanctity of the family units these couples head.

Marital status and sexual orientation of couples may, in addition, serve as a proxy—though not perfectly correlated for (i) religious orientation (or lack thereof) and/or (ii) likelihood of the couple being active members in a faith community that discriminates on the basis of sexual orientation and/or marital status in their acceptance of members. The discriminatory CSS certification process for prospective foster parents arguably then potentially, through indirect means, violates the First Amendment religious freedom rights of at least a segment of those rejected couples who would not be certified by CSS based on their marital status and/or sexual orientation.[41]

Lutheran Child and Family Services of Illinois amicus in the instant case pointed out that

> Prospective parents can be deterred from pursuing foster or adoptive parenting if they believe that they will not be welcomed and respected due to their sexual orientation. . . . And in many parts of the country, objecting organizations may be the primary or only foster agencies available to LGBTQ parents.[42]

Importantly, the Lutheran Child and Family Services of Illinois amicus pointed out that "LGBTQ youth make up a disproportionately large percentage of children in foster care."[43] The Lutheran Child and Family Services of Illinois

---

(United States Supreme Court), Brief for Lutheran Child and Family Services of Illinois in Support of Respondents (City of Philadelphia et al.) (August 20, 2020) at p. 4.

40 The UN Convention on the Rights of the Child (UNCRC), an international legal instrument (to which the US is a signatory but a State that has not yet ratified the treaty) sets out that children have, among other fundamental rights, the right to religious freedom (see UNCRC Article 13). Further, the US Constitution does not restrict religious freedom rights to only adults.

41 Some same-sex and unmarried couples may yet identify as Catholic though their couple relationship is not accepted by that faith community, while many other such couples may have left the Catholic religious community, converted to another religion or abandoned religion to varying extents.

42 Fulton et al. v City of Philadelphia et al. No. 19–123. Decided June 17, 2021 (United States Supreme Court), Brief for Lutheran Child and Family Services of Illinois in Support of Respondents (City of Philadelphia et al.) (August 20, 2020) at p. 7.

43 Fulton et al. v City of Philadelphia et al. No. 19–123. Decided June 17, 2021 (United States Supreme Court), Brief for Lutheran Child and Family Services of Illinois in Support of Respondents (City of Philadelphia et al.) (August 20, 2020) at p. 2.

concluded in this regard that "Depriving LGBTQ youth of the possibility of placement in a large group of potentially affirming foster homes can rob them of urgently needed safety and stability, while sending them a harmful message about their own identities."[44] The aforementioned amicus also makes the critical point that non-discrimination rules are not motivated by religious animus but rather the best interests of children in the child welfare system including those children in desperate need of a foster placement.[45] Lutheran Child and Family Services of Illinois in fact argues that "non-discrimination rules work against all kinds of prejudice, including religiously motivated animus."[46]

### *USSC Contention Three*

The USSC contended that Philadelphia's Fair Practices Ordinances did *not* apply to CSS's implementation of its foster care services under contract to the City. The USSC explained its position in this regard thus:

> Certification[47] is not "made available to the public" in the usual sense of the words. Certification as a foster parent is not readily accessible to the public; the process involves a customized and selective assessment that bears little resemblance to staying in a hotel, eating at a restaurant, or riding a bus. The District Court's contrary conclusion did not take into account the uniquely selective nature of foster care certification.[48]

*Counter-argument*: The fact that the certification of prospective foster couples is a selective process (involving various stages of screening) does not mean that those screening processes properly and constitutionally can be discriminatory based on marital status and/or sexual orientation per the religiously based preferences of the agency contracted to provide this public service. Indeed, one could argue that the public interest served by a non-discriminatory foster family vetting service is of even greater import than ensuring open non-discriminatory access to a hotel or public transport as significant as the latter is no doubt. This in that discrimination in the foster family certification process may have devastating effects on a child's short- and long-term welfare depriving

44 Fulton et al. v City of Philadelphia et al. No. 19–123. Decided (June 17, 2021) (United States Supreme Court), Brief for Lutheran Child and Family Services of Illinois in Support of Respondents (City of Philadelphia et al.) (August 20, 2020) at p. 2.

45 Fulton et al. v City of Philadelphia et al. No. 19–123. Decided (June 17, 2021) (United States Supreme Court), Brief for Lutheran Child and Family Services of Illinois in Support of Respondents (City of Philadelphia et al.) (August 20, 2020) at p. 3.

46 Fulton et al. v City of Philadelphia et al. No. 19–123. Decided (June 17, 2021) (United States Supreme Court), Brief for Lutheran Child and Family Services of Illinois in Support of Respondents (City of Philadelphia et al.) (August 20, 2020) at p. 3.

47 Referring to certification of prospective foster couples as suitable under State statutory criteria requirements.

48 Fulton et al. v City of Philadelphia et al. No. 19–123. Decided (June 17, 2021) (United States Supreme Court) Syllabus at p. 3.

that child potentially of a supportive foster placement. The harms done in the latter instance are likely to be, to some extent at least, irreparable especially if the child spends years in the child welfare system outside of a family setting as occurs all too often.

### *USSC Contention Four*

> The contractual non-discrimination requirement burdens CSS's religious exercise and is not generally applicable, so it is subject to "the most rigorous of scrutiny. . . . A government policy can survive strict scrutiny only if it advances compelling interests and is narrowly tailored to achieve those interests. . . . The question is not whether the City has a compelling interest in enforcing its non-discrimination policies generally, but whether it has such an interest in denying an exception to CSS.[49]
>
> CSS seeks only an accommodation that will allow it to continue serving the children of Philadelphia in a manner consistent with its religious beliefs; *it does not seek to impose those beliefs on anyone else* (emphasis added). The refusal of Philadelphia to contract with CSS for the provision of foster care services unless the agency agrees to certify same-sex couples as foster parents cannot survive strict scrutiny and violates the Free Exercise Clause of the First Amendment. The Court does not consider whether the City's actions also violate the Free Speech Clause.[50]

*Counter-argument*: It is here argued, in contrast, that even on a strict scrutiny standard, the CSS claim of infringement of its First Amendment rights cannot stand in the first instance. CSS in declining to certify same-sex or unmarried couples (the latter whether same-sex or heterosexual) as foster couples who meet all State requirements for certification but are not considered acceptable based only on CSS religious tenets *is imposing* its religious views on (i) the prospective foster couples falling into the aforementioned categories arbitrarily excluded by CSS from certification and indirectly on (ii) the children denied a foster placement as a result of the foster family shortage to which the aforesaid CSS policy and practice contributes. There is a compelling public interest in sending the message to the public that same-sex and unmarried couples are not on that basis considered unsuitable as foster or for that matter adoptive or biological parents. CSS in acting as an agent of the government in accepting the city of Philadelphia's contract to provide foster care services, including certification, owes a duty of professional care[51] to both the prospective foster parents and the children in need of foster

49 Fulton et al. v City of Philadelphia et al. No. 19–123. Decided (June 17, 2021) (United States Supreme Court) Syllabus at p. 3.

50 Fulton et al. v City of Philadelphia et al. No. 19–123. Decided (June 17, 2021) (United States Supreme Court) Syllabus at p. 3.

51 For a discussion of professional standards in the provision of foster care services, see Fulton et al. v City of Philadelphia et al. No. 19–123. Decided (June 17, 2021) (United States Supreme Court), Brief for Lutheran Child and Family Services of Illinois in Support of Respondents (City of Philadelphia et al.) (August 20, 2020) at pp. 11–14.

placement who come to the attention of CSS. On the respectful view here that duty of care cannot be fulfilled to professional standards where the certification process is tainted by discrimination whether religiously or otherwise based. The First Amendment was intended to protect individual and collective religious and free speech rights, it was not intended as a basis to undermine the rights of families and children to their own First Amendment rights and to family privacy.

Furthermore, on the view here (i) CSS has no *constitutional right* to act as an agent for the State in the certification process for prospective foster couples notwithstanding the many years that CSS has done so in the City of Philadelphia and (ii) certainly *no constitutional right* to implement the certification process on behalf of the government relying in part on religious bias. To accept the latter as protected under the Free Exercise Clause of the First Amendment is, it is here argued, to eliminate the distinction between Church and State. The latter would be to the detriment of (i) the welfare of prospective foster couples falling into a distinct class (unmarried couples and/or same-sex couples) and (ii) that of children desperate for a foster placement who are denied a placement that may have been possible had CSS applied non-discriminatory certification criteria as required under statute and as do all other foster care services in the City of Philadelphia (aside from CSS) including those that are religiously based.

It will be recalled that, according to the United States Supreme Court (USSC) in *Fulton*, it is precisely "Because CSS believes that certification of prospective foster families is an *endorsement* of their relationships, [that] it will not certify unmarried couples—regardless of their sexual orientation—or same-sex married couples (emphasis added)."[52] It is here argued then that the *refusal ipso facto* of CSS to certify unmarried couples—regardless of their sexual orientation—or same-sex married couples as foster couples is in fact discriminatory speech communicated to the public in regard to the *alleged* unsuitability of said couples to provide a proper foster family setting that meets necessary standards. Those standards in this regard however, on the view here, as applied by CSS are improperly not State standards. Indeed, the USSC in *Fulton* readily concedes in the *Fulton* opinion that "The religious views of CSS inform its work in this system"[53] and that includes certification of foster parents.

In short then, it is here contended, that the USSC *Fulton* ruling *did* encompass the Free Speech issue (notwithstanding the Court's clarification that "The Court does not consider whether the City's actions also violate the Free Speech Clause"[54]). That is non-certification as a foster couple, by CSS's own reckoning, *communicates* to the public that unmarried couples (regardless of sexual orientation) and same-sex couples are automatically precluded from certification

52 Fulton et al. v City of Philadelphia et al. No. 19–123. Decided (June 17, 2021) (United States Supreme Court) Syllabus at p. 1.

53 Fulton et al. v City of Philadelphia et al. No. 19–123. Decided (June 17, 2021) (United States Supreme Court) Opinion at p. 2.

54 Fulton et al. v City of Philadelphia et al. No. 19–123. Decided (June 17, 2021) (United States Supreme Court) Syllabus at p. 3.

by CSS. The latter is *speech about the CSS religious position* and not about the qualification criteria set out by the State under statute for fostering children. It is hence *not* speech, on the contention here, that is consistent with the responsibility of carrying out, on behalf of government, the public function of certification of prospective foster couples. Such discriminatory speech frustrates the right of prospective couples who are qualified to foster under the criteria set by State statute to receive certification from CSS as an agency performing a public governmental function. Further such speech, on the view here, promotes a bias against the LGBT+ community as foster and adoptive parents (and by implication also as biological/genetic parents(s)). Hence also for that reason, such speech by CSS is, on the respectful view here, not in the public interest.

On the analysis here, CSS religiously based views on the purported lack of legitimacy of the relationships of unmarried couples and of same-sex couples are (i) irrelevant to its *public function* on behalf of the City of Philadelphia in certifying prospective foster couples and (ii) do *not* trigger CSS First Amendment speech protection *in that context.* On the respectful view here, the United States Supreme Court in *Fulton* disregarded the compelling public interest in requiring CSS—as an *agent of government* in this instance—to perform its certification process regarding foster couples (a public function) in a manner consistent with State stipulated non-discriminatory criteria/standards and City policy/regulation. Instead, the Court, it is here contended, erroneously applied a First Amendment shield *essentially to government* (since CSS was acting as an agent of government) engaged in discriminatory speech and practice damaging to a certain class of prospective foster couples, prospective foster children and the LGBT+ community more generally.

The current author respectfully contests the USSC's view in *Fulton* that the City's failure to offer CSS a religious exemption in certifying *qualified* unmarried and/or same-sex couples as prospective foster parents (should such a couple apply) creates undue "religious hardship" *for CSS.* She does so on the grounds that religiously based discriminatory considerations are *not* properly a part nor a necessary part of the foster couple certification process in the first instance. If CSS found that the absence of a discretionary religious exemption (granted by the City Commissioner or that person's delegate) creates "religious hardship" for the agency in its functioning on behalf of government in the provision of certain foster care services, it was, on the analysis here, CSS's moral and ethical responsibility to withdraw from the foster family certification enterprise. This since, on the view here, with respect, such religious considerations *resulting in discrimination based on sexual orientation and/or marital status* are inimical to the duty of care owed to clients under the State statute and the professional standard for the provision of social work services. There is no compelling public interest in providing *to any* religiously based private agency a religious exemption for discriminatory practices (i.e. relating to marital status or sexual orientation of couples or otherwise) in the carrying out of the *public function* of the certification of prospective foster or adoptive couples as an agent of government. The failure of the City to offer CSS a religious exemption is not discrimination against religion or a particular religion but rather the realization of the proper separation of Church and State in providing certification processes of prospective foster couples. There is, on the view here, no legitimate *non-religious* reason to preclude prospective foster (or adoptive couples) from certification based only on marital status and/or sexual orientation. Hence, the CSS automatic bar on certifying such couples is, on the respectful view here, unconstitutional religious discrimination in the provision of a service provided by an agent of government in this context.

On the view here, the City's contract with CSS can be read/interpreted to be constitutionally sound in that the failure to grant CSS an exemption is consistent with s. 3.12 of the contract titled "Rejection of Referral."[55] This in that CSS had no legitimate non-religious reason to *ipso facto* preclude unmarried and same-sex couples from certification as foster couples. The current author adopts the City's position that a discretionary exemption applies to the placement of the child in a particular family not to freedom to deem couples as ineligible for certification as foster parents based on marital status and/or sexual orientation of the couple. *The guiding principle in such cases of exemption from placement referred to must be an objective assessment by the Commissioner or his or her delegate of the best interests of the particular child separate and apart from any religious considerations of the foster agency.* Where such compelling best interests of the child can be shown based on the child's history and current emotional status and concerns, then a discretionary exemption might be offered not to place the child with the couple to which the child was referred. That couple may be unmarried or same-sex orientation. In other instances, such a same-sex and/or unmarried couple might be the preferred couple for a particular child (for instance conceivably likely to best meet the needs of an older child who identifies as a member of the LGBTQ community but has issues with self-acceptance). *In that regard then, it is something of a misnomer to refer to such an exemption from a referral as a religious exemption. On the view here, the discretionary exemption to a certification and/or a specific referral in regard to a particular placement, when enacted on the basis of the principle of the child's best interests, is a constitutional neutral, generally applicable provision of the contract of CSS with the City of Philadelphia.* In the latter instance, in a meaningful sense the exemption belongs to the child to serve that child's best interests and not the foster agency.

On the respectful analysis here, the fact that the City of Philadelphia did *not* contemplate offering a discretionary religious exemption to CSS in regard to the provision of certification services to same-sex or unmarried couples is *not* discrimination against a particular religion. Rather, it reflects the fact that CSS would be guided in its dealings with same-sex and/or unmarried couples by religious considerations as incorporated in the Catholic faith as opposed to only the principle of the best interests of the child. However, the best interest of the child is, on the view here, the exclusive appropriate professional standard in providing

55 Fulton et al. v City of Philadelphia et al. No. 19–123. Decided (June 17, 2021) (United States Supreme Court), Opinion, Cited at p. 7.

foster services of any sort as opposed to also the inherent religious, political or other biases or preferences of the private foster care service contracted to act as an agent of government in offering foster care services.

The USSC's opinion in *Fulton* furthermore arguably places vulnerable families in need of government services in a position of undeserved uncertainty and distress:

> Accepting CSS's invitation to establish a constitutional right of government services contractors to opt out of contract requirements that conflict with their faith would have extraordinary consequences. . . . Government contracting agencies and vulnerable children, families and individuals in need of help would face uncertainty and confusion because they would not know what providers would be willing to serve them, provide particular services, or provide services when needed if providers could discriminate, decline to provide specific contracted-for services or decline to provide those services on particular days for religious reasons.[56]

The current author is in accord with amicus KidsVoice that the United States Supreme Court ruling in *Fulton* erred in not considering the discretionary exemption as a neutral contract term but does so for the aforementioned reasons.[57] Finally, the current author concurs with KidsVoice that:

> Decisions regarding how local and state governments contract for social services when delegating government duties to private providers should prioritize meeting the needs of the vulnerable children, families and individuals in need of help, not upon the needs of providers who, if they disagree with contract terms, could choose to forego involvement.[58]

The underlying argument in this chapter's case analyses then has been that the democratic rule of law, when not perverted by political, religious or other bias, operates inherently to defend the compelling general public interest including, as envisioned by U.S. Constitution, protecting the vulnerable from discrimination under the law. Where the courts sidestep the issue of compelling general public interest in protecting also the most vulnerable and marginalized from inequities under the law, democracy and its fundamental human rights foundation itself are in peril. The courts in a democracy are the last bastion in protecting the

56 Fulton et al. v City of Philadelphia et al. No. 19–123. Decided (June 17, 2021) (United States Supreme Court), Brief of Amicus Curiae KidsVoice (August 20, 2020) at p. 2.

57 Fulton et al. v City of Philadelphia et al. No. 19–123. Decided (June 17, 2021) (United States Supreme Court), Brief of Amicus Curiae KidsVoice (August 20, 2020) at pp. 2–3. For a discussion of the complications of a "workaround" see Brief of Amicus Curiae KidsVoice *id.* at pp. 12–13.

58 Fulton et al. v City of Philadelphia et al. No. 19–123. Decided June 17, 2021 (United States Supreme Court), Brief of Amicus Curiae KidsVoice (August 20, 2020) at p. 16.

compelling public interest in the realization of equity in the implementation of constitutional guarantees for the powerful and powerless alike. To fulfill this mission is not judicial overreach but rather the indicia of a robust democracy with a well-functioning independent judiciary.

## References

### *Materials*

Centers for Disease Control and Prevention (CDC). *Early Release* (October 29, 2021) 70 Laboratory-Confirmed COVID-19 Among Adults Hospitalized with COVID-19—Like Illness with Infection-Induced or mRNA Vaccine-Induced SARS-CoV-2 Immunity—Nine States (January–September 2021) www.cdc.gov/mmwr/volumes/70/wr/mm7044e1.htm.

Fulton et al. v City of Philadelphia et al. No. 19–123 (Decided June 17, 2021) (United States Supreme Court), Brief for Lutheran Child and Family Services of Illinois in Support of Respondents (City of Philadelphia et al.) (August 20, 2020).

Indiana University, COVID-19 Frequently Asked Questions www.iu.edu/covid/faq/index.html#vaccine-req (accessed August 13, 2021).

SCOTUSblog Klaassen v. Trustees of Indiana University: Application for Injunctive Relief Denied by Justice Barrett (August 12, 2021) www.scotusblog.com/case-files/cases/klaassen-v-trustees-of-indiana-university/ (accessed October 30, 2021).

UN Convention on the Rights of the Child (UNCRC) www.ohchr.org/en/professionalinterest/pages/crc.aspx (accessed August 31, 2021).

### *Cases*

Fulton et al. v City of Philadelphia et al. No. 19–123 (Decided June 17, 2021) (United States Supreme Court).

Hamilton v. Regents of the University of California, 293 U.S. 245, 264 (1934).

Jacobson v. Massachusetts, 197 U.S. 11 (1905).

United States Court of Appeals for the Seventh Circuit, No. 21–2326 Ryan Klaassen et al. v The Trustees of Indiana University (Decided August 2, 2021).

United States District Court for the Northern District of Indiana, Ryan Klaassen et al. v The Trustees of Indiana University, Complaint for Declaratory and Injunctive Relief (June 21, 2021).

United States District Court for the Northern District of Indiana, Ryan Klaassen et al. v The Trustees of Indiana University, South Bend Division, Opinion and Order, Cause No. 1:21-CV-238 DRL (July 18, 2021).

# 7 Concluding Remarks

## On the Role of the Courts in Upholding the Democratic Rule of Law

We have examined in the preceding case discussions a range of First Amendment cases in which the courts have spoken. They have done so; depending on one's perspective, for better or worse. In so doing, the courts have upheld the democratic rule of law as a means to resolve controversies while not foreclosing the opportunity for any still aggrieved party to litigate another day, theoretically at least, with a more on point test case and new arguments. In so doing, the courts have also shaped the understanding by the populace of constitutional rights. All the selected cases previously here discussed implicate the public interest more generally rather than simply the interest of the parties involved. It is with that in mind that the current author refers to the opinion of the United States Supreme Court (USSC) in *Whole Woman's Health et al. v Austin Reeve Jackson, Judge, et al.*[1] The case concerns the potentially unconstitutional imposition on the women of Texas of a new abortion law, one arguably largely politically inspired to appeal to a certain largely religious segment of the Republican voter base in violation of women's right in Texas to make private decisions informed by their own conscientious beliefs. The case highlights the role of the courts in upholding the democratic rule of law and the consequences when arguably the Court ducks and weaves in a highly contentious case thereby leaving on the face of it (based on USSC precedent) an unconstitutional statute to stand, at least temporarily with no legal remedy available.

*Whole Woman's Health et al. v Austin Reeve Jackson, Judge, et al.*[2] concerns a Texas statute that bans abortions after six weeks of pregnancy with no exceptions for rape or incest though there is a limited exception for medical emergencies. Six weeks is the time at which cardiac activity of the unborn can be detected. The USSC declined to offer the injunctive relief requested by the petitioners and did

1 In the United States Supreme Court, Whole Woman's Health et al. v Austin Reeve Jackson, Judge, et al., On Application for Injunctive Relief, 594 U. S. ____ (2021) (Chief Justice Roberts joined by Justice Breyer and Justice Kagan dissenting).

2 In the United States Supreme Court, Whole Woman's Health et al. v Austin Reeve Jackson, Judge, et al., On Application for Injunctive Relief, 594 U. S. ____ (2021) (Chief Justice Roberts joined by Justice Breyer and Justice Kagan dissenting).

DOI: 10.4324/9781003153764-7

so without receiving full briefing and argument by the parties.[3] That relief would have stayed the law pending the outcome of litigation on the substantive and procedural issues the Texas statute implicates. The USSC, at the same time, did *not* rule on the merits of the plaintiffs' case generally or the constitutionality of the Texas law at issue:

> we stress that we do not purport to resolve definitively any jurisdictional or substantive claim in the applicants' lawsuit. In particular, this order is not based on any conclusion about the constitutionality of Texas's law, and in no way limits other procedurally proper challenges to the Texas law, including in Texas state courts.[4]

The vote was 5 to 4 with only Justice Roberts siding with the three justices who are generally characterized as the liberals on the Court. The upholding of the new Texas abortion statute, even temporarily, is an anomaly in that USSC case precedent prohibits banning of abortions prior to fetal viability usually thought to occur between 22 and 24 weeks.[5]

The Supreme Court of the United Sates in *Whole Woman's Health et al.* stated that:

> The applicants now before us have raised serious questions regarding the constitutionality of the Texas law at issue. But their application also presents complex and novel antecedent procedural questions on which they have not carried their burden (emphasis added).[6]

The procedural complexities the Court was referring to relate to the fact that the Texas abortion statute at issue ostensibly deputizes private citizens to enforce the statute at issue. More specifically, the statute has as its procedural purpose to empower private citizens to enforce the aforementioned abortion statute by their suing for ten thousand dollars any person who aids and abets an abortion in the State of Texas that is to occur after six weeks of pregnancy. The Supreme Court of the United States noted that "*The State represented that neither it nor*

3 *Whole Woman's Health et al. v Austin Reeve Jackson, Judge, et al.* 594 U. S. ____ (2021) was referred to the USSC as part of the so-called shadow docket with the plaintiffs seeking emergency relief. The shadow docket sidesteps the normal appeals processes before arriving at the USSC. See American Bar Association "Supreme Court "Shadow Docket" Under Review by U.S. House of Representatives" (author: Samantha O'Connell).

4 In the United States Supreme Court, Whole Woman's Health et al. v Austin Reeve Jackson, Judge, et al., On Application for Injunctive Relief, 594 U. S. ____ (2021) (Chief Justice Roberts joined by Justice Breyer and Justice Kagan dissenting) Syllabus at p. 2.

5 Compare NPR online. Supreme Court Upholds New Texas Abortion Law, For Now. (Nina Totenberg) (September 2, 2021).

6 In the United States Supreme Court, Whole Woman's Health et al. v Austin Reeve Jackson, Judge, et al., On Application for Injunctive Relief, 594 U. S. ____ (2021) (Chief Justice Roberts joined by Justice Breyer and Justice Kagan dissenting) Syllabus at p. 1.

***its executive employees possess the authority to enforce the Texas law either directly or indirectly*** (emphasis added) "[7] Given the foregoing then, on the analysis here, the State of Texas in actual fact, through the construction of the procedural aspects of the new abortion law (i) created the illusion of rendering private citizens independent actors *acting under colour of law* in filing punitive law suits against aiders and abetters of abortion in Texas as relates to aborting an unborn after six weeks of pregnancy (such lawsuits, on the view here, in actual fact constitute *the State enforcing the new abortion statute indirectly* which the State itself concedes it has no authority to do); (ii) created the illusion that such plaintiffs having legal standing in such cases despite their having, in most instances, no personal connection at all to the case and no prospect of personally suffering direct harm from the attempted or completed abortion and (iii) created a situation where in fact the presumed, but in most cases non-existent legal interest of the private citizen plaintiff, grounded as it is on the said Texas abortion statute, actually represents a State interest. Thus, it is here argued that though civil lawsuits by one private person against another are normally private matters, here this is not the case. *The suing party is, per the new Texas abortion statute, actually acting in a public capacity as an agent of the State supposedly endowed by authority under law to file such a lawsuit under colour of law*. It is the statute that allegedly allows for such suits though the plaintiffs in most instances will *not* have any personal connection to any of the parties sued or the pregnant woman or girl and will not have suffered any direct personal injury because of the actions taken by the respondents in aiding and abetting an abortion. The statute was crafted thus to allow the suing party to act in furtherance of the State's self-perceived interests and policy objectives where normally that private party would have no legal standing to sue the aider and abetter of abortion that is to take place in Texas in the first stage of pregnancy after six weeks. However, on the analysis here, the State of Texas *cannot constitutionally* under the new Texas abortion statutory scheme, notwithstanding its peculiar procedural aspect, given that *Roe v Wade*[8] is still "good law," evade responsibility for interfering with the current constitutional right of women in Texas seeking an abortion prior to fetal viability. This is *not* to say that in the proper case where substantive and procedural issues are advanced and litigated that the constitutionality of *Roe v Wade*[9] is beyond challenge regardless of its long-standing entrenched status as *stare decisis.*

As a practical matter, it was possible for the USSC in *Whole Woman's Health et al.*[10] to have, temporarily at least, blocked the new Texas abortion statute (thus

7 In the United States Supreme Court, Whole Woman's Health et al. v Austin Reeve Jackson, Judge, et al., On Application for Injunctive Relief, 594 U. S. ___ (2021) (Chief Justice Roberts joined by Justice Breyer and Justice Kagan dissenting) at pp. 1–2.

8 Roe v. Wade 410 U.S. 113, 164 (1973).

9 Roe v. Wade 410 U.S. 113, 164 (1973).

10 In the United States Supreme Court, Whole Woman's Health et al. v Austin Reeve Jackson, Judge, et al., On Application for Injunctive Relief, 594 U. S. ___ (2021) (Chief Justice Roberts joined by Justice Breyer and Justice Kagan dissenting).

enjoining the filing of any abortion lawsuit where the plaintiff, a private citizen acting as supposed agent of the State under colour of law—the new Texas abortion statute, cannot establish legal standing based on (i) a personal meaningful connection to the woman or girl seeking the abortion and/or to others directly involved in the case and relating to (ii) a compelling showing that the plaintiff would allegedly be seriously harmed in some way should the abortion be attempted or completed). Thus, the current author respectfully disputes the view of the USSC majority ruling in this case that it is unclear against whom (which enforcement agent) the injunctive relief should be issued when in fact it is the State of Texas that has through the new abortion law ascribed to itself authority it does not have. Further, no one can (including then those in effect purportedly lawfully deputized as agents of the State for this purpose), on the view here, subvert current constitutional law in the context at hand of abortion nor presumably in any other context:

> Indeed we have made clear that since the State cannot regulate or proscribe abortion during the first stage . . . the State cannot delegate authority to any particular person . . . to prevent abortion during that same period (emphasis added).[11]

Thus arguably (i) no State, given USSC case precedent regarding abortion, *currently* has the authority to subvert the woman's or girl's recognized contentious constitutional right to abortion "during the first stage"[12] and further (ii) the State then cannot in this regard delegate such an authority since it is an authority the State does *not* itself possess in the first instance. Yet in *Whole Woman's Health et al. v Austin Reeve Jackson, Judge, et al.*,[13] this arguably is precisely what the Texas statute purports to do—namely delegate the subversion of a USSC established/recognized constitutional right to private persons ostensibly acting as agents of the State under colour of law (by filing suits to hinder or stop the exercise of the said constitutional right). On the respectful view here, the Court allowed in this case, at least temporarily, the *illusion of lawful delegation by the State of alleged legal authority to private persons (rendering them ostensibly agents of the State) to subvert a to date recognized constitutional right (as established under USSC case law), namely the right to abort a non-viable unborn.*

11 In the United States Supreme Court, Whole Woman's Health et al. v Austin Reeve Jackson, Judge, et al., On Application for Injunctive Relief, 594 U. S. ____ (2021) (Chief Justice Roberts joined by Justice Breyer and Justice Kagan dissenting) Syllabus at p. 1.

12 It is beyond the scope of this work to analyze whether such an abortion right in fact is embodied in the Constitution or was judge-crafted through USSC case law, and it is not necessary for the purposes of this current work to do so.

13 In the United States Supreme Court, Whole Woman's Health et al. v Austin Reeve Jackson, Judge, et al., On Application for Injunctive Relief, 594 U. S. ____ (2021) (Chief Justice Roberts joined by Justice Breyer and Justice Kagan dissenting).

The current author thus in accord with the dissent in *Whole Woman's Health* et al.[14] holds that the State cannot lawfully delegate private persons, as it is doing, to subvert constitutional law in this case. This since the State does not itself retain that authority which it wishes to delegate to private citizens in their filing of lawsuits under the new Texas abortion law. On the view here, the plaintiffs *prima facie* have no legal standing if unconnected to a particular abortion case in a meaningful and substantive way and do *not* in fact constitutionally act under colour of law notwithstanding their invocation of the new Texas abortion law.[15] *The new Texas abortion statute does not by itself confer legal standing on private citizens to file such lawsuits to interfere with the exercise of abortion rights in Texas since that law is, on the view here, currently unconstitutional.* The statutory scheme is, as discussed, arguably *an illusion* since the State has no authority in the first instance which it can delegate to private citizens so as to purportedly cloak them with the necessary legal standing to be able to file lawsuits against aiders and abetters of abortion in the first stage of pregnancy where those abortions are to be conducted in the State of Texas. Thus it is, in the final analysis, on the argument here, the State itself that is acting *unconstitutionally* and *ultra vires as an enforcer* of the contested statute using private citizens as nothing more than a kind of smokescreen.[16] This by the State endorsing the statute and allowing it to create a *chilling effect* in Texas, as it was no doubt intended to do, on lawful means to accessing abortion in that State in the first stage of pregnancy. The evidence is that the new Texas abortion statute has had just that "chilling effect" on abortion providers and others. It is here argued then that it was the State of Texas (the executive's) responsibility itself in the first instance to litigate *against* the statute rather than facilitating its implementation. The State thus can be enjoined from continuing in this (respectfully on the view here) dereliction of duty in acting in the public interest *in upholding the democratic rule of law as set out in USSC constitutional precedent* in the abortion context (that constitutional case precedent not being immune from challenge in the proper future case, however).

14 In the United States Supreme Court, Whole Woman's Health et al. v Austin Reeve Jackson, Judge, et al., On Application for Injunctive Relief, 594 U. S. ____ (2021) (Chief Justice Roberts joined by Justice Breyer and Justice Kagan dissenting).

15 It is not surprising then this author maintains that "the sole private-citizen respondent before us [the USSC in the Whole Woman's Health et al. case] has filed an affidavit stating that he has no present intention to enforce the law." In the United States Supreme Court, Whole Woman's Health et al. v Austin Reeve Jackson, Judge, et al., On Application for Injunctive Relief, 594 U. S. ____ (2021) (Chief Justice Roberts joined by Justice Breyer and Justice Kagan dissenting), Syllabus at p. 2.

16 Thus, on the respectful view here, the USSC erred in contending that "it is unclear" whether the Court could intervene (compare In the United States Supreme Court, *Whole Woman's Health et al. v Austin Reeve Jackson, Judge, et al.*, Syllabus at p. 1 in that the State of Texas is arguably acting to create an undermining of the Constitution in such a way that its statutory scheme poses a threat that *is already having dramatic effects in curtailing access to abortion for women in the State of Texas in their first stage of pregnancy (On the plaintiffs' view constituting constitutional harm).*

The cases analyzed in this work highlight the crucial role of the courts in (i) upholding the democratic rule of law; (ii) ensuring that the larger public interest is served by protecting constitutional rights including the rights and interests also of the most vulnerable and (iii) maintaining the public peace by providing a civil forum for resolution of sensitive and key highly contested controversies while always preserving the potential for reconsideration of the issues when the legal and/or material facts change and/or the understanding of the issues and equity interests implicated shift. *Whole Woman's Health et al. v Austin Reeve Jackson, Judge, et al.*[17] alerts us that the courts' role in preserving the democratic rule of law is not something that the public can take for granted and stay silent on. Rather that role of the court must be cherished and actively protected. When the court's role is challenged for example by a State ostensibly evading judicial review (as on the respectful view occurred in the *Whole Woman's Health et al. case)*,[18] it is imperative that the public, regardless of the members' diversity of views on the core issue in the case, exercise their First Amendment right and speak out in protest on the court's unwillingness *in effect* to intervene (i.e. here to temporarily enjoin a statute in the interim, a statute which *conflicts with existing constitutional precedent*—waiting instead for a full hearing on the merits).[19] This to communicate to the courts that the public expects the courts to act vigorously to defend the Constitution from subversion whether the latter is by way of statutory scheme[20] or other crafty means alleged to be lawful.[21] It is key to the democracy itself that there exist in practice a meaningful "ability to ask the Judiciary to protect an individual from the invasion of a constitutional right—an invasion that threatens immediate and serious injury."[22] That "ask" must allow for a possible legal remedy. The current author is in accord thus also with the comment in the dissent by Sotomayor, J in *Whole Woman's Health et al.* that "the

17 In the United States Supreme Court, Whole Woman's Health et al. v Austin Reeve Jackson, Judge, et al., On Application for Injunctive Relief, 594 U. S. ____ (2021) (Chief Justice Roberts joined by Justice Breyer and Justice Kagan dissenting).

18 In the United States Supreme Court, Whole Woman's Health et al. v Austin Reeve Jackson, Judge, et al., On Application for Injunctive Relief, 594 U. S. ____ (2021) (Chief Justice Roberts joined by Justice Breyer and Justice Kagan dissenting).

19 "*[T]he Act is a breathtaking act of defiance—of the Constitution*, of this Court's precedents, and of the rights of women seeking abortions throughout Texas." (*In the United States Supreme Court, Whole Woman's Health et al. v Austin Reeve Jackson, Judge, et al.*, Opinion, Dissenting, Sotomayor, J at p. 3, emphasis added).

20 "By prohibiting state officers from enforcing the Act directly and relying instead on citizen bounty hunters, the Legislature sought to make it more complicated for federal courts to enjoin the Act on a statewide basis." (See *In the United States Supreme Court, Whole Woman's Health et al. v Austin Reeve Jackson, Judge, et al.*, Opinion, Dissenting, Sotomayor, J at p. 3.)

21 "The Court should not be so content to ignore its constitutional obligations to protect not only the rights of women, but also the sanctity of its precedents and of the rule of law" (see *In the United States Supreme Court, Whole Woman's Health et al. v Austin Reeve Jackson, Judge, et al.*, Opinion, Dissenting, Sotomayor, J at p. 4).

22 In the United States Supreme Court, Whole Woman's Health et al. v Austin Reeve Jackson, Judge, et al., On Application for Injunctive Relief, 594 U. S. ____ (2021) (Breyer, J, Opinion (dissenting) at p. 3.

Act [referring to the new Texas abortion law] is a breathtaking act of defiance—of the Constitution, [and] of this Court's precedents"[23] and, the current author would add, and the high court's response an example also of the Court missing the opportunity to reinforce the democratic rule of law.

## References

### *Materials*

American Bar Association www.americanbar.org/groups/committees/death_penalty_representation/publications/project_blog/scotus-shadow-docket-under-review-by-house-reps/ (accessed September 12, 2021).

NPR online. Supreme Court Upholds New Texas Abortion Law, for Now. (Nina Totenberg) (September 2, 2021) www.npr.org/2021/09/02/1033048958/supreme-court-upholds-new-texas-abortion-law-for-now (accessed September 10, 2021).

### *Cases*

In the United States Supreme Court, Whole Woman's Health et al. v Austin Reeve Jackson, Judge, et al., On Application for Injunctive Relief, 594 U. S. ____ (2021) (Chief Justice Roberts joined by Justice Breyer and Justice Kagan dissenting).

Roe v Wade, 410 U. S. 113, 164 (1973).

23 In the United States Supreme Court, Whole Woman's Health et al. v Austin Reeve Jackson, Judge, et al., On Application for Injunctive Relief, 594 U. S. ____ (2021) (Sotomayor, J Opinion (dissenting) at p. 3.

# Index

Note: Page numbers followed by 'n' indicate a note on the corresponding page.